PRAISE F[OR]
The Reckoning by P[...]

"Bishop successfully weaves a story that is both entertaining and revealing about a critical time in Middle East history. He is at his very best as he lays the groundwork for the fatal collision in that apartment. And he does an admirable job of showing how British police officers faced the difficult task of maintaining order between Jews and the Arabs whose resistance set the stage for later bloody confrontation"
—*Washington Post*

"Bishop's book has all the suspense and detail of a good novel."
—*Boston Globe*

"Mr. Bishop's depiction of Stern's downfall is masterful."
—*The Economist*

"What [Bishop] does, thanks to tireless research and powerful storytelling, is show how a ruthless murderer of civilians became an unnecessary martyr."
—*New York* magazine

"Bishop's fast-paced, well-written work sheds considerable light not only on how and why Stern was killed but on the final, violent years of the British mandate in Palestine."
—*Publishers Weekly*

"Clearly representing the point of view of the colonial British authorities, the author largely avoids demonizing or making heroes of either of his main protagonists, a failing of most English and Israeli accounts of the period."
—*Library Journal*

Also by Patrick Bishop

NONFICTION
THE WINTER WAR (with John Witherow)
THE PROVISIONAL IRA (with Eamon Mallie)
THE IRISH EMPIRE
FAMOUS VICTORY
FIGHTER BOYS: SAVING BRITAIN 1940
BOMBER BOYS: FIGHTING BACK 1940–1945
3 PARA
BATTLE OF BRITAIN
GROUND TRUTH – 3 PARA: RETURN TO AFGHANISTAN
TARGET TIRPITZ
WINGS

NOVELS
A GOOD WAR
FOLLOW ME HOME

THE
RECKONING

Death and Intrigue in the Promised Land—
A True Detective Story

PATRICK BISHOP

HARPER

NEW YORK · LONDON · TORONTO · SYDNEY

HARPER

A hardcover edition of this book was published in 2014 by HarperCollins Publishers.

THE RECKONING. Copyright © 2014 by Patrick Bishop. All rights reserved. Printed in the United States of America. No part of this book may be used or reproduced in any manner whatsoever without written permission except in the case of brief quotations embodied in critical articles and reviews. For information, address HarperCollins Publishers, 195 Broadway, New York, NY 10007.

HarperCollins books may be purchased for educational, business, or sales promotional use. For information, please e-mail the Special Markets Department at SPsales@ harpercollins.com.

Originally published in Great Britain in 2014 by William Collins, an imprint of HarperCollins*Publishers*.

FIRST HARPER PAPERBACKS EDITION PUBLISHED 2015.

The Library of Congress has catalogued the hardcover edition as follows:

Bishop, Patrick (Patrick Joseph), author.
  The reckoning : death and intrigue in the promised land—a true detective story / Patrick Bishop. — First edition.
    pages cm
  ISBN 978-0-06-226782-5 (hardback) — ISBN 978-0-06-226783-2 (paperback) — ISBN 978-0-06-226784-9 (ebook) 1. Stern, Abraham, 1907–1942—Assassination. 2. Lohame herut Yisra'el—Biography. 3. Revisionist Zionists—Palestine—Biography. 4. Palestine—Politics and government—1917–1948. I. Title.
  PJ5053.S865Z54 2014
  892.4'8509—dc23
  [B]
                                                                          2014024717

ISBN 978-0-06-226783-2 (pbk.)

15 16 17 18 19   OV/RRD   10 9 8 7 6 5 4 3 2 1

IN MEMORY OF RICK BEESTON
AND
IAN MACKENZIE

Contents

Author's Note

I have not tried to impose any orthodoxy on spellings of Jewish and Arab personal and place names, which inevitably vary in transliteration. To keep things simple I have left some as they appear in contemporary documents, while those that might seem confusingly archaic have been updated. In writing the story I found it had a habit of straying from the path to dart down some fascinating alleyway. To keep the narrative moving, I have sometimes explored these byways in the source notes. Consulting them may also help to answer questions arising from the text.

Glossary

Balfour Declaration
Statement issued by the British foreign secretary Arthur Balfour in November 1917 that the government favoured the idea that Palestine would one day be a 'a national home for the Jewish people'.

Betar
Militaristic youth organisation of the Revisionist movement. Particularly strong in Poland.

Haganah
'The Defence'. Militia founded in 1920 to defend 'Jewish lives, property and honour'. Under the control of the left-leaning Zionist establishment.

Havlagah
Policy of self-restraint in the face of Arab attacks. Favoured initially by the Haganah and the Yishuv's leaders but opposed by the Revisionists.

Irgun Zvai Leumi
The 'National Military Organization', which broke away from the Haganah in 1931 in protest at its unpreparedness in the face of Arab violence. Revisionist in outlook.

Jewish Agency
The body officially representing the Yishuv to the British administration of Palestine and the outside world.

xii · PATRICK BISHOP

Lehi

'Fighters for the Freedom of Israel'. The name of the splinter group which followed Avraham Stern after the 1940 split with the Irgun.

Mapai

Left-wing political party led by David Ben-Gurion and the dominant political force in the Yishuv.

Palmach

Elite unit of the Haganah.

Revisionist movement

Founded by Ze'ev Jabotinsky in 1925 to demand a 'revision' of Zionist policies towards the British mandate. Its militarism and capitalist sympathies created sharp differences with the Yishuv's establishment.

White Paper

The 1939 document drawn up by the British to decide the future of Palestine. Its proposal for strict limits on immigration, if implemented, would effectively have doomed the aspiration for a Jewish state and it was fiercely opposed by all Zionists.

Yishuv

The Jewish community in Palestine.

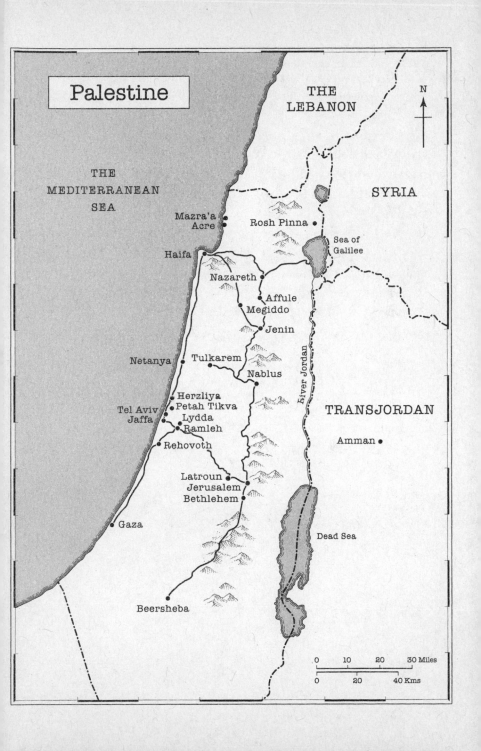

Palestine

THE LEBANON

N

THE
MEDITERRANEAN
SEA

SYRIA

Mazra'a
Acre

Rosh Pinna

Sea of
Galilee

Haifa

Nazareth

Affule
Megiddo

Jenin

Netanya

Tulkarem

Nablus

River Jordan

TRANSJORDAN

Herzliya
Petah Tikva
Tel Aviv
Jaffa
Lydda
Ramleh

Amman

Rehovoth

Latroun
Jerusalem
Bethlehem

Dead Sea

Gaza

Beersheba

0	10	20	30 Miles
0		20	40 Kms

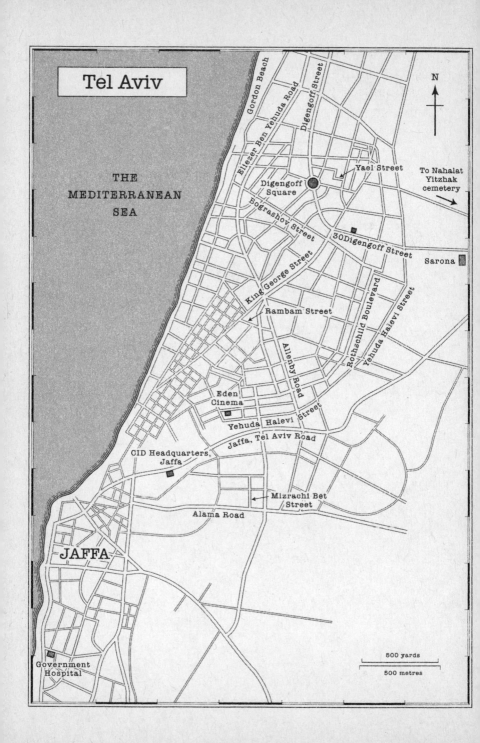

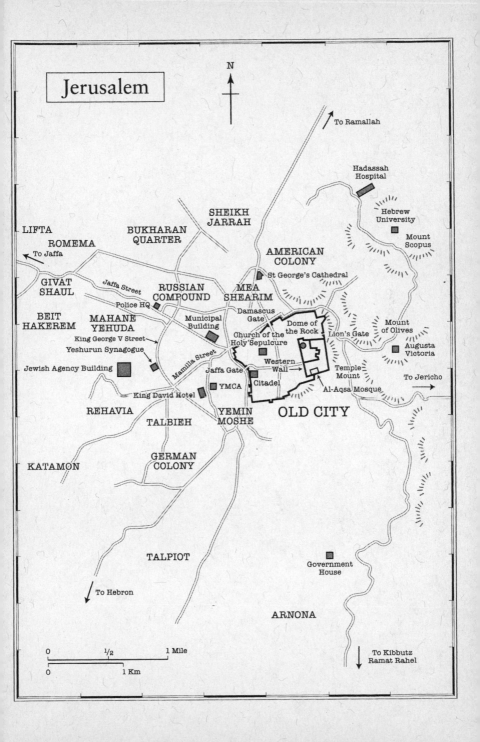

THE RECKONING

Prologue

'Where to Rest My Tired Head?
Where to Hide My Shivering Flesh?'

Avraham Stern was asleep on a makeshift bed in a corner of the living room. A few feet away, curled up on a couch, lay a slim, dark woman. Rain rattled on the window panes of the tiny rooftop flat and cold seeped through the thin walls. Four storeys below, the streets of Tel Aviv lay silent, blanketed in the darkness of the wartime blackout.[1]

At six o'clock there was a scratching at the door. The woman stirred. Her name was Tova Svorai and she was Stern's landlady and now his sole protector. She glanced over at him and saw he was already awake. They both knew what the sound meant. It was the signal announcing a visit by one of their few remaining contacts with the outside world, a girl called Hassia Shapira. But what was she doing here? Her instructions were to stay away, in case British detectives were watching and followed her to the flat. The clock on the cabinet ticked ominously. One, two, three seconds passed. Eventually Stern nodded. Tova rose and padded the few steps across the chilly tiles to the hallway, opened the door and pulled Hassia inside.

She was full of apologies. The police were everywhere but she had to risk coming. She was carrying a vital letter, one that might save Stern's life. He calmed her and led her to Tova's bed, telling her to get under the covers and keep warm until it was light and she could slip away. Then he sat down at the small square table in the hallway to read the message that Hassia had considered so important. It was indeed a lifeline. A former ally who had become an enemy was now offering him sanctuary. It was a generous and unexpected gesture, but Stern's mind was made up. There would be no running away

1

and no going back. In his neat hand he wrote a polite rejection. It declared: 'I am not one of those who voluntarily give themselves up to the police.'

Dawn broke just after seven o'clock. It was Thursday, 12 February 1942.

By 7.30, daylight was showing through the shutters, painting bars of light on the drab walls. It was safe now for their visitor to leave. Tova unlocked the door and Hassia descended the staircase and stepped outside. Mizrachi Bet Street was in the middle of Florentin, a neighbourhood of small factories and workshops and cheap apartment blocks. The working day had begun. The people who lived here were recent immigrants and Yiddish, Romanian and Polish mingled in the chatter, laughter and shouts drifting up to the flat.

Tova put out the breakfast things and boiled a kettle for tea. Stern paced to and fro, from hallway to living room and back again. He was thirty-four years old, slightly built, and five feet six inches tall. His thick, dark hair was swept back from his brow in a widow's peak above high cheekbones and grey, deep-set eyes that mesmerized his followers.

They sat down in the gloomy half-light to their breakfast of bread, cheese and jam, eating in silence. Both had much to think about. A few miles away Tova's husband, Moshe Svorai, lay under armed guard in a hospital ward, recovering from gunshot wounds sustained during his capture by British detectives. She had not dared to visit him for fear that she would be followed and would lead Stern's pursuers to his hideaway.

He was now the most wanted man in Palestine. His picture was blazoned across the newspapers and on billboards all over the country and there was a thousand-pound reward upon his head.* This slim, introspective figure was the man behind the wave of violence currently rocking Palestine. At the start of the year his

* The equivalent of a thousand pounds sterling and a very substantial sum.

followers had pulled off a wages snatch, killing two innocent bystanders in the process. When two of the perpetrators were caught, he declared war on the police. His men lured detectives to an apartment in Tel Aviv then triggered a bomb that killed three officers. In the ensuing manhunt, two members of the group were mortally wounded and two more captured.

These outrages dismayed Stern's fellow Jews. The Jewish Agency, which spoke for most of them, led the outcry, offering its whole-hearted support 'in order to track down the murderous gang and free Palestine … from the nightmare of hold-ups and assassinations'. The words invoked images of Prohibition-era Chicago and were chosen carefully to puncture Stern's grandiose self-image. In his short life he had morphed from promising scholar and poet to aspiring Zionist theorist to underground fighter. Now he seemed to think of himself as a warrior prophet, taking the name 'Yair' in homage to the leader of the Zealots who killed each other rather than surrender to the Romans. In the course of the journey he had formed an unshakeable conviction – that Britain was the main enemy of the Jews and the chief obstacle to the creation of a new Israel. The outbreak of the war had done nothing to change his mind. When his former comrades in the underground went off to fight alongside the British, Stern tried to undermine them by allying himself with their enemies, seeking deals with Fascist Italy and Nazi Germany.

His ambitions challenged not just Britain but the Zionist establishment and together, it seemed, they had defeated him. His organization was in ruins. Men he had regarded as brothers had given themselves up and the rest had been arrested or had gone to ground.

They finished breakfast, and Tova cleared away the plates. Stern sat down again at the small table and began writing, as he did most mornings, filling long strips of paper in neat, scholarly script. He had been writing poems to pass the long hours. One verse, at once self-pitying and defiant, read:

> Mad pouring rain
> And ardent bitter cold
> Where to rest my tired head?
> Where to hide my shivering flesh?

He sat hunched at the table, thin, dark and lonely. The pen scratched over the paper. All he could do was wait.

Three miles away, on the north-east outskirts of Tel Aviv, Assistant Superintendent Geoffrey Morton of the Palestine Police was setting off to work. He lived in Sarona, a cluster of attractive stone villas and bungalows on the edge of the city. He walked down the pathway to the waiting car, dressed in plainclothes detective's civvies: tweed jacket, grey flannels and trilby. His wife, Alice, a strong, intelligent woman, who taught at the Jaffa High School for Girls, was at his side.

Morton and Stern were almost exactly the same age. Physically they could hardly have been more different. Morton was over six feet tall, slim and well muscled with big, size-ten policeman's feet. He had blondish hair with a long face and a cleft chin that hinted at stubbornness. His eyes sloped down at the corners, giving him a slightly melancholy air. They were, however, quick to light up. He looked upon the complicated scene around him with dry amusement and the almost equine face split frequently into a grin. Stern and he nonetheless had things in common: they were both ruthless, ambitious and utterly convinced of their own righteousness.

The saloon carrying the Mortons hummed southwards along the highway on the six- or seven-minute journey. To the left stretched a landscape of palm trees and low stone houses, through which camels and donkeys and Arab men and women in long, loose clothing made their unhurried way. To the right gleamed the white Bauhaus-style apartment houses and office blocks of Jewish Tel

Aviv, a brand-new city, whose streets and boulevards were already choked with traffic.

Morton's reputation at that time was at its peak. He was intelligent, hard-working, famously brave, and to all appearances heading for the top. Since late 1939 he had commanded the Tel Aviv area Criminal Investigation Department, charged with countering Jewish and Arab political violence. With the start of the war, this work had taken on great importance. Britain was on the defensive everywhere and in the eastern Mediterranean the situation was getting worse. In Egypt, a hundred miles to the south, British forces were bracing for a renewed assault from the west by Rommel and the Afrika Korps.

Morton believed he was only a few steps away from removing one cause of concern. The Stern group's rampage was an affront to law and order in Palestine. If it managed to get backing from the Nazis it might develop into a more serious threat – a fifth column operating in the rear of British forces as they prepared for the next German advance.

Thanks to Morton, though, the group was on its knees. Sixteen days earlier, he had led a raid on a flat in central Tel Aviv where some of Stern's most dedicated followers were holed up. He had burst through the door and shot down three of them, including Tova Svorai's husband, Moshe. The raid had convinced some of the group to surrender and others had been rounded up. Without Stern, however, Morton's victory could not be complete. But where was he?

The big saloon stopped outside police headquarters, a bleak three-storey concrete block on the main road between Arab Jaffa and Tel Aviv. The couple got out and Alice set off for the high school, to give her first lesson of the day. Morton headed for his office, to await what he hoped was vital information.

The big prize was within his grasp. Some days before he had laid a trap which, if it came off, would complete the destruction of the Stern Gang. Two of the men he had shot in the raid had since died. The survivors, Moshe Svorai and the group's master bomb-maker

Yaacov Levstein, were recovering in the detention ward of the Government Hospital in Jaffa. They were in the charge of Sergeant Arthur Daly, an Irishman who spoke good Hebrew. Soon after the prisoners arrived, Daly had come to Morton with a plan. He proposed offering to act as a go-between with the detainees and their families. He had succeeded in winning Levstein's confidence and had been running messages to his mother. Disappointingly, the letters revealed nothing. But now Svorai had decided to make use of the sergeant's services. Might he perhaps provide a clue that would lead to the leader of the gang?

Morton had barely had time to settle behind his desk when the news he was awaiting came through. Shortly after ten o'clock his car pulled up outside 8 Mizrachi Bet Street. His big feet clattered up the fifty-nine steps to the door of the rooftop apartment. The details of what happened next would be endlessly contested. There were, though, two undeniable facts. Minutes after Geoffrey Morton entered the flat, Avraham Stern was dead and Morton had shot him.

At the time, the exact circumstances of the shooting scarcely seemed to matter. For the British, a dangerous enemy had been taken out of the game and a difficult case was closed. For the Jews, a gangster whose activities had brought shame on the community had been eliminated. Morton and his men were deluged with praise. But what seemed like an end was only a beginning. In death, Stern would prove far more menacing than he had ever been in life. The shots Morton fired would echo down the remaining years of British rule in Palestine and reverberate through the titanic events that shaped the birth of Israel. If you listen carefully, you can still hear them today.

ONE

'There Are Few Who Do Good and Many That Do Evil'

On the morning of 3 March 1938, a slim figure dressed in the blue and silver frock coat and white-plumed cocked hat of a Governor General of the British Colonial Service stood on the deck of HMS *Endurance* looking east towards the fast-approaching shore of the Holy Land. Haifa harbour had been dressed up for the occasion. Union Flags and bunting fluttered from ships and buildings. Chiaroscuro light effects added to the drama as the sun made intermittent appearances, darting in and out from behind the dark rain-clouds stacked up over Mount Carmel.

For Sir Harold MacMichael, the arrival in Palestine to take up his post as High Commissioner represented a considerable change in his fortunes. At the age of fifty-five, his career had been going nowhere. He had spent most of his working life in one of the empire's least congenial corners, imposing a semblance of order on the natives of Sudan. He immersed himself in its culture, spoke fluent Arabic and was admired for his scholarship, evident in such works as *Brands Used by the Chief Camel-Owning Tribes of Kordofan*. He was equally at home in the drawing rooms of the empire's elite. His mother, Sophia, was the sister of George Nathaniel Curzon, sometime Viceroy of India, whose hauteur had been immortalized in a famous piece of doggerel while he was still an undergraduate at Oxford.*

---

* My name is George Nathaniel Curzon/I am a most superior person/My cheeks are pink, my hair is sleek/I dine at Blenheim twice a week.

Ability and high connections had brought few obvious benefits. Departmental jealousies and bureaucratic rules stalled his progress and after nearly three decades in Sudan, the Colonial Office's reward was to shunt him sixteen hundred miles further south to be governor of Tanganyika. There he stewed for three years, uninspired and unfulfilled, treating the post as 'a disagreeable interlude before a more suitable position' came along.[1]

Then, in December 1937, a message from London offered a way out of the cul-de-sac. The High Commissioner of Palestine, Sir Arthur Wauchope, was moving on. Would MacMichael, the Colonial Secretary Sir William Ormsby-Gore wondered, be interested in replacing him? The answer was yes. And now he was entering his new domain, with all the pomp and circumstance that the empire could muster.

Endurance docked at a few minutes before nine o'clock. The rain had come to a respectful halt and the sea glittered in bright sunshine. Sir Harold, with Lady MacMichael and his daughter, Araminta, by his side, walked down the carpeted gangway and into the harbour's No. 3 Shed, transformed into a reception hall for the arrival ceremony. The officials and notables gathered to greet him stood to attention while the band of the Second West Kent Regiment played the national anthem and the warship's seventeen guns boomed out a salute. Sir Harold then mingled with the company, delighting those standing near him by chatting in Arabic to the mayor of Haifa, Hassan Bey Shukry.

Before the First World War the area had been under Ottoman rule, a backwater of a backward empire, unregarded by any of the major colonial powers. Britain's presence there stemmed from a slight-looking document issued in November 1917, which would have seismic consequences for the region and, indeed, the world.

The Balfour Declaration was less than seventy words long. It was made public in a letter from the Foreign Secretary Arthur James Balfour to the Jewish peer Lord Rothschild, a shy, bearded giant who preferred zoology to the family banking business. It stated: 'His

Majesty's Government view with favour the establishment in
Palestine of a national home for the Jewish people, and will use
their best endeavours to facilitate the achievement of this object, it
being clearly understood that nothing shall be done which may
prejudice the civil and religious rights of existing non-Jewish
communities in Palestine, or the rights and political status enjoyed
by Jews in any other country.'

The formula passed through many hands before it was finally
approved, yet no amount of drafting could resolve the contradiction
at its heart. At the time there were roughly 60,000 Jews in Palestine,
a mixture of Zionist pioneers trying to build a modern state on
historic territory and the poor and pious, who wished to end their
days on sacred soil. They were outnumbered twelve to one by Arabs,
the great majority of whom were Muslims.

Britain's motives for giving the first international endorsement
of mass Jewish immigration to Palestine – with the implicit goal
of establishing some sort of political entity there – were complicated. Among them was the fact that the war was stuck in a
bloody stalemate and pro-Zionist declarations were thought
useful to coax a reluctant United States into the fray. Possession
would provide a land bridge to the oil-producing areas of Iraq,
which now had great potential strategic importance. Persuasive
figures in the British political establishment, Winston Churchill
among them, also held the sincere conviction that the Jews
deserved a home of their own. Altruism might bring its reward.
Surely Jewish immigrants to Palestine would feel a debt of gratitude to their benefactors and cooperate closely with British plans
for the area?

It was obvious that mass immigration would cause huge social,
economic and political upheaval. How such a feat of human engineering would be achieved without friction, tension and – very
probably – bloodshed was neither explained nor even addressed.
Britain was in a hurry to finish the war and the consequences could
be dealt with later.

A month after the Balfour Declaration one major obstacle to its implementation was removed. The Ottoman Empire had sided with Germany in the war. Unbeknownst to its enfeebled ruler, Sultan Mehmed V, the British and French had in 1916 hatched a future carve-up of his Arab possessions, a shady bargain known as the Sykes–Picot Agreement. In 1917, British forces advanced from Egypt to secure their portion. On 11 December their commander Sir Edmund Allenby entered Jerusalem's Old City on foot to take its surrender. Palestine soon belonged to Britain by right of conquest and, at the 1919 Versailles peace conference, it hung onto it. Britain's governance was formalized when the League of Nations granted it the Mandate to rule Palestine in 1922.

Fifteen years on, a territory that had been acquired in a spirit of hasty opportunism was starting to feel like an accursed burden. When MacMichael accepted the post, the Colonial Secretary William Ormsby-Gore left him in no doubt of what he had got himself into. 'I am very grateful indeed to you for consenting to take on what I must admit is the hardest and toughest job under the Colonial Office,' he wrote. 'The various problems of Palestine [are] among the most difficult that the empire has been confronted with in its history.' Given that Britain's domains included the vast human mosaic of the Indian subcontinent, Canada and Australia, widely scattered footholds on the shores of the world's oceans and large chunks of Africa, this was saying something. Palestine represented only a tiny sliver of the great imperial pie. The populated area was less than 150 miles from north to south and no more than fifty miles wide. But as the British had learned with Ireland, the smallest morsels could cause the greatest heartburn. As with Ireland, it was the inhabitants who were the problem. 'The human material, both Jewish and Arab is particularly difficult,' lamented Ormsby-Gore. 'The country is full of arms and bitterness and there are few who do good and many that do evil.'[2]

There had been trouble from the start. With intoxicating swiftness, the Zionists' dream of a Jewish state had become a practical proposition. From 1918 Jews flocked to Palestine, most of them refugees from an Eastern Europe shaken up by revolution and the aftershocks of the First World War and rancid with anti-Semitism. They brought energy and modern attitudes and skills and came armed with money, buying up large swathes of cultivable land, mainly from Arab proprietors.

For the Arabs of Palestine, rooted in the stasis of centuries, the rush of change was shocking and then threatening. Anti-Jewish riots broke out in Jerusalem in 1920 and the port city of Jaffa in 1921. They were stoked by a sandy-haired, lisping rabble-rouser, Haj Amin al-Husseini, the Grand Mufti of Jerusalem, and, by virtue of his office, the leading Muslim legal authority. The Mandate's rulers remained serene. They were used to this sort of thing. Then in August 1929 came an explosion of violence that could not be ignored. In a week of murder, rape and arson 133 Jews lost their lives. In suppressing the pogrom, 116 Arabs were killed. British complacency evaporated.

London dispatched a commission to investigate, the first of many that would wrestle with the Palestine problem. Essentially, it addressed Arab grievances and recommended reining in Jewish immigration and restricting land purchases. It was a vain proposal. Not only would it prove unworkable. The British had revealed that their commitment to the Balfour Declaration was faltering and from now on Jewish suspicions and disillusionment would grow.

In the meantime, though, it was the Arabs who were causing the trouble. MacMichael would be taking over in the middle of a full-blooded uprising. Hitler's rise to power in Germany had triggered a new Jewish exodus. In 1935 more than 60,000 Jews arrived in the country, and more were trickling in illegally. There were now about 430,000 in Palestine – roughly a third of the total population.[3] It only needed a spark to ignite Arab anger and that came in April 1936 when the murder of two Arabs by Jewish extremists in retaliation for the murder of two Jews sent violence rippling through the country.

Arab bands, reinforced by mercenaries and sympathizers from Syria and Iraq, attacked Jews, policemen and soldiers. They felled telegraph poles, ambushed cars and blew up railway lines and the oil pipeline that ran through Palestinian territory on its way from Mesopotamia to Haifa. A general strike lasted for six months. The rebellion was coordinated by the Arab Higher Committee, a collection of notables dominated by the Mufti. Their demands were simple: an end to Jewish immigration and land sales and a representative council that would pave the way for an independent Arab state.

London responded with another commission, led by Lord Peel. It arrived in October 1936 and there was a lull while it went about its work. Its report was published in July 1937 and came up with a drastic but inevitable-seeming solution – the partition of Palestine into an Arab and a Jewish state. The Jews gave qualified backing to the plan. The Arabs rejected it outright and now, as the security arrangements for MacMichael's onward journey to Jerusalem made plain, the revolt was back in full swing.

Just before ten o'clock the High Commissioner's party boarded a special train. The authorities were expecting trouble. As the engine steamed slowly away from the harbour, it was preceded by a flatbed trolley, mounted with a machine gun manned by soldiers of the Royal Scots Fusiliers. Others stood guard at regular intervals along the track. For the first few miles three Royal Air Force aircraft weaved in formation overhead.

No matter how fiercely the rebellion burned, it was clear that the Jews were in Palestine to stay. As the special train passed Tel Aviv and clattered onto the spur line that climbed up to Jerusalem, it came within sight of the settlement of Rehovot. It was the home of the scientific research centre run by Dr Chaim Weizmann, the Russian-born Manchester University chemistry lecturer who was Zionism's most effective lobbyist in Britain and the president of the World Zionist Organization. A few days earlier he had been visited by 'William Hickey' of the *Daily Express* – the pseudonym of the influential boulevardier Tom Driberg. The journalist had been impressed by the 'sun-bathed orange groves, orchards, Riviera-like gardens, the white-walled Institute where seventy scientists from many countries are working, the garden city beyond ...'[4] In the subsequent piece, Weizmann had delivered his judgement on the partition plan. He was prepared to accept it 'on the "half a loaf" principle' and believed that 'with slight improvements, most Jews' would do the same.

Even so, he made it clear that the territory allotted to the Jews was not nearly big enough to absorb Europe's persecuted masses. 'No territory you could produce would hold them,' he said. 'There are five or six million of them – in Germany, Hungary, Romania, Poland. You can't fight a tidal wave. All we can do is salvage the children. Concentrating on young Jews, I anticipate bringing one and a half million of them into Palestine in the next twenty years.'

When Driberg suggested that this was fanciful, Weizmann retorted: 'It may be sentiment but we have converted the sentiment into dynamic power.' It was the English, he said, who were sentimental – 'sentimental about the Arabs. They admire picturesque inefficiency. It is the tourist attitude. We may be spoiling the landscape but five years ago all this was bare desert.' Driberg was convinced. 'It is this spectacular success of the Zionist colonisation,' he concluded, 'that has made the clash acute. The Arabs are in retreat from the land.'

It was true that many British officials had a soft spot for the Arabs, a combination of affection shot through with condescension. Before taking the job, MacMichael had sought the counsel of Sir Robert Brooke-Popham, until recently commander of the Royal Air Force in the Middle East. He had given freely of his advice. 'One sees the Arab seated under a tree and playing on his pipes to encourage his sheep and goats to graze,' he mused.[5] 'One goes down to Tel Aviv and one sees all the bustle and blatancy of a mushroom-like town. From the purely economic point of view, far more wealth is being produced and circulated in Tel Aviv than by any number of Arabs playing to their goats. But one may be permitted to wonder which method really does more ultimate good in the world, and I fancy the Arab is feeling the same sort of thing.'

His paternalistic sympathy was matched with a Victorian belief that to spare the rod was to spoil the child. 'As of course you know, what the Arab appreciates is swift punishment,' he wrote. 'Any delay he regards as weakness.'

MacMichael did know. His high, donnish forehead, receding chin and quiet manner disguised an outlook that was as hard and sharp as flint. Familiarity with colourful, oriental cultures did not incline him to leniency towards colourful, oriental rebels. He had a strict sense of racial hierarchy with the Sudanese of the Upper Nile who lived in a state of 'semi-simian savagery' at the bottom and the British at the top. MacMichael, wrote a historian of the Anglo-Egyptian Sudan, combined 'great intelligence, extensive study and experience [and] a commanding ability in debate' with 'a rigidity of standards, and a public presence of icy reserve'.[6] He brought to every problem 'logic, orderliness, orthodoxy' and a keen awareness of protocol. The daytime temperature in Khartoum averaged 99 degrees Fahrenheit, yet he insisted on his officials being properly attired in jackets and ties when dealing with natives, for 'any informality of dress and manner ... might be resented and undermine authority'.

MacMichael's orthodoxy was one of the main reasons he had been chosen for the Palestine job. With the Arab revolt showing no signs of abating, London needed a man who could be relied on to follow instructions and take hard measures. That had not been the style of his predecessor. Wauchope was unpopular with his officials, the military and ultimately his chiefs back in London, whose belief that he was too soft on the rebels had hastened the decision to retire him.

As Ormsby-Gore made clear in his welcoming letter, there could be no question of backing down in the face of force. 'We have to remain in Palestine for strategic reasons and for reasons of political prestige,' he declared. He did not hide from MacMichael his opinion of Wauchope's administration, which had been 'weak and poor to say the least of it'. The situation required 'firm' as well as 'wise' handling.

A tougher strategy against the rebels was already evident. During Wauchope's absence on sick leave his Chief Secretary, a genial, indiscreet but above all efficient Cornishman called William Battershill, moved to impose some grip. The government approved his request for a crackdown and on 1 October 1937 those members of the Higher Committee who had not already fled were rounded up, put on a British warship in Haifa and deported to the Seychelles. The Mufti, who Battershill discovered on first greeting him 'had a hand like a piece of damp putty',[7] took refuge in Jerusalem inside the Haram al-Sharif. The compound enclosed the Dome of the Rock, the shrine that marks the spot from where Mohammad made his night journey to heaven on the white steed Buraq and a place so bristling with religious sensitivities that it was a no-go area for British hobnailed boots. From there he soon escaped, disguised as a woman by some accounts, and made his way to French-controlled Lebanon, to carry on agitating.

Martial law was imposed and henceforth rebels were tried by military courts which could impose death sentences for the mere possession of a firearm. The Palestine garrison had been steadily reinforced since the troubles and was now 20,000-strong.

The most important element in the struggle against unrest was not the army but the police. The Palestine Police Force (PPF) was set up in 1920 with a core of British officers controlling a much larger native force of Arabs and a smaller number of Jews. It had failed to prevent, and struggled to contain, the persistent outbreaks of violence. Late in 1937 two colonial police veterans, Charles Tegart and David Petrie, were brought in to devise a strategy against the revolt and to carry out reforms.

Their most dramatic proposals were to build a network of re-inforced concrete forts at key points around Palestine and a barbed-wire barrier along its northern and eastern frontiers to stem the flow of arms, fighters and supplies from Lebanon, Syria and Iraq. They also called for the strengthening of the Criminal Investigation Department. It was clear that the police would continue to play the lead role in gathering information about political subversion in Palestine. They, after all, lived in the place and were kept up to date on the moods and machinations of the Arab and Jewish communi-ties via their local employees. The RAF had a permanent presence in the country and air force intelligence officers made some contribu-tion to the information picture. The army units, though, came and went, and military intelligence resources had anyway been drasti-cally run down after the war. On the recommendations of Tegart and Petrie, the CID would be transformed into a vigorous, system-atic and efficient service aimed at penetrating the workings of the multiple organizations – Jewish and Arab – that threatened to undermine the rule of the Mandate.

The authority of the British was being challenged everywhere. It was essential to demonstrate confidence and resolve and remind the local populations where the balance of power lay. As MacMichael's train laboured up the switchback track that led through the stony slopes of the Jerusalem hills, three RAF aircraft appeared overhead once more, swooping and wheeling through the thunderclouds glowering over the Holy City. By the time it pulled into Jerusalem station at 2 p.m., the heavens had opened and when the band of the Black Watch had played a few bars of the national anthem Sir Harold and his party were whisked off to Government House.

There, in the ballroom, 200 guests were waiting. Sir Harold's finery was matched by the costumes of many of the assembly. Soldiers, policemen and airmen were in full dress uniform. Prince Naif, son of King Abdullah, Emir of the British protectorate of Transjordan, wore Bedouin costume. The *Palestine Post*'s reporter declared that it was the assembled patriarchs, priests and rabbis who 'presented the most striking picture, rivalled only by the Moslem religious dignitaries in their red tarbushes, white turbans and black capes'.[8]

They stood as Sir Harold signed the royal commission of appointment and Chief Justice Trusted, wearing full-bottomed wig and purple cape, gave his welcoming speech. According to the *Post*, it was 'very brief and delivered with deliberation and emphasis'. After paying tribute to each of Sir Harold's four predecessors in Palestine, he concluded with an observation with which the new High Commissioner was by now all too depressingly familiar: 'Many major problems await your excellency's consideration,' he rumbled, 'and we cannot doubt that you are faced with an arduous task.'

Sir Harold's reply was short and frank. He was not going to make a speech as he had only been in Jerusalem for half an hour and was starting work in a country of which he knew 'practically nothing'. That night, in a twelve-minute broadcast to the people he now governed, he again protested his ignorance, saying he was 'sure of little but the incompleteness of my own knowledge of conditions and personalities'. He nonetheless laid down the principles on which he would govern. The first was 'the duty to maintain the authority of His Britannic Majesty and the firm establishment of law and order'.

This uncompromising message was softened by a declaration of his good intentions to all. 'The motives that will actuate me will be simple ones of good faith and honest endeavour to do what is best for all concerned with firmness and impartiality,' he said. 'Nor does impartiality present difficulties for me, for the problem is not one upon which I have any preconceived ideas or bias.'[9]

It was not impartiality, though, that the Arabs and Jews wanted from the British. As MacMichael would soon learn, each side would be clamouring for his undivided support. After delivery, the speech was re-broadcast in Arabic and Hebrew. There was nothing much in it to indicate to the listeners that this cold, efficient man held the key to the Palestine conundrum. Looking back over the day, the

Palestine Post was reduced to taking comfort in superstition. 'There were three good omens in connection with His Excellency's arrival in Haifa,' it reported on its front page. 'A rainbow was seen over the Bay of Acre as the *Enterprise* drew near the harbour. As Sir Harold entered the transit shed, a dove flew the length of the building. An old Arab proverb welcoming an honoured guest says "when you came, the rain came".'[10]

TWO

'This Was the Job for Me'

The rainbow that arced over Haifa that day would have been visible to Geoffrey Morton as he went about his duties controlling the city's traffic during Sir Harold's arrival and departure. He was not the sort of man to believe in omens. Life was good. He was thirty years old, fit, happy and second in command of the Haifa urban district. His service record was crammed with seventeen commendations and in the 1937 New Year's Honours' List he became the first recipient of the new Colonial Police Medal in recognition of 'distinguished and valuable services'. He had got where he was not through luck but by hard work and determination.

Haifa was a good posting, the most attractive city in Palestine. It faced onto the Mediterranean which sparkled like a sheet of sapphires in the bright daylight and glowed like molten gold in the setting sun. To outsiders it seemed blessedly civilized, a relief after Tel Aviv's perpetual building works and Jerusalem's unedifying religious rivalries, which were enough to put some of the devout among the Mandate's rulers off God for ever. When the Arab revolt erupted, though, Haifa had felt the shock waves.

Morton was there for the start of the trouble. One morning in May 1936 he was dispatched to deal with a crowd of Arabs who were gathering in the souk. They waved knives and sticks and shouted anti-Jewish and anti-British slogans and were soon surging through the streets towards the District Commissioner's offices in the middle of town.

When the main body was blocked by a police cordon, a break-away band of troublemakers regrouped on Kingsway, one of Haifa's main streets, and began stoning Jewish cars. Morton was one of the small squad sent to deal with them. He was wearing a steel helmet – standard riot issue. As he stood in the lee of a building discussing the situation with a fellow officer, someone dropped a coping stone from three storeys up, which caught him square on the head.

He was knocked unconscious but when he came round he carried on with his duties. The requested reinforcements did not materialize. The mob was getting ever more threatening. The senior officer present, Inspector G. F. 'Dinger' Ring, decided it was time for action. The Palestine Police had a detailed drill for dealing with mobs. Ring yelled out a proclamation in Arabic, calling on the rioters to go home or face the consequences. The Arabs responded with a shower of missiles. He now ordered the designated marksman in the party, Sergeant 'Nobby' Clarke, to move to the next step. He 'went through the rifle drill as calmly and efficiently as if we were giving on the parade ground a demonstration of our humane methods to a delegation from the League of Nations,' Morton recalled.[1]

First Clarke held a cartridge aloft to leave the crowd in no doubt of what was coming and give them time to do the sensible thing. The gesture had no effect. He loaded the round into the breech and thrust the bolt home. There was another pause, then Ring gave the order to take aim – but to wound, not to kill. 'Slowly and deliberately' Clarke drew a bead on the knees of the mob's ringleader. Morton saw several stones and sticks hit the sergeant's body 'but he stood there, steady as a rock, resisting the irresistible instinct to flinch and duck'. Morton speculated later that perhaps a missile had spoiled Clarke's aim or the victim had been stooping to pick up a stone when he was hit. Whatever the reason, an instant after the order to fire, the ringleader 'lay, 20 yards away in front of the mob, stone dead, with a neat, round hole between the eyes'. The gunshot was followed by 'a split second of petrified silence and then by the vague sounds of myriad feet running for dear life'. Moments later 'there was not a soul to be seen, and that particular riot was over'.

In later life Morton recounted this incident – and many more like it – with relish. He liked the smell of danger. He welcomed the psychological challenge inherent in every confrontation between the forces of law and order and the mob. Inevitably the police were outnumbered and, though armed, would be overwhelmed if the rioters went on the rampage. By keeping their nerve, though, and reading the mood of the crowd, good policemen should be able to impose their will on far superior forces. Service in the Palestine Police would give him many opportunities for matching his will and skills against the enemies of British rule.

Like many in the force, he had arrived there almost by chance. Geoffrey Morton was the second son of William Jackson Morton, a lively character who seemed to embody the vigour, public-mindedness and optimism of early twentieth-century Britain. He was the manager of a busy branch of United Dairies, whose horse-drawn carts supplied London housewives with their daily milk and butter. The premises were in Urlwin Street, Lambeth, south London, next to the yellow-brick arches of a railway viaduct that carried commuters and shoppers back and forth between Blackfriars Station a mile or so away on the north bank of the River Thames and the southeast suburbs of London. Mr Morton lived a few dozen yards from his place of work with his wife, Sarah, two sons and daughter and a maid in a large nine-room terraced house. Their home was a middle-class outpost in a boisterously working-class area. It faced onto Camberwell Road, a wide, traffic-ridden street that during the day was lined with barrows selling fruit and vegetables manned by coarse, chatty costermongers. The many pubs, music halls and cinemas ensured that the area was equally lively at night.

At first sight, William Morton appeared a man of monumental respectability. He attended the local Anglican church on Sundays and was an enthusiastic Freemason. For thirty years he sat as a Conservative member on the London County Council, the powerful municipal body that ran many of the capital's services, and, as a lay magistrate, dispensed justice to the drunks and delinquents of the borough. When the war came in 1914, he was forty-three, too old for the colours. He signed up instead as a special policeman, rising to command the auxiliaries in Lambeth and neighbouring Southwark. On his death in 1940, the local newspaper described him as 'one of the best-known figures in South London'.[2]

Behind the austere frontage of conformity, though, there gleamed a sense of fun. Edward VII was on the throne when Geoffrey was born and William Morton shared his sovereign's enjoyment of card games and long, smoke-filled evenings. Like the monarch, he did not allow his wife's strict sense of rectitude to interfere with his own enjoyable routines of meeting friends and visiting music halls.

Later in his own life Geoffrey Morton would give an exhaustive account of his professional career. He said very little about his boyhood and adolescence – as if it had no bearing on who he was or what he became. He left nothing on record concerning his brother, Arnold, four years his senior and a 'black sheep' who disappeared early from the family story. Much more is recorded about his younger sister, Marion, an ambitious, spirited girl who went on to become a teacher and an international standard netball player.

He started at his first proper school aged eight in January 1916. Every morning he set off from Camberwell Road on the two-mile journey to St Olave's Grammar School, an impressive red-brick building, adorned with stone bas-reliefs of philosophers and poets, which sat on the south bank of the Thames next to Tower Bridge. 'Stogs', as it was known to generations of pupils, was founded in 1571 to provide free education to boys from modest homes. The curriculum in 1916 included scripture, Latin, Greek, French, German, Spanish, English grammar and literature, history, geography, arithmetic, algebra, geometry, trigonometry, chemistry, physics and botany. Great store was set on the values of the rugby field and the cricket pitch. Olavians filled the ranks of the professions. They were lawyers and bankers, accountants and teachers and doctors. They also served the empire as soldiers, sailors and administrators.

The list of distinguished Old Boys was long. It seemed unlikely that Geoffrey Morton would ever be among them. 'He has been somewhat disappointing,' recorded his form master, Mr Midgley, when Geoffrey had been at the school barely six months. 'His work has shown ability but he is not consistently keen.'[3]

The school's ethos was Victorian and Edwardian – forward looking, but intensely patriotic and nostalgic for an imagined chivalric past. Its solid brick walls could not shield it from the very modern war being fought across the Channel. Stogs men were floundering in the khaki mud of Picardy, and dying at the same rate as everyone else. In Geoffrey's first year, the school magazine was full of death notices and unsparing accounts of the fighting. 'In the Royal Army Medical Corps we see the most terrible side of war,' wrote an Old Boy, Leslie Hocking.[4] 'We see strong men pass us on their way up the trenches and a few hours later it is our duty to fetch some back as terribly disfigured and mangled corpses.' Hocking was killed before his account appeared.

The conflict was on the doorstep. Britons could no longer rely on the surrounding seas to insulate them from violence when the country went to war. In the summer of 1915 Zeppelin airships started to drop bombs on London. In 1917, a raid demolished homes in Albany Road, a few hundred yards away from the Mortons' house, killing ten and injuring twenty-four.

Occasionally, Geoffrey responded to his teachers' urgings to try harder. The rallies were brief. Now and again he shone at French and German. His best subject was English grammar. In everything else he was towards the bottom of the class. He was particularly weak at scripture. William Morton's conventional piety had failed to rub off on his son and Geoffrey's indifference to God would persist all his life.

He left St Olave's in December 1922, three months after his fifteenth birthday. His penultimate report carried a wounding parting shot from the headmaster, William Rushbrooke. 'Failure in effort is culpable,' he pronounced. 'He can't smile a path to success.'[5]

Geoffrey's smile was one of his most noticeable characteristics. In the school photographs he always wears a shy grin that makes him seem vulnerable and very young. This immaturity was also commented on by the teachers. 'He is often childish and silly in his behaviour,' his last class master, L.W. Myers, observed in the same report.

Geoffrey's subsequent amnesia about his schooldays can be explained as a simple unwillingness to recall a period of prolonged failure. Qualifications came to mean a lot to him. In his police career he accumulated many yet he left St Olave's with none. In a recording made at the end of his life he confessed to being 'embarrassed' by this.[6]

Stogs boys were expected to stay until they were at least sixteen, when they sat for the School Certificate, which was an essential requirement for a halfway decent job. He never explained the early departure, but it is unlikely that money was the problem. The school fees were modest and the family's circumstances were comfortable enough to fund Marion's education through school and university. The likeliest reason was that there seemed little point, to parents and teachers, perhaps to Geoffrey himself, in staying on.

Without his 'school cert' he could expect only a dead-end job. He found one at the meat and poultry market at Smithfield in the City of London, where, each day, from the early hours, porters in blood-stained overalls humped carcasses from cold stores to butchers' vans. He worked as a clerk for a provisions merchants, no more than a 'general dogsbody' he would say later.[7]

At some point he quit Smithfield and started work as a low-level manager with his father's firm, United Dairies. It was scarcely more rewarding than clerking. He soon decided that his 'future lay elsewhere' but where exactly he had no idea.

In the early summer of 1926, chance pointed him in the right direction. Beyond the dairy walls, a great national crisis was brewing. Britain was in the throes of a social upheaval that seemed to some the prelude to a possible revolution. In May, the General Council of the Trades Union Congress called a general strike in an attempt to block proposals to cut miners' pay and increase their hours. Nearly two million workers responded. The government set up volunteer units to maintain essential services. Tens of thousands of conservative-minded males stepped forward to do their bit to keep the country running, including Geoffrey Morton.

When the strike was announced he joined one of the expanded special police units that sprang up to assist the forces of law and order. They were untrained, unarmed save for a whistle to summon help and wore civilian clothes with only an armband to denote their authority. On the second day of the strike he turned up at the nearest police station and awaited instructions. The main drama of the day was an attempt by strikers to blockade the London County Council tramcar depot at Camberwell Green and paralyse local transport. One tram had managed to break through and travel half a mile to the Elephant and Castle, a busy road junction. It had been halted by pickets and Morton and a 'burly constable' were sent to the scene of the trouble.

When they arrived, he wrote, they found 'a large crowd of men – several thousand of them – centred around a stationary tramcar to which they had clearly conceived a marked antipathy. All professional transport workers were on strike, so that the presence of the tram meant that it must be manned by volunteers – or blacklegs as the strikers would have called them.'[8]

Morton 'saw smoke and flames rise from one end of the vehicle, to be greeted by an ironic cheer from its attackers'. Preoccupied by the spectacle of the burning tram, the strikers had not noticed the pair arrive. Despite the number present, Morton's hefty companion 'wasted no time. He did not trouble to draw his baton, but with a verve and determination which should assuredly have earned him his cap for England at Rugger, started to elbow his way through the mob towards the tram, with the strikers giving way right and left beneath the impetus of his progress.'

Morton followed in the constable's wake, 'safe in the vacuum created by his passage'. As the crowd registered the arrival of the police, the missile-throwing faltered. One man remained oblivious, and 'brought his arm back over his shoulder, nearly hitting my policeman on the nose as he did so, and launched a bottle containing a colourless fluid at the tram. As the missile flew from his hand some instinct must have warned him of impending danger for, with a look of horror on his face, he turned his head and saw the huge bulk of the constable towering over him.' The rioter blurted out an apology only to be 'answered by a laconic: "Too late, mate!"' The constable's baton, 'which had materialised as if by magic, came down smartly on the bottle-thrower's unprotected left shoulder. In another second he had disappeared behind us, the baton was back in its pocket and we were on our way once more.' Soon reinforcements arrived, the rioters were dispersed and order was restored.

Despite the jaunty tone of this account, the incident made a deep impression. Writing many years later, after a long and incident-packed police career, Morton declared he had 'never anywhere witnessed a more effective display of sheer police sense than that given by that ordinary, uniformed, duty constable in dealing with that mob'. The arrival of reinforcements had relieved him of the need for a further display of initiative but Morton was convinced that 'had they not arrived I am sure that my friend was prepared, as a simple matter of duty, to place himself squarely between the tram crew and the rioters, who would only have got at their intended victims over his dead body'.

The episode had given him an intoxicating taste of the possibilities of police work. It offered power, a whiff of danger, opportunities for heroics in the discharge of duty, and above all adventure and a way out of the tedium of his current existence.

When the strike ended after nine days in utter defeat for the trade unions, Geoffrey stayed on in the 'specials'. Nothing he did subsequently, though, matched the excitement of those first days. During the next three years of service he carried out mundane police duties, doing well enough to rise to the rank of sergeant. He was still stuck in his boring job. Every day he scanned the small ads in the newspaper looking for a way out, but the prospects of finding one were dwindling. At the end of 1929 the Great Depression settled on the country and millions were out of work.

In the late summer, advertisements began to appear calling for recruits to the Palestine Police Force. The anti-Jewish rioting of August had demonstrated the urgent need for more British officers. The Colonial Office was offering adventure, comradeship, sport and sunshine and an absence of academic qualifications was no handicap. It seemed the answer to Morton's prayers. 'The more I thought about it,' he wrote, 'the more I was convinced that this was the job for me. It had everything, and surely I had quite a lot to offer in return – I was fit and strong, reasonably literate and willing to learn.'[9]

He set off to apply in person at the offices of the Crown Agents for the Colonies at Number 4, Millbank, Westminster, overlooking the Thames. He left after a brief interview with 'an acute feeling of depression'. Preference was being given to ex-servicemen and being a sergeant in the specials did not compensate for his lack of military experience.

The walk home through the dreary streets of autumnal south London only intensified his determination to escape. A few months later more recruiting ads appeared. This time Morton did not apply in person but simply sent for the application forms, and filled them in with no mention of the previous setback. He was summoned for a brief interview and a medical, both of which he passed. He was in. On a bitterly cold morning in February 1930, together with twenty-nine other embryo policemen, he set sail from Southampton for Port Said, Egypt. The boat was the *Esperance Bay*. It was, he said later, a good name. 'Esperance' meant 'hope', the spirit sustaining all of them as they headed off to their new lives.[10]

The force they were joining had an exotic, frontier feel. They wore the kalpak, a high-crowned astrakhan cap, a legacy of the Ottoman era, and the rural sections patrolled the dusty fields, parched hills and stone-walled villages of the territory on horseback. The British contingent contained a high proportion of adventurers and risk-takers. It seemed to some of its members that they had joined a sort of British version of the French Foreign Legion, whose ranks were filled with men who had enlisted to escape or forget.

'Between us,' wrote Morton, 'we represented every conceivable stratum of life in the British Isles, from the heir of an impoverished Earl, products of exclusive public schools and graduates of famous universities to professional bruisers, coalminers, regular soldiers and really tough Tyneside Geordies who played a better game of football in their bare feet than they did with boots on.'[11]

The PPF had been set up as a gendarmerie, whose main function was as shock troops ready to bash the heads of unruly locals at times of unrest. The British element kept to themselves, treated their Palestinian colleagues with a condescension bordering on contempt and were not required to have any knowledge of either Arabic or Hebrew. Morton noted that 'the policeman of any rank who took the trouble to learn even a smattering of everyday language in the vernacular was looked upon … with scorn, only very slightly tinged with respect or envy.'[12]

It would take Morton some time to settle into his calling. By the time of MacMichael's arrival he was an up and coming young officer, winning the attention of his superiors with his efforts on the front line in the fight to suppress the Arab revolt. As the spring advanced it was clear that violence was not only intensifying. It was no longer an Arab monopoly.

On the hot afternoon of Monday, 11 April 1938, a crowded train stood ready to depart from the Iraq Petroleum Company pipeline terminal in Haifa Bay where oil from the Iraq fields ended its journey across the desert. There were several hundred passengers on board, most of them Arab workers who were returning home at the end of their shifts. Just before 4 p.m. an Arab sergeant of the Palestine Police was patrolling nearby when someone pointed out two suspicious-looking packages on board the train. He told the driver to delay departure while he removed the parcels. They were placed next to a guardhouse where one of them exploded, killing a Druze police constable. The second then went off, mortally wounding an Arab bystander.

Shortly afterwards, three buses taking Jewish workers from a nearby building site back to Haifa passed by. The Arabs decided that the Jews were to blame for the explosions. They started hurling stones and a small riot ensued with both sides exchanging missiles.

Now a police team from Haifa arrived on the scene. They were led by Sergeant Walter Medler, a conscientious and popular twenty-seven-year-old. By 5.15 p.m. calm had been restored and passengers were waiting to re-board the train. Then Sergeant Medler made another discovery. Stuffed under one of the seats was a sack, tied at the neck with string. Medler picked it up, threw it out of the window and ducked. Nothing happened. He stepped from the train and began, warily, to untie the string. A second later Medler was dead. So, too, was Constable Michael Ward, a twenty-two-year-old only recently arrived in Palestine who was standing behind him. The explosion, it was learned later, was caused by a time bomb – quite a sophisticated device by the standards of the time and place.[13]

It had been Medler's bad luck to be called to the oil terminal. As a junior sergeant at the Haifa police station he worked under Geoffrey Morton, acting as his deputy on many operations. That day Morton had taken a squad on a duty that was becoming part of their regular routine. Twenty miles to the south of Haifa at Wadi Hawareth, Bedouins were being evicted from land they had grazed their livestock on for generations. It had been sold over their heads to Jews who planned to build a kibbutz and the police were there to intervene in the likely event of trouble. It was to Morton and many other policemen 'one of the more distasteful tasks' they were asked to perform.[14] Normally, Morton would have taken Medler with him and left his senior sergeant, Jack Bourne, behind to deal with emergencies. He wrote later that on this day, however, 'for some reason which in retrospect I have never been able to understand, I decided to take Jack Bourne with me to Wadi Hawareth and to leave Wally Medler in charge in Haifa'.[15] The eviction went off without incident. Morton returned from a long and dispiriting day to be told Medler and Ward were dead. The death of comrades was almost a routine event by now, but the news hit Morton very hard. Medler was not just a valued colleague but a close friend. He came from Norwich where his father was a wholesale fruit merchant and went to the city's Junior Technical College, a pioneering academy for the sons of ordinary families, but left early to work in a solicitor's office. Then, according to the local newspaper report on his death 'the opportunity of seeing something more of the world and the prospects of advancement attracted him to the Palestine [Police]'. His hopes had been realized. In 1935 he became the youngest sergeant in the force. He was a good sportsman and the police welterweight boxing champion.[16]

Even allowing for the generosity shown to the newly (and violently) deceased it is clear that Medler was an exceptional man. 'Trim and neat in figure, whether in charge of a traffic escort or on the sports field, in giving evidence in court or in the boxing ring, Walter Medler bespoke his character' ran the appreciation by 'BWF' in the *Palestine Post*. He was 'an omnivorous reader, yet not a bookworm, a popular messmate and comrade ... the all-round athlete who had time for good books, good concerts, good contacts and wholesome entertainment'. Medler's rank, BWF concluded, might be that of 'second class sergeant', but 'his rank among his many friends was "prince"'.[17]

Morton, like most of his colleagues, took a cheerfully fatalistic view of life and death but the loss of his friend brought on an uncharacteristic fit of the blues. 'Haifa lost much of the savour it had previously held for me,' he wrote. 'I was lonely and miserable and found it difficult to concentrate on my work.'[18] After hearing the news he went to say his farewell to his friend in the mortuary. A silver pencil, splintered by the explosion, was sticking out of his breast pocket. He took it and kept it as a memento for the rest of his life.[19] Among Morton's papers is a photograph of Wally Medler. It is

a well-framed shot showing him sunbathing with another policeman, Arthur Brument, next to the ruins of a Crusader castle on the
Mediterranean at Athlit, just south of Haifa. Even though it is in
monochrome you can almost feel the heat of the burning sand and
admire the depth of the two men's suntans.

Who had planted the bombs? The likeliest culprits were right-
wing Zionists, angered by the campaign of murder and arson being
waged by the Arab rebels against the Jews of Palestine. In the face of
Arab aggression, the instinct of the Zionist establishment was to
exercise *havlagah* – to show restraint and to suppress the desire to
hit back. Such a stance was both moral and practical. Retaliation
would almost certainly mean killing innocent Arabs along with the
guilty, and undermine Zionism's claim to high ethical standards
both in its aims and in its conduct.

In showing restraint the leaders of Palestine's Jews also hoped to
gain political advantage. The great majority of Zionists, left and
right, believed that their interests lay in cooperating with the empire.
By holding back they were relieving the hard-pressed security
services of an extra burden. Their good behaviour, they calculated,
might persuade the British to look more favourably on their ambitions for statehood.

As the Arab revolt rumbled on and the murder of innocent
Jews persisted, patience with *havlagah* began to wear thin. The political divisions of the Jews in Palestine corresponded to the politics
of the countries they had left behind. The ideologies of old Europe
were mirrored in the numerous parties and organizations that flour-
ished in the Holy Land and the political spectrum contained
communists, socialists and those whose aesthetic and beliefs
bordered on fascism.

The ideological centre of gravity of the Yishuv, as the Jewish
community in Palestine was known, lay firmly on the left. The
dominant political force was the Mapai, in Hebrew the acronym for
the Workers' Party of the Land of Israel, and the dominant political
figure was its leader, David Ben-Gurion. He was born David Grün

in 1886, in the Polish town of Płońsk inside the Russian Empire. His father, Avigdor, was a lawyer and enthusiastic Zionist and at the age of fourteen David founded a youth club to study the Hebrew language and promote emigration to Palestine. In 1906, after studying at Warsaw University, he practised what he preached by setting off to pick oranges on one of the earliest Jewish settlements in Palestine at Petah Tikva – the 'gate of hope'. And it was hope, not fear, that drove him and the other young Zionists of Poland and Russia to Palestine's shores. 'For many of us, anti-Semitism had little to do with our dedication,' he wrote. 'I personally never suffered anti-Semitic persecution … we emigrated not for negative reasons of escape but for positive reasons of building a homeland.'[20]

Ben-Gurion was an atheist but looked and sounded like an Old Testament prophet. He seemed to exude a pacific tranquillity, yet all his life was a fighter, starting from the day in 1908 when he took up arms to defend the agricultural settlement in the Galilee, where he was now living, from Arab attack. He was an idealist but also a superb political tactician. By 1935 he had established himself as both the head of Mapai and also the chairman of the Jewish Agency, which had been recognized five years earlier by the British as the legitimate representative of the Jews of Palestine and therefore the *de facto* government of the Yishuv.

His main ideological opponent was also brilliant, driven and charismatic. Whereas Ben-Gurion radiated calm, Ze'ev Jabotinsky hummed with restless energy. He had a chin that stuck out like the prow of a ship and a mouth like a downturned scimitar. His dark eyes scrutinized the world from behind wire-rimmed spectacles with ruthless intensity. He was a remarkable writer and speaker, expressing himself in statements and utterances that seemed to have been chiselled from stone.

He had been born Vladimir Zhabotinsky in 1880 in the lively cosmopolitan city of Odessa, in the Russian Empire. His parents brought him and his sister up with little reference to their Jewishness. He was converted to Zionism by an event that transformed the lives of many young Jews. In April 1903 in Kishinev,* a city on the south-eastern borders of the Russian Empire, Christian mobs embarked on a pogrom, killing forty-seven Jewish men, women and children while the Tsarist police looked on. The incident was shocking not only for the amount of blood shed but because of the conduct of Jewish males, who ran away or hid when the rampage began.

The massacre taught Jabotinsky a lesson. It was summed up in a slogan: 'Jewish youth, learn to shoot!' He followed his own prescription, founding Jewish self-defence units across Russia. In the First World War he was a founder of the Jewish Legion, created to fight alongside the British against the Turks in Palestine. The move was designed to win British support for the establishment of a Jewish state. Jabotinsky admired the British Empire and would have preferred to work with it, but Palestine's rulers regarded him as a troublemaker. They imprisoned him and finally banished him in an – inevitably unsuccessful – attempt to shut him up.

Jabotinsky's style was emphatic and impatient. His vision of Zionism rejected gradualism and compromise and exalted action. He preached that every Jew had the right to enter Palestine, that only active retaliation would deter the Arabs and that only Jewish armed force would ensure a Jewish state.[21]

The need for some sort of military force had been recognized since Zionist settlers first began arriving in Palestine. After the anti-Jewish riots of 1920, a paramilitary organization, the Haganah (Defence), had been established under the loose control of Mapai and with the tacit acceptance of the British. The organization would eventually come under the overall control of Mapai and the Jewish Agency to form the 'secret army of the Left', as a British report put it.[22] In its early days, though, it lacked structure and resources and its failure to protect Jews during the pogrom that erupted in the summer of 1929 led to demands for more vigorous action. In 1931 a group that included many Jabotinsky supporters broke away.

* Modern-day Chişinău, the capital of Moldova.

Eventually the secessionists would form a new underground militia known as the Irgun Zvai Leumi, or National Military Organization. Its philosophy and aims were summed up in its badge, which showed a hand clutching a rifle superimposed on a map with the outline of an Israeli state stretching far across the Jordan and bearing the slogan 'Raq Kach' – Only Thus.

The Irgun's underground status bred a secretive and conspiratorial culture. According to a British intelligence report, the organization combined 'totalitarian tendencies' with 'violent nationalism' and 'a hearty dislike for socialism'.[23] The last attitude guaranteed a difficult relationship with the overwhelmingly left-wing institutions of the Yishuv. Its members were young, avid and quarrelsome and the potential for schism was strong. In the spring of 1937 a passionate debate on future strategy produced the first big split. One side proposed uniting with the Haganah to form a single Jewish military body. The other argued that their approaches were incompatible and that the Irgun should remain independent. The issue was decided in a referendum, with each side arguing its case at secret meetings of local groups. The Irgun divided down the middle with half returning to the Haganah.

The 1800 who stayed put were mostly hardline Revisionists and the majority had served in the Betar, the movement's youth organization whose members, with their fondness for uniforms and parades, resembled the Italian boy fascists of the Balilla. The link with the Revisionists was made explicit when Ze'ev Jabotinsky was installed as the new Irgun's supreme commander – essentially a figurehead role since the British had barred him from Palestine. It was from this quarter that the opposition to maintaining *havlagah* was strongest. Ben-Gurion was adamant that abandoning restraint would be a moral and political error. Jabotinsky, too, was reluctant at first to condone reprisals as he was hoping the British might allow the emergence of an official Jewish military force. His followers, though, were straining at the leash. From the beginning of the Arab revolt the Irgun carried out sporadic, unauthorized tit-for-tat reprisals. On the early morning of 14 November 1937 came a wave of attacks which showed that they had finished with *havlagah* for good.

Following the killing of five young men from a kibbutz near Jerusalem, a wave of gunfire rippled across the city. Five Arabs, two of them women and all of them innocent of any obvious involvement in the uprising, were killed. The attacks brought a horrified reaction from the Yishuv. The *Palestine Post* could barely bring itself to believe that it was Jews who had carried them out but, if that were the case, 'the depraved wretch or wretches would have to be excommunicated'. Whoever was responsible must be 'found, faced and dealt with'.[24]

The operation had in fact been planned by David Raziel, the Irgun's twenty-six-year-old Jerusalem commander. He was quiet, strongly religious and committed to the notion of 'active defence'. This was presented as a military doctrine by which Arab aggressors were targeted before they could launch anti-Jewish attacks. In practice it translated into indiscriminate bombings and shootings aimed at any Arab who was to hand. After 'Black Sunday', as the Jerusalem outrages became known, the Palestine Police rounded up a number of suspected Irgun members. The anti-Arab campaign, now sanctioned by Jabotinsky who realized he had no means of stopping it, continued nonetheless and the tempo of operations increased.

The bombs on the train at Haifa in April 1938 appeared to be part of the campaign. But instead of murdering Arabs, they had killed Wally Medler and Michael Ward. Until now, Geoffrey Morton's police activities had mainly involved dealings with Arabs. The incident had brought him into painful contact with what was the emerging, and would eventually be the dominant, threat to law and order in Palestine – the activities of dissident Jews. According to Morton the Irgun issued leaflets admitting their responsibility for the bombs 'but stating that [they] had been intending to kill Arabs and not British police'. He was 'not able to derive any consolation from this explanation'.[25]

In his autobiography which appeared in 1957, and in another unpublished account of his police career in Palestine written just before he died, Morton gave great emphasis to the incident. As well as losing his friend he had gained an enemy, a figure who would come to dominate his life. Preoccupied with the Arab uprising, Morton knew little about the Irgun, which anyway had only a small presence in Haifa. He now 'took the opportunity to find out all I could' about them.[26] In the process he 'heard for the first time of the man' who was reputed to be the brains behind the killings. 'His name', he revealed with a flourish, 'was Abraham Stern.'*

In the later memoir, completed in 1993, three years before his death, he gave a slightly expanded but no less dramatic version. 'Intelligence sources reported that one Abraham Stern, who was known to be their ballistics expert, was responsible for devising and setting this booby trap', he wrote. 'It was a name I had not heard before. I was to remember it.'[27]

This account varies in some minor details from the earlier one. The main assertion, though, is the same: Avraham Stern was the man behind the bomb that killed Wally Medler and Michael Ward. The detail that the bombs were aimed at Arabs rather than police-men would soon be overlooked as, within eighteen months, the Irgun widened the scope of their operations and British officers came under attack.

Morton was right to blame the Irgun for the bombing. But was it true that Avraham Stern was behind it? There is no surviving official documentation on the killings of Medler and Ward. Much of the Mandate's paperwork was destroyed or scattered in the process of departure.

The most complete record of activities of the Palestine Police CID – the department that dealt with the Jewish underground – was collected by the Haganah, who had many members and sympathizers among the government's Jewish employees. It is made

* British officials tended to refer to him as Abraham rather than Avraham Stern.

up of documents secretly copied under the noses of the Mandate's rulers and papers captured after the British left and is now housed in a library in Tel Aviv. The boxes contain no material about the Haifa bombings. When, later, Avraham Stern's name does begin to appear in intelligence reports, there is no mention of his being suspected as the brains behind this operation.

That does not, of course, mean that British intelligence officers did not believe Stern was the culprit. If they did, they were wrong. It was true that Stern knew something about ballistics. Together with David Raziel, he had produced a 240-page small-arms manual entitled *The Gun*.[28] He had no known expertise in explosives, however. There was a bigger problem, though, in linking him to the killing of Wally Medler. Avraham Stern was not in Palestine when the bombs went off.

THREE

'Let Fists Be Flung Like Stone'

On 8 April 1938, Avraham Stern wrote from Warsaw to his wife Roni in Tel Aviv. 'My heart aches that I misled you and didn't return when I said I would … but I am dealing with important matters and I must finish them. I get the feeling that for us, this trip is the most important one of all.'[1]

Stern had left Palestine for Poland at the end of January. The visit would turn out to be another protracted absence of the sort that was placing a strain on his marriage but the excuse was genuine; the mission was indeed important. He was acting as an envoy for the Irgun, liaising with high-level Polish officials who seemed willing to cooperate with one of the Revisionists' boldest and most visionary schemes. There were three million Jews in Poland and the government was keen to reduce the numbers. When the Irgun proposed a plan to encourage Jews to emigrate to Palestine they had responded positively. They had gone even further and appeared willing to allow military training for young Jewish Poles and to facilitate the export of weapons to the Irgun's armouries in Palestine. Stern was effectively the Irgun ambassador in Poland and deeply involved in all aspects of the transaction. It seems unlikely that he would divert from these duties to organize an anti-Arab outrage at 1500 miles remove, even if it had been logistically possible.

Stern was a very busy man. He was also a dutiful son and during his trips to Poland made time to visit his parents in Suwalki, 150 miles north-east of Warsaw near the border with Lithuania. It was there that he had been born on 23 December 1907, three and a half months after Geoffrey Morton arrived in the world. More than a century later, Suwalki has not changed all that much. The long main street is lined with pastel-painted, stucco-fronted public buildings, shops and dwellings – the sort of thing you can see anywhere in the thousand-mile swathe of territory between the Baltic and the Balkans.

There is nothing to indicate that Suwalki once had a thriving Jewish community – that the large yellow-washed apartment block on the high street housed the old Jewish hospital or a smaller, more elegant structure next to the town hall used to be a Jewish high school.[2] Stern's home is marked, however. Set into the wall of a building just off the main street is a tablet of liver-coloured marble. The faded lettering on it records that this was the birthplace of 'Abraham Stern – Yair', the 'poet and linguist' who was 'killed in action in Tel Aviv'. The town council was persuaded to put it there some thirty years ago by Stern's younger brother, David, in return for him renouncing any claim to the house.[3]

The building is now a bank. In 1907 it was a bourgeois villa, the residence of Mordechai Stern, a dentist, and his wife Hadassah-Leah, known as Liza, a midwife in the Jewish hospital. Its windows look out onto the town hall and a large park. There in the summer you could take coffee, eat an ice cream, read a Warsaw newspaper, while bees buzzed over the flowerbeds and a cooling breeze stirred the leaves on the trees. 'Oh, the park!' remembered Leslie Sherer, a contemporary of Stern's. 'An oasis of fresh air and tranquillity. To sit down on a bench and close your eyes and listen to the "klop, klop" of horses' hooves on the stone pavement.'[4]

The calm classicism of the architecture gives an impression of solidity and order. But in early twentieth-century Suwalki the fields began just on the other side of the elegant *portes-cochères* and beyond them lay the thick forests and vast lakes of one of the wildest stretches of north-eastern Europe.

The town's position was unfortunate. The area was an endlessly contested borderland and had at various times been part of Polish,

Russian and Prussian territory. When Avraham was born it lay within the Russian empire and had done so since 1815. It was a military post and Tsarist troops were garrisoned in the gaunt brick-built barracks on the outskirts. Jews began arriving in the town in the early nineteenth century and before long, according to the historian of the Jewish community Shmuel Abramsky, 'constituted the vital pulse of the region's economic life'.[5]

Their energy and confidence was reflected in a crop of new buildings. In 1821 the first synagogue was built. Soon there were Jewish schools for boys and girls and Bible study centres. The elderly were looked after in the old folks' home. The sick were treated in the Jewish hospital on the city's main thoroughfare and the dead buried in a large cemetery on the edge of town, near the Czarna Hańcza river.

There was little friction between Jew and Gentile, though neither community mixed outside of business. 'It can be said [wrote Shmuel Abramsky] that relations between Jews and Christians were generally tolerable from the founding of [Suwalki] until World War 1. There was no continuous tradition of fanatic anti-semitism. In fact there were no conflicts of interests between Jews and non-Jews.'

Zionism had taken root early in Suwalki. In 1881 a prominent local businessman and Talmudic scholar, Eliezer Mordechai Altschuler, set up the first Zionist foundation, Yissud Hama'ala, to raise funds for a colony in the Promised Land. The following year he set off on an exploratory mission. He left behind a land of woods and water on which the industrial age was rapidly encroaching and landed in a parched, backward world, sunk in medieval squalor. The collision with reality failed to dent Altschuler's enthusiasm – one of the essentials of Zionist belief was a contempt for mere facts. He wrote home that, on the journey from the coast to Jerusalem, 'I descended from my wagon many times and fell to the ground and embraced it, and kissed the stones with burning lips.'[6] Eventually, a colony was established and Suwalki was linked to the Promised Land.

It was in this society, invigorated by prosperity and the stimulus of new ideas, that Avraham Stern passed his early childhood. His father Mordechai's days were spent in his surgery on the ground floor. Liza went to and from the hospital a few blocks away, where she oversaw the births of most of the city's Jewish babies. According to her grandson Yair Stern, she 'was the powerful force in the family'.[7] Avraham was known as 'Mema', a nickname he used in letters to those closest to him for the rest of his life. In 1910 a brother, David, was born. Their upbringing seems to have been a stable and contented one and David's daughter, Amira, remembered her father talking fondly of the early days in Suwalki.[8]

In August 1914 came the first tremors of the earthquake that would destroy old Europe. By the following June, Suwalki was in German hands. When the Germans arrived, Mordechai was in the East Prussian capital, Königsberg, either receiving medical treatment or seeking supplies for his practice according to different accounts. He returned home to an empty house. Liza had fled with Avraham and David across the Lithuanian border to her father's home in Vilkomir. Mordechai was arrested and sent to a detention camp.

The flight brought to an end the longest period of stability that Stern would ever know. For the next six years he was a refugee, reliant on the charity of a succession of relations or, after his mother decided to return to Suwalki, more or less having to fend for himself. He spent some of his exile with an uncle in Petrograd, which was still in a state of revolutionary ferment. Twelve-year-old Avraham worked for the local student cooperative in return for food. He made extra money selling cigarettes. He enrolled at a school and learned to play the piano. He also joined the Pioneers, the Communist Party's version of the Boy Scouts.

He lived beyond the control of adults, hanging out with young revolutionaries and visiting the Mariinsky and Alexandrinsky theatres. When his parents wrote demanding his return, he played for time, asking to be allowed to finish the school year. In the summer of 1921 he could stall no longer and made his own way home. Without money or documents he was reduced to hopping freight trains, and arrived in Poland illegally, smuggled over the border in a sack on the back of a farmer.

He was barely out of childhood yet he had already had great adventures and witnessed historic events. At first family life was strange and restricting. Father, mother and son found it difficult to reconnect. According to Stern's biographer, Ada Amichal-Yevin, Mordechai Stern was a distant figure who sat alone reading and 'never … found a path to the heart of Avraham'.[9] Avraham Stern's son, Yair, formed the impression from conversations with Liza that he was 'not a father who [cared] a lot about his children'.[10] Liza, too, seems to have been too preoccupied with work and a busy social life to engage very closely with her son.

Avraham went to the Jewish Gymnasium on Kościuszko Street just down the road from his home. He had to learn Polish anew, but he had a gift for languages and was soon impressing his classmates with his eloquence. 'He had his own way of building sentences,' one of them remembered. 'He had a captivating way of speaking.'

Avraham Stern stood out from the start. He was a show-off with a compulsion to perform. He organized amateur theatricals and took the best parts. In 1925 he played the title role in his own production of *King Lear*. He thrilled the Gentile girls at the Polish high school with a poetry reading, and managed to conduct a protracted flirtation with three of them, wooing them with examples of his own poetry. He preferred the company of girls to playing football or swimming in the Czarna Hańcza river with his schoolmates. He seems to have set out to be special. According to his biographer, 'although he did not behave towards his friends arrogantly, they felt a distance – a certain secret and unexplained space between him and them'. This was seen in the way he dressed – sharply, as observed by the beady-eyed headmistress of the Polish girls' school who noted disapprovingly the ring that flashed on the young Jew's finger as he read verses to her impressionable Christian charges. It also showed in the way he froze out anyone who displeased him, behaving as if they did not exist.

In one respect, though, Stern conformed with his contemporaries. Suwalki was a Zionist town. The chaos that rocked the borderlands after the war had deepened the belief that this was no place for Jews. At home and at school the message was repeated. Mordechai and Liza were fervent Zionists. The Gymnasium's principal, Binyamin Efron, made sure his pupils were indoctrinated in the new faith. The regular curriculum was supplemented by ten hours of Jewish subjects – history, literature, the study of Hebrew and the Bible. Zionists were aspiring, at one level, to be normal – but in a Jewish way. In the land of Israel they would be farmers and sportsmen and soldiers. Contemporary Jewish military heroes were in short supply. Jewish boys had to reach far into the past for role models.

They called their football team after the Maccabees, the rebel army that drove out Hellenized usurpers and restored the Jewish state of Judaea, 160 years before the birth of Christ. If young Avraham Stern did not play football, he felt the excitement in the air and wanted to share in it. When the Zionist Boy Scout movement, Hashomer Hatzair ('The Youth Guard'), opened a branch in Suwalki, he became its first leader.

In 1925 the government subsidy to the school was cut and it was forced to close. Most of Avraham's classmates made arrangements to continue their education elsewhere in Poland. Even before the announcement of the closure, the Sterns had been considering sending their son to Jerusalem to finish his studies. A Zionist charity supplied a grant which helped towards the costs. At the age of eighteen, Avraham Stern had already experienced enough dramas to last a lifetime. In December 1925, he left Suwalki with his friend Pinhas Robinson to embark on a new adventure.

The pair landed in Haifa on New Year's Day 1926. Stern had no doubt he had made the right decision. In March he wrote to Meir

Kleif, a friend in Suwalki: 'I arrive full of hopes and reverentially touched this land … upon which I intend to build a new life full of song, sun and joy … I was like an innocent foolish and happy child as I ate and drank from what is ours, when I walked on our land and under our sun … the land was so pretty that my soul filled with hope and faith in a better future.'[11]

The boys went to Jerusalem where they enrolled at the Hebrew Gymnasium in the Bukharan quarter, a lively area of the new town growing up outside the Old City walls. Many of the pupils had been born in Palestine and raised in a culture of boisterous informality. Avraham, with his good manners and correct clothes, brought a whiff of the old world to the classroom. He seems to have enjoyed the distinction, teaching the other pupils ballroom dancing and sentimental Polish songs.

The dandyish pleasure in his appearance, the light-hearted love of theatricals and music were a genuine and enduring side of Avraham Stern's nature. But they combined with a sense of destiny and a conviction that a violent struggle was looming that would settle the fate of the Jews. Both aspects of his character were displayed at one of the school's end of term entertainments. He was chosen to recite a poem, and he selected 'In the City of Slaughter' by Hayim Nahman Bialik, a Ukrainian Jew, which described in harrowing detail the 1903 Kishinev pogrom that had radicalized Jabotinsky and transformed the outlook of many Jews.

The poem's anger is aimed not just at the perpetrators but at the men of the Kishinev ghetto and their passive acceptance of their fate. These 'sons of Maccabees' had looked on from their hiding places where 'Crushed in their shame they saw it all/They did not stir nor move/They did not pluck their eyes out/They beat not their brains against the wall'. The poem is a lament but also a call to arms. The dead of Kishinev must be avenged and the shame of those who cowered must be wiped away. Henceforth, says Bialik, 'Let fists be flung like stone!/Against the heavens and the heavenly throne!'[12]

In October 1927 Stern gained a place to study Hebrew literature and classics at the Hebrew University. Among his year's intake was a slim, open-faced seventeen-year-old with chestnut hair and bright brown eyes. Roni Burstein was the daughter of once wealthy but now impoverished émigrés from the Ukraine. Stern was captivated and was soon chatting her up. According to his son, Yair, 'he approached her and started to talk to her and at the beginning she thought he was a Sephardi Jew because his face was dark ... but then when he found out she was of Russian origin he started to speak Russian to her and quote Russian poets. She nearly fell down.' He 'started courting her and a big love story began'.[13]

The prevailing political atmosphere on Mount Scopus, among faculty and students alike, was liberal and leftist. The adolescent attraction Stern had felt in his Petrograd days for revolutionary communism was long forgotten. His main interests were artistic and he had yet to develop a coherent political outlook.

That changed with the riots of August 1929. Any complacency that might have remained among the Yishuv about the scale and dangers of the task they had set themselves was swept away by the massacres. In Hebron, where a small community of Jews had lived in peace with their neighbours for centuries, Arab mobs killed, maimed and raped, leaving at least sixty-five dead.

These events had the same effect on the Jews of Palestine as the Kishinev pogrom had on the Jews of Central Europe.

The events of August sent convulsions through the Yishuv. They revealed an alarming truth: the Haganah – the Defence – had failed in its prime task. It had lacked the organization or the means to shield the Jews from what was clearly going to be a continuing threat. Its leaders now set about training recruits and acquiring arms, unhindered by the British who, in light of their own failure to protect their charges, had conceded the notion that, in certain circumstances, the Jews had the right to defend themselves.

Stern was among the new recruits. The Haganah sent him first to a guard post in Jerusalem, then to a village in southern Galilee. By now the trouble was over and there were no weapons available even if violence were to flare up again. On guard duty, Stern passed the hours of darkness staring out into a night scented by the cooling earth, his head filled with melancholy thoughts. He felt, he wrote later, 'alone and abandoned ... so distant, a stranger ... everyone is far from me. Only death is near; only he has not forgotten me.'[14]

After a month in the countryside he returned to Jerusalem. By then, Roni had left for a study course in Vienna and for the next year Avraham would have to rely on the power of his words, poured out in hundreds of letters, to keep the romance going. In October he went to visit his aunt in Alexandria on the train that clacked along the coast, stopping every few miles at Jewish settlements. He described the journey in a letter to Roni's mother. The colonies were surrounded by orchards and plantations, making a 'sea of green' that 'filled his soul with joy and happiness', he enthused. But, simultaneously, the bucolic sight, glowing with vitality, aroused thoughts of death: 'I thought how happily I would give my life so that all of Palestine could bloom like these orchards ... we love Eretz Yisrael more than our lives ... we are ready to give ourselves and our lives to her.'[15]

At this stage his attachment to Zionism was still romantic rather than practical. In a short time his outlook would change and be replaced by a determination to make his poetic vision of 'Eretz Yisrael' – the 'Land of Israel' in something like its biblical dimensions – a reality. Career and security, even his love for Roni, would take second place to his pursuit of this end, no matter how distant it might seem. As he wrote to his younger brother David in Suwalki in November 1930, 'reality is not what it is and appears to be, but what force of will and longing for a goal may make it'.[16] This belief in the supremacy of willpower carried him through the rest of his life, colouring almost all his actions, a system of belief that simultaneously made compromise impossible yet opened the way to courses of action that seemed to contradict the spirit of the dream.

Despite the shock of August 1929, the Haganah remained a defensive organization and firmly under the control of the left-leaning Zionist establishment. Stern's political opinions were hazy and coloured by his poetic imagination rather than hard fact. Events were shaped not by economics and social factors but by heroes and great sacrificial deeds. Among his inspirations were Jewish warriors of antiquity such as Simon bar Kokhba, who rose up against the Romans, and Elazar ben Yair, who in AD 73 or 74 led the Jews of Masada who chose to kill each other rather than surrender to Caesar's forces. But they also included modern nationalist figureheads such as Giuseppe Garibaldi who, with a thousand dedicated men, had created modern Italy, and Jozef Pilsudski who in 1918 founded a new independent Poland after 123 years of foreign domination. Stern admired men of destiny, almost regardless of ideology. He could find positive attributes even in Mussolini, Stalin and Franco. In time he would come to believe he was a man of destiny himself.

These were men who did not shrink from violence and Stern's poetry reveals a fascination with bloodshed and death. He might seem a dandy aesthete, but his imagination was filled with visions of sacrificial violence: 'As my father carried a prayer shawl to Sabbath synagogue, I carry sacred pistols,' he wrote in a 1929 poem.[17]

Stern's attitudes led him naturally towards the Revisionist movement. Its image was self-consciously heroic. It rejected the gradual, democratic approach of Weizmann and Ben-Gurion, which relied on Britain to realize the Zionists' dreams. If Jews wanted a state, the Revisionist message ran, they would have to take it for themselves. It appeared to have a strong leader in Ze'ev Jabotinsky, whose impatience and disregard for obstacles put him in almost permanent conflict with the Zionist establishment.

But Stern was above all an individualist. The discipline and structures of a political organization made him uneasy and he had an aversion to accepting orders. When, in 1931, radical elements inside the Haganah – most of them Revisionists – broke away to form what would become the Irgun Zvai Leumi (IZL), Stern did not rush to join them.

He was eventually recruited by David Raziel, a fellow student at the Hebrew University. Two years younger than Stern, Raziel was reserved and taciturn. He was committed to action and contemptuous of restraints. At the same time he had a firm grasp of practicalities and did not share the quasi-mystical enthusiasms of his friend.

Stern joined the Irgun early in 1932 and underwent a short junior officer's course. His first contribution was to write a poem, 'Anonymous Soldiers', which subsequently became the Irgun anthem, with a melody composed by Roni Stern. Two of the verses sum up the essence:

> We are soldiers without names or uniforms
> Our companions are terror and death
> We will serve in the ranks for the rest of our days
> Only discharged with the last of our breath.

> On days that are red with blood and atrocities
> On black nights dark with despair
> We'll raise our flag in the towns and cities
> On that flag 'Protect and Conquer' will appear.

At this stage these visions bore little resemblance to the activities of Stern and his comrades. He was mostly engaged in propaganda and political agitation, co-editing the Irgun magazine which preached unyielding resistance to Arab demands.

Stern was popular with his liberal-minded professors and his good manners and charm overcame misgivings they might have about his politics. In 1932, however, his activities brought him into conflict with the Hebrew University's authorities. The chancellor, Judah Leon Magnes, an American-born liberal rabbi, intended to use the place to foster good relations between Jews and Arabs. When he appointed Norman Bentwich, the former Mandate attorney general who combined Zionism with sympathy for Arab aspirations, to the new Chair of International Peace, Stern helped to organize a protest. One demonstration had to be broken up by British troops at bayonet point. Even though Stern was not present he was suspended for several weeks.

Late in 1933 he left Palestine for the University of Florence, to study classical literature on a scholarship provided by the Mussolini government. Aboard ship he met a young academic called Isaiah Berlin, whose family had fled Latvia for Britain and who was now installed as a philosophy don at Oxford University. Berlin had just made his first visit to Palestine and they discussed the political situation. He found Stern utterly opposed to any accommodation with the Arabs. 'We will fight and fight,' he told him. 'And if blood has to be shed ...' He shrugged expressively.[18] His studies were interrupted when, the following spring, he was visited by the Irgun leader Avraham Tehomi who offered him the chance to do something significant for the cause.

He asked him to act as the Irgun's agent, organizing the purchase of arms from Italian and Polish sources. Stern accepted eagerly. From now on, he would divide his time between Palestine and Europe. He roamed Poland, Romania and Italy posing either as a book salesman or a journalist, a correspondent for the *Palnews* weekly news magazine. His new work brought him into the Revisionist network in Europe, giving him great opportunities for building both a reputation and a following.

The movement was developing a distinct, radical political identity that put it increasingly at odds with the left. In 1935, Jabotinsky's differences with Weizmann led him to pull his supporters out of the World Zionist Organization, and to set up the New Zionist Organization. This would now be the political face of Revisionism. It was supplemented by a militaristic youth organization, Betar, whose main strength was in Poland though branches had also been opened in Palestine.

Revisionism was, nonetheless, a movement rather than an ideological and organizational monolith, an 'orchestra', in Jabotinsky's description, with himself as the conductor.[19] He was the towering figure but his authority was far from dictatorial. Banned from Palestine, he had to watch events unfold there from Europe and America. He was nominally the Irgun's 'supreme commander'. He was unable, though, to exercise close control over policies and personalities.

Stern agreed with Jabotinsky that the aim of Zionism should be to flood Palestine with European immigrants who would establish a Jewish state inside broad borders that stretched across the Jordan river. They would achieve the goal by force of arms if necessary. But when he first caught sight of the great man in January 1935 in Kraków, at a Betar international assembly, he was not impressed. He wrote to Roni that Jabotinsky was 'ageing. This is not the same person who could once rouse the masses to follow him.'[20] Over the next few years his disenchantment would deepen as he grew frustrated with Jabotinsky's flexible approach. Despite its treatment of him, Jabotinsky remained an admirer of the British Empire and imagined a future Israel as Britain's ally in the region. For Stern, though the Arabs might be their immediate foe, the real enemy was the British who loomed behind them, blocking the road to a Jewish state. Over the next years he would turn against Jabotinsky, thus establishing a pattern of traumatic ruptures with colleagues that would last throughout his life.

Stern's long periods abroad made it difficult to maintain his relationship with Roni. Nor did it help that he sent repeated, almost brutal, reminders to her that in the competition between love and duty the cause would always come first. The demands of his job would justify any disruption to their plans. She was nonetheless expected to be waiting, to minister to him humbly and lovingly when he decided that time allowed.

He finally proposed to her – eight years after they first met – during a visit to Tel Aviv in October 1935, but made it clear that the nature of the life he had chosen made it impossible for them to have children. For the time being, at least, she accepted his terms. 'You are everything for me, beloved one,' she wrote, 'child and husband.'[21] He immediately set off on a two-month trip to Athens, Bucharest and Warsaw, returning in time for the wedding, which was due to take place on 31 January 1936 at Ramat Gan, in the house of Roni's cousin. When the ceremony was due to begin there was still no sign of Avraham. It was a Friday and the hour of Shabbat was approaching. The wedding canopy was just being dismantled when, according to Yair Stern, the guests 'saw a herd of cows coming towards the place of the wedding ... and out from the cows comes the bridegroom, with flowers that he collected in the fields for his bride'.[22] The wedding photographs show a radiant Roni, wearing white and smiling at the camera, with her dapper husband standing proudly by her side.

The couple had three months together before Avraham departed once more for Poland. For the next three years he would shuttle back and forth between Europe and Palestine, boarding a ship at Haifa for the Romanian port of Constanta then proceeding by rail for Warsaw via Bucharest and Lvov. For much of the time in Warsaw he lived out of a suitcase, staying in cheap hotels and short-let apartments, spending his evenings in the Silver Rose and Europe cafés, arguing with friends and comrades over glasses of vodka and dishes of pickled herring. In the autumn of 1937 he was wafted into a higher social sphere. The charming, passionate young man caught the eye of a lawyer, Henryk Strassman, and his wife, Lily. Henryk was a senior official in the Polish Ministry of Justice, a lecturer in criminology at Warsaw University and a reserve officer in the Polish army. The couple were wealthy, well connected and Jewish. They had been assimilationists but the rise of Hitler and the mounting anti-Semitism of their fellow Poles converted them to Zionism. Lily soon fell under the spell of Stern who, she said, 'enslaved my spirit with his simple and succinct talk'.[23] She put her wealth and influence at his disposal. She opened the Yarden Club in Poznanska Street in central Warsaw to host Zionist gatherings. In addition, the Strassmans backed two new newspapers, *Jerozolima Wyzwolona* (Liberated Jerusalem) and the Yiddish-language *Di Tat* (The Deed).

They also introduced him to important figures in the Polish government. Stern's direct manner inspired confidence and cut through red tape. 'Matters that normally would require prolonged deliberations ... were settled simply and without signatures,' wrote Ada Amichal-Yevin. Some of the officials he came into contact with became friends, among them Witold Hulanicki, the art-loving Polish consul in Jerusalem who helped arrange passports for Betar youths bound for Palestine and overcome the obstacles that the British were always throwing up in an attempt to stem the flow of Jewish immigration.* This was a heady experience. A Jew from the provinces, not yet out of his twenties, was moving easily in the highest circles and by his skill and charm striking valuable deals with a government whose outlook was increasingly anti-Semitic. It reinforced his conviction that anything was possible and persuaded him that help for the great project could be found in the most unlikely-looking quarters. This belief would cause him great trouble later on.

There were plenty who could attest to the young Stern's magnetism. Lily Strassman herself described her decision to follow Stern in almost mystical terms. 'It's difficult for me to explain that this was not a simple matter of persuasion,' she said. 'I wasn't religious. But it was as if the finger of God had pointed him in the direction he had taken and to me to follow him.'[24] Many of Stern's acolytes were to use similar language in describing their dealings with him. Consciously or otherwise, their testimony has a scriptural ring to it, with them the disciples and Stern the Christ-like teacher. By now he was thinking and behaving as someone anointed for great things, a man who could not be expected to be constrained by the normal rules of discipline or behaviour. He conducted much of his business without reference to the Irgun command in Palestine, much less to Ze'ev Jabotinsky.

* Hulanicki's connection did him no good. He would be abducted and shot dead by Stern's followers in February 1948.

The Polish connection was essential to Jabotinsky's vision. His grand plan was to arrange a mass exodus of 40,000 young Jewish males from Poland and elsewhere to Palestine, to form the core of a liberation army to wrest Palestine from the Arabs and challenge British rule. From late 1936, Betar members started training at clandestine military camps. Stern was closely involved in the process. Initially he teamed up with the man running the early courses, a Polish Jew named Avraham Amper. Then, through his contacts, he persuaded the Polish military to provide premises and instructors for three-month programmes. From the outset he seems to have regarded this as a personal project, one that would give him a power base independent of Jabotinsky, and he did his best to keep the details from him. By early 1939, the scheme had grown to the point where the Poles were providing a rigorous military education not only for local Jews but for visitors from Palestine. One young volunteer, Yaacov Levstein, remembered a twenty-four-hour rail trip from Constanta to Kraków, from where he went to a training base in the Tatra Mountains on the border with Czechoslovakia. The instructors were 'Polish army officers, some of them veterans of Pilsudski's legions, some former members of the pre-World War One Polish underground, and the rest Polish army career officers'.[25] The instruction was divided into underground tactics and conventional war fighting. The underground training involved 'terrorist bombing, conspiracy, secret communications … sabotage was taught on a scientific basis. Many hours were devoted to calculating the quantities of explosives needed for destroying targets.'

The lectures were accompanied by live exercises. 'Every day we would go out to the woods … the vicinity roared with thunderous explosions, automatic fire and gun shots … we would go out at dawn on a long hike and come back at night, tired, frozen and dirty but joyous and hopeful.'

Avraham Stern would turn up during the course or at the passing-out parade and deliver speeches that moved not only the Jews but their Polish instructors. Levstein remembered him speaking 'to us of his plan for national liberation and explained that if we did not act expeditiously the British would implement their plan of putting our country under Arab rule and reducing the Yishuv to a ghetto they could easily control'.

Yaacov Polani, another veteran of the course from Palestine who stayed on for a while afterwards as a Betar instructor in Poland, later told his British interrogators that Stern was believed to be using the training for his own ends. The programme was supposed to provide a professional military cadre which would remain in the ranks of the Betar and come under Jabotinsky's overall control rather than that of the Irgun. Stern, however, was 'busy organising what he called "the reservoir" ... people who would get military training and on arrival in Palestine would join the [Irgun]'.[26] This manoeuvre 'did not find favour in the eyes of the Revisionist Party and a number of people were expelled from Betar for joining Stern's activities'. When Betar leaders appealed to Jabotinsky to urge Stern to desist 'he got certain promises from Stern but very vague ones'.

In effect, Stern was creating the nucleus of a band of followers who could later be relied upon to carry out his plans. Some stayed on in Poland until the German invasion, then, by one means or another, made their way to Palestine where they naturally gravitated to Stern. Among them was Avraham Amper, a quiet man who followed orders unquestioningly, and Yitzhak Tselnik, who was effectively Stern's deputy at the time of his death.

Stern's ambition also created problems with the Irgun leadership in Palestine. Following the split in the ranks in April 1937, when half the members had returned to the Haganah, his old friend David Raziel had emerged as the commander-in-chief of the hard-line rump. During his stays in Palestine, Stern took charge of propaganda and worked with Raziel to produce a statement of the new group's principles, the first of which was that 'the fate of the Jewish nation will be decided by Jewish armed force on the soil of the homeland'.

Stern was loquacious and sophisticated, Raziel was taciturn and dour. They were both, though, dedicated to violent action, as Raziel had demonstrated in his response to the Arab uprising. The attacks on Arabs in Jerusalem on 14 July 1937 that signalled the end of *havlagah* had been followed by many more bloody reprisals. In the summer of 1938 the British hanged a young Betar member, Shlomo Ben-Yosef, for his part in an unsuccessful ambush of a bus full of Arabs near Rosh Pinna in the north of the country. Raziel ordered a wave of bombings and shootings. They were directed not at Mandate forces but at Palestinian civilians. In one attack, mounted on 6 July 1938, an Irgun man disguised as an Arab porter carried milk cans into the Haifa souk. He left them in a quiet corner and disappeared. A few minutes later they exploded, spewing fire and shrapnel into the shoppers. Twenty-three Arabs were killed. A few weeks later a similar attack in the same place killed thirty-nine. Stern had no moral objection to such outrages. By now, though, he believed that the effort was misdirected, and that the violence should be aimed at the British.

He also opposed what he saw as Raziel's deferential attitude towards Jabotinsky. In November 1938 Jabotinsky called a meeting in Paris with the aim of merging Betar with the Irgun. Raziel went along with the plan but Stern was bitterly critical of it. He avoided an outright confrontation with Jabotinsky but let his feelings be known to Raziel. Behind his back he took soundings of Irgun members in Palestine to gauge whether they were willing to break away from the partnership with the Revisionists and reject Jabotinsky's authority altogether. Stern's machinations on this occasion came to nothing. It was clear, though, that further confrontations with his comrades were inevitable and that sooner or later Stern would be going his own way.

FOUR

'A Soul for a Soul and Blood for Blood'

In the spring of 1939 Roni Stern was living a dull life in Tel Aviv, giving piano lessons while waiting for her husband to make one of his intermittent appearances from Poland. From time to time her routine was brightened by an invitation to a party given by a man who lived around the corner from her apartment in Nevi'im Street in the centre of the city. Efraim Ilin was only twenty-seven years old but he was already one of Tel Aviv's liveliest characters. He was employed as a tax clerk in the port. The job provided a cover of respectability as well as access to shipping traffic and he used it to build up a profitable business smuggling in illegal immigrants and weapons. Ilin's sympathies were with the Irgun. His parties, though, were a social and political pot-pourri. In his flat in Chen Boulevard, many of the leading players in Palestine's tumultuous affairs rubbed shoulders, drinking, gossiping and dancing to gramophone records of the latest tunes.

Among the guests were officers of the Criminal Investigation Department of the Palestine Police Force. After nearly three years the Arab revolt was losing momentum, worn down by the ruthless efficiency of the Mandate forces and the death or capture of key leaders. The CID was now spending an increasing amount of time investigating Jewish armed groups, and the Irgun in particular. An invitation from Efraim Ilin provided an opportunity to meet the Yishuv's power brokers as well as those with links to the underground in convivial surroundings and to forge contacts that might provide valuable information and lead to useful alliances. Roni's presence at the parties was encouraged by her husband and his Irgun associates for similar reasons.[1]

Among the regulars at Ilin's soirées were three of the CID's brightest officers. Arthur Giles was a child of the empire, born in Cyprus in 1899 to a family of soldiers and clergymen. He served in the Royal Navy in the First World War before joining the Egyptian Police Service where he acquired the honorific title of 'Bey', by which he was known to everyone. Giles Bey spoke Arabic, Greek and Turkish and was regarded as a brilliant policeman. In 1938 he decided his career would benefit from a change of scene and in March he was appointed head of the Palestine CID.

Dick Catling was a wiry, energetic twenty-seven-year-old. Like Geoffrey Morton he had joined the Palestine Police to escape the soul-destroying lack of opportunity in 1930s Britain. He came from a family of Suffolk farmers and butchers but decided to seek his fortune in London. 'The only work I could find to do was in the City of London in a wholesale textile warehouse,' he recalled. 'I worked there for three and a half years and on most days at lunchtime I would wander down to the Pool of London and look at the ships, and say to myself, I really must get into one, and go away as soon as I can because this is all too depressing.' One day, returning home to Suffolk, his train stopped at Ipswich. 'There was another train on the other side of the platform and I looked out of my window and saw sitting in this other train a young man with whom I was at school. I hopped out and went across and said Parker, haven't seen you since we were at school. He told me he was off to Palestine to join the police there, so I returned to my train and thought, well, if Parker can go to Palestine, surely I can.'[2] Now, four years after arriving, he was one of Giles Bey's brightest young detectives and relishing the challenges involved in penetrating the complicated and constantly changing world of Jewish political and military activism. It was 'an extraordinarily fascinating battle of wits', he said long afterwards. 'We had to get up very early in the morning if we were going to come out on top.'[3]

Catling's guide through the thickets of the Jewish political demi-monde was another East Anglian. Tom Wilkin was three years older than Catling and, like him, came from an ordinary home. His family lived in the Suffolk seaside town of Aldeburgh where they were publicans, grocers, drapers and shoemakers.[4] He seems to have served in the Suffolk constabulary before joining the Palestine Police in 1931. Early in 1933 he went with a policeman friend to a ball at the Eden cinema, a Moorish-style venue in the centre of Tel Aviv, to celebrate the light-hearted Jewish festival of Purim when people wear fancy dress and make merry. Among the revellers was a blonde, pretty young woman wearing a long flowing dress and a black mask. Wilkin nonetheless recognized her as the same girl he had tried unsuccessfully to chat to at the Tarshish café overlooking the sea a few days earlier. Wilkin was a low-ranking inspector of police who lacked the polish of the young officers from old British regiments who populated Tel Aviv's bars and hotels. He was slightly-built, had reddish hair and wore a rather unconvincing moustache. He was understandably nervous about making another approach to this sophisticated belle but his friend assured him that fate had clearly decreed that they should meet. They danced and talked. The young woman told him that she gave English lessons. Wilkin wanted to improve his Hebrew and they agreed to meet again. Thus was born an intriguing and unlikely love story that would endure until Wilkin's violent death eleven years later.

The woman in the mask was Shoshana Borochov. She was the daughter of Dov Ber Borochov, a Russian-born Marxist-Zionist whose ideas helped shape the attitudes of the Yishuv's left-wing establishment. Despite the high level of fraternization between Mandate officials and the Jews of Palestine, liaisons were frowned upon. Jewish parents were uneasy with their daughters consorting with Gentiles who seemed increasingly unsympathetic to their cause. The authorities, meanwhile, were concerned that soldiers and policemen would find that their loyalties were divided in the inevitable conflict between heart and duty. Shoshana and Tom defied the taboos despite family disapproval and official discouragement. They were not the only ones. Despite mounting tension between the Jews and the British, a surprising number of romances sprang up. Dick Catling had a Jewish girlfriend for a while, a Tel Aviv rabbi's daughter whose sister went out with another policeman.

Wilkin's Hebrew lessons were more than a ruse to win time with Shoshana. He was a natural linguist and was soon speaking the language fluently. He was intellectually curious and had a voracious interest in Jewish history and culture. Shoshana was from the Yishuv's elite and introduced him to her circle. From these encounters Wilkin made his own friends, including businessmen like Ilin whom he met at a reception held by the mayor of Tel Aviv, Israel Rokach, and leading figures in the Jewish Agency and the Haganah. They were impressed by his good manners and genuine willingness to see their point of view, though when Ilin once challenged him over the 'immorality' of the stringent British restrictions on Jewish immigration he defended the Mandate line robustly.[5] Wilkin was careful not to advertise the range and quality of his contacts. 'He was a very close man … a secretive man if you like,' Catling remembered. 'He worked quietly and, more often than not, alone.'[6]

Wilkin's chief, Giles Bey, was equally energetic in cultivating all the players in his domain, Arab and Jew, no matter where they were placed in the political spectrum. He would meet anyone and sit talking for hours, uncensoriously exploring their opinions in an apparent spirit of impartiality. It was a technique that his brighter subordinates – notably Catling – adopted and used to great effect.

The word soon spread that Giles Bey was a policeman to be trusted. This reputation attracted some surprising approaches, none more so than a communication he received at the end of 1938 from David Raziel. Raziel was in a delicate position. The Irgun were now engaged in a continuing campaign of reprisals against Arabs. At the same time, they were the main organizers of illegal immigration to Palestine, a traffic that was swelling weekly as the circumstances of Europe's Jews grew ever more desperate. Both activities placed a

burden on the Mandate's law and order resources and attracted the
unwelcome interest of the Palestine Police in the Irgun's operations
and members.

The CID played an extremely important role in the affairs of the
Mandate. Its field of activities was broad and included monitoring
all aspects of political life in Palestine. Its reports were crucial in
determining the views of Sir Harold MacMichael and the analyses
and recommendations he sent back to the Colonial Office. The
department was very well informed about the machinations of
established Jewish organizations. Much of the information came
from friendly sources inside the Jewish Agency and the Vaad Leumi
– the Jewish National Council, which represented all the main
factions of the Yishuv. The authorities also engaged in systematic
phone tapping from listening posts based at the Jerusalem
headquarters and the CID's four district headquarters. Yishuv
organizations – and particularly the Haganah – were equally well
informed about the workings of the Mandate. Jewish policemen
and Jewish officials routinely passed on information to the
Haganah's intelligence service, the Shai. The Irgun's equivalent
section, Meshi, also had its moles. According to Yaacov Levstein,
who became one of Stern's most loyal lieutenants, 'from its
inception Meshi did not spare any efforts to infiltrating the CID and
making use of its employees, who provided us with first-hand
information on political affairs, lists of men about to be arrested,
copies of various documents etc.'[7]

Raziel's feelings towards the British were ambivalent. Unlike
Avraham Stern he had not arrived at the conclusion that it was they
who were the chief obstacle to a Jewish state and were therefore the
Irgun's prime enemy. Like Jabotinsky, Raziel retained the hope that,
despite Britain's anti-immigration policy and periodic appeasement
of the Arabs, in the right circumstances it could still bring its weight
down decisively on the side of the Jews. At the end of 1938 it seemed
that the right circumstances were approaching. Another world war
was looming and Britain would need all the help it could get. An

offer of military cooperation might be parlayed into unequivocal support for a Jewish state. Raziel decided that the time had come to reach out to the Mandate authorities. He made his overture in a letter to Giles Bey in which he wrote that he was 'not an enemy of Great Britain in Palestine'. Indeed, he admired British culture and believed that Britain had 'a friendly attitude towards my people'. The Jews in Palestine were surrounded by hostile Arabs and needed the support of a European ally. The Irgun might 'criticize the methods of the government'. But 'we do not intend to uproot their rule'.[8]

Giles's response has not survived. However, within a few months of the letter being sent the Mandate's policy had swung onto a new course which dealt a blow to Jews who believed in Britain's good intentions. As 1939 dawned, war with Germany seemed not merely probable but inevitable. This realization forced a reassessment of British policy in Palestine. The Arab revolt had attracted widespread support in neighbouring Iraq, Syria and Egypt. It was vital to keep them on side in the coming fight. Two divisions of British troops who might be needed elsewhere at any minute were tied up fighting the Arabs. Some settlement would have to be found before the balloon went up.

Early in 1939 representatives from the Arab, Muslim and Jewish worlds were invited to London to settle the future of Palestine. The conference opened on 7 February in St James's Palace and it was clear it was doomed from the start. The Arabs refused to sit with the Jews and each delegation arrived at a different entrance to avoid embarrassing encounters. Prime Minister Neville Chamberlain's speech had to be delivered twice – at 10.30 for the Arabs and at noon for the Jews.

It was obvious from the outset that British policy was shifting decisively in favour of the Arabs. As the pointless meetings ground on, the Irgun intensified their attacks on Arabs. They were joined now by 'special squads' of the Haganah who had decided that a policy of restraint was no longer tenable if they wished to represent themselves as defenders of the Yishuv. On 27 February 1939, bombs exploded across the country killing thirty-three and wounding nearly sixty. Most of the casualties were in Haifa, where bombs were planted in the eastern railway station and the souk. The Haganah's calculation that the actions would have at least the acquiescence of the Yishuv proved correct. In his weekly intelligence report, Giles noted that the bloodshed had not been condemned by mainstream Jewry, who appeared to believe that it might force a change of heart by Malcolm MacDonald, the Colonial Secretary. 'There is no doubt that the Jewish public now believe that their case has been assisted by these outrages and the hands of the perpetrators have been strengthened thereby,' he wrote.[9]

It was not to be. With no agreement between the parties, the government announced its own plan. The White Paper detailing the provisions was issued on 17 May, making it painfully clear that in the coming conflagration Britain had decided it needed the Arabs more than it did the Jews.

The White Paper's message was that, with 450,000 Jews now settled in Palestine, the Balfour Declaration had achieved its aim and Britain was washing its hands of the Mandate. It had never been the intention to create a Jewish state against the will of the Arabs. In consequence Jewish immigration would be limited to 75,000 over the next five years and thereafter would depend on Arab consent. Sales of land to Jews would also be subject to heavy restrictions. It set a ten-year timetable for the establishment of an independent state in which Arabs and Jews would share government.

The White Paper was a shocking document for Zionists of every stripe. The terms meant that Jews could never form a majority in Palestine, putting an end to the dream of a Jewish state. But it was not just the future significance of the policy that caused dismay. It was the implications for the present.

Jews were pouring out of Germany but all over the world doors were being slammed in the refugees' faces. And now the British were drawing the bolts across the gateway to Palestine – the land they had designated as a home for the Jews.

Cries of protest rang out from all quarters. The *Manchester Guardian* called it 'a death sentence on tens of thousands of Central European Jews'.[10] In Palestine, David Ben-Gurion's Jewish Agency denounced the 'Black Paper' as a 'breach of faith ... a surrender to Arab terrorism, a delivery of England's friends into the hands of its enemies'. The *Palestine Post* editorial declared that 'acceptance of this policy would be tantamount to national suicide'.[11]

In Jerusalem and Tel Aviv crowds took to the streets setting fire to government buildings and clashing with the police and army. In Jerusalem two British policemen were shot, one fatally, after confronting a 5000-strong mob. In London, on 18 May, Malcolm MacDonald nonetheless told the House of Commons that he had been assured by Sir Harold MacMichael that the situation was 'generally quiet'. This prompted the tiny red-haired Labour member for Middlesbrough, Ellen Wilkinson, to ask him: 'what is it like when it is not quiet?' MacDonald made no reply.[12]

Avraham Stern was in Warsaw when the news of the White Paper broke, busy with the training camps, which now had full Polish support, and planning the mass exodus to Palestine. It was brought to him by Nathan Yellin-Mor, a former schoolteacher who was his co-editor on *Di Tat*. According to Yellin-Mor he took the British U-turn coolly, telling him that it might in fact be good news for 'it will deal a mortal blow to the Jewish Agency, the National Council and the Zionist leadership – all those who link their future and the future of the nation to a partnership with Britain'.[13] That list now included Jabotinsky. Stern's break with him was out in the open since he had denounced him in a press conference in Warsaw on 6 March, as a 'former activist following a policy of complacency towards Zionism's problems'.

Within forty-eight hours, Stern found himself thrust into a position from where he could attempt to apply his own solutions. The Irgun's anti-Arab attacks had exhausted any goodwill Raziel might have bought himself with the British by his friendly overture to Giles. As the Yishuv boiled with rage over the White Paper, the CID moved to decapitate the organization. On the morning of 19 May, Raziel set off to Haifa for a meeting with Pinhas Rutenberg, a former Russian revolutionary, who, as well as setting up Palestine's electricity generating network, was a founding father of the Haganah and a leading Yishuv fixer. The likely purpose of the rendezvous was to further enhance cooperation between the Irgun and the Haganah. It never took place. In order to avoid the British checkpoints that had sprung up on major roads, Raziel decided to fly. He boarded an aeroplane at Sde Dov, just north of Tel Aviv. The aircraft made an unscheduled stop at Lydda a few miles away. The passengers deplaned and were directed into a waiting room where their documents were checked. A few minutes later British policemen appeared and David Raziel was arrested and taken off to the nearby detention camp at Sarafand.

When the Irgun leadership met to respond to the crisis, they chose Hanoch Strelitz,* the Jerusalem commander, to replace him. Strelitz was born in Lithuania in 1910 and moved to Palestine with his family at the age of fourteen. He was a Hebrew language scholar who had been with the Irgun from the start and commanded the Haifa unit at the time of Wally Medler's death. He was popular with his men. 'He had a great influence over us and we loved him as a teacher and a leader,' remembered Yaacov Polani, who had received his basic training from him.[14] Despite his scholarly manner, Strelitz was a hardliner who had been one of the first to argue for the end of *havlagah* and the start of reprisals when the Arab revolt broke out.

Strelitz's first act as commander-in-chief was to widen the scope of Irgun operations. They would continue to kill Arabs. But from now on, in light of the treachery revealed in the White Paper, they would also attack British targets. The first actions would be largely symbolic in nature with the aim of winning over the Yishuv to the

* Like most Jews in Palestine, Strelitz swapped his European name for a Hebrew one and would be better known as Hanoch Kalai. For the sake of consistency I have used the names by which the figures in the story were known to the British authorities at the time.

Irgun's way of thinking. Words were as important as deeds and a skilled propagandist was needed to direct the campaign. A message was sent to Avraham Stern that it was time to come home.

The order could not have been more inconvenient. For one thing Roni had just arrived from Palestine. Anticipating that he would be in Poland until at least the end of the year, Stern had rented a house in the Warsaw suburbs and sent for her to join him. She duly quit her music teaching job, sublet the Tel Aviv apartment and boarded the boat for Constanta. More importantly, he was on the verge of closing several crucial deals. The finishing touches were being put to a large weapons consignment, part of which had been donated free by the Poles. He was also involved in buying, on very favourable terms, the Polish passenger ship *Pilsudski*, which he hoped would provide the transport for the 40,000 recruits for the liberation army plan.

Though Stern was becoming increasingly resistant to discipline, the order could not be ignored. He and Roni prepared for an immediate return. Before they left, Lily Strassman took Roni shopping for clothes. Stern had decreed that his wife dress only in Zionist colours and in accordance with his wishes she bought a blue coat. As they headed south the patriotic wardrobe expanded. In Lvov he bought her blue and white shoes and in Costanza a blue and white blouse.

According to Roni, his nerves were on edge throughout the voyage. What if the police were waiting for him at Haifa? But they passed through immigration unchallenged and were soon ensconced in the Yarden Hotel in Tel Aviv's Ben Yehuda Street, a broad boulevard that ran parallel to the sea. Stern was still cautious. He told Roni not to leave the hotel in case she ran into friends who would want to know why she was back from Poland so soon. He, too, stayed inside, slipping out at nightfall to meet his Irgun cohorts. After two weeks the couple moved out to an apartment on Rothschild Boulevard, rented in Roni's maiden name.[15]

Strelitz appointed Stern as his deputy with responsibility for propaganda as well as the intelligence section. He was also to act as the main link between Palestine and the European organization and to oversee the considerable funds brought in from the Irgun-organized illegal immigration. Stern was soon at work explaining the rationale of a spate of deadly attacks on Arabs. On the morning of 29 May an Irgun squad led by a firebrand called Moshe Moldovsky entered the village of Bir Adas on the coastal plain near Jaffa apparently looking for 'gangsters'. They shot dead five Arabs, four of them women. Jabotinsky had opposed mounting attacks to protest at the White Paper and first heard about the operation from a British newspaper. He dispatched an angry letter to Strelitz demanding an explanation. It read: 'An order: *The Times* reports that at Bir Adas four women were killed with the use of a revolver and those who were shot were found not outside the house but inside. That means that they intended to target the women. If this is a lie you must immediately deny it. If it is true you must punish those responsible and inform me what the punishment is.'[16]

There was no denial and no one was punished. The account of the incident put out by Stern was a fiction in which a group of their men had chased off an Arab band that had been sheltering in Bir Adas and went on to 'conquer' the village. The bulletin mentioned nine wounded Arabs but no dead women.[17] Stern turned the event into a great symbolic victory, which had taken the struggle into the Arab heartland. 'Our enemy today is the Arabs,' he wrote. 'By our reprisals ... first within the Hebrew Yishuv, then on the borders of the Arab area and in the end by penetrating to pure Arab areas like Bir Adas we will uproot the feet of the hateful Arab spy.'[18] His attitude towards the Arabs was simple. The issue of who owned Palestine would be decided by force and rightly so. The Arabs had after all won the land by conquest and intended to rule it for ever. Now it was time for the Jews to win it back.

The logic was that every Arab was an enemy and therefore a legitimate target. On the same day as the Bir Adas action another operation was mounted in Jerusalem which showed that Strelitz and Stern had now abandoned any pretence that Irgun violence was directed only at the guilty. It was devised by Roni Burstein's twenty-one-year-old cousin Yaacov 'Yashke' Levstein, who had chosen to study chemistry at the Hebrew University in order to gain expertise in bomb-making. He had also learned how to handle explosives at an Irgun training camp in Poland. The plan was to plant bombs in the Arab-owned Rex cinema during an evening showing of a Tarzan film, when the auditorium would be packed. The operation would be carried out by four men and three women from the Irgun cell in Jerusalem. They were chosen because of their dark looks, which enabled them to pass as Arabs, and, as Levstein gleefully recounted, they played their parts to perfection. One, Mazlia Nimrodi, 'was groomed like an Arab, perfumed, his hair sleeked, a colourful hand-kerchief in his chest pocket, his shoes glistening. He had expensive English cigarettes in his pockets, an Arab favourite.'[19]

Nimrodi was a Sephardi tailor who spoke Arabic. He had sewn the special jacket packed with explosives which would cause the initial blast. The other members of the team posed as courting couples. The women each carried a box of 'chocolates' inside which was a tin containing a charge of gelignite, nails and metal shards. Just before the film began, Nimrodi got up from his seat in the stalls, leaving his jacket hanging on the back of the seat in front of him, and left the cinema. Seven minutes later, at 8.30 p.m., the bomb exploded. The couples in the balcony then threw their chocolate-box bombs into the screaming, panic-stricken mass below.

The attack killed five and wounded eighteen, among them a Jewish boy and girl. The Irgun claimed responsibility for the blasts but showed no sympathy for the injured Jewish couple who had gone to the pictures 'to enjoy themselves in the company of Arabs'.[20]

In June and July, the Irgun carried out random attacks on Arabs in Jerusalem, Haifa and Tel Aviv. Stern thoroughly approved of the policy, though there is no evidence he ever threw a bomb or pulled a trigger himself. His job was to publicize the mayhem and to explain the purpose behind it. By now he had a well-established *nom de plume.* He was 'Yair', in homage to Elazar ben Yair, one of the leaders of the Jews of Masada.

The original Yair's followers were a minority inside the Jewish community whose uncompromising beliefs and sacrificial deaths provided a heroic example for their weaker brethren to follow. The modern Yair presented the Irgun in a similar light in newspaper articles, leaflets and broadcasts by a clandestine radio station, Radio Liberated Zion, which broke into the airwaves of Palestine to abuse the Yishuv establishment, and glorify Irgun actions. A typical bulletin described the activities of 29 June in flat, military communiqué-style form: 'At 5.30 a.m. an Arab was killed by our men at Jaffa–Tel Aviv Road near Nahlat Benyamin Street ... another Arab was killed near the orchards of Sheikh Mouness ... an Arab carriage was fired at by our men in the vicinity of Beit Shearim. Four Arabs were killed and one wounded and died later.' It noted that, in the southern district of Palestine alone, Irgun men had, in the space of an hour, managed to kill fourteen Arabs.

Their industry was in sharp contrast to the Haganah approach. The concerted action between the two organizations in February had been short-lived and efforts to create a joint strategy had come to nothing. Stern's propaganda presented the Haganah as timid, even treacherous. On this occasion they 'failed to follow our steps and did not go into battle'. Instead, in Haifa, they 'handed over to the police a Jew who was believed to be shooting an Arab'.

The Irgun's random killings were 'not acts of despair and not acts of revenge ... These were fighting acts of persons who believe that the Jewish kingdom must be created by force.' Their deeds had divine approval. The 'unknown soldiers' (a nod to Stern's poem of the same name) were obeying 'the ancient Jewish command, issued by God himself in his holy Torah: "A soul for a soul and blood for blood."'[21]

Stern was preaching to a largely hostile audience. If, as Giles Bey believed in February, the Yishuv had tolerated anti-Arab outrages in the hope that they might force the British to reconsider their new policy of abandoning the Mandate and making the Jews of Palestine subject to the laws of democracy, they did not do so now. The bloodshed had brought no gains and with the mainstream Jewish organizations committed to a programme of non-violent protest in the form of strikes and boycotts, the Irgun's actions were widely deplored.

Giles's weekly intelligence report of 28 June noted a leaflet distributed by 'The Daring Ones' whom he took to be a group on the left wing of the Labour party. It denounced the Irgun as a 'gang of despised hooligans' who were 'raging through the country. Through the wireless and in loathsome leaflets they boast of their heroic deeds.' It went on to list some of the Irgun's recent actions: 'They murder an Arab family in Byar Adas [sic]. They murdered Arabs passing on their business through Tel Aviv. They killed and wounded Arabs passing through Jewish quarters ...'

These 'conquerors', it went on, 'stain the splendour of our clean war for the liberty of the nation with the blood of innocent people'. The real aim of their campaign, the authors asserted, was to 'establish a reign of internal terror, throw down national discipline, divide the Yishuv, throw mud at the elected bodies and sow anarchy'.[22] Stern and Strelitz regarded any criticism of their methods as an act of aggression. Early in July, Moshe Smilansky of the Farmers Association wrote an article in the mainstream *Haaretz* newspaper stating that Jews who 'committed acts of terrorism against innocent and defenceless Arabs ... merely brought degradation on Jewry'. Attached to the article was a declaration headlined 'Thou Shalt Not Kill' signed by 200 prominent members of the Yishuv. A few days later the newspaper's editor received a letter from the Irgun 'press section'. It demanded that he publish a response comprised of biblical quotations justifying acts of vengeance or face 'proper action'. The editor bravely refused.[23]

Stern's propaganda machine also issued threats against Jewish members of the Palestine Police. A leaflet urged them to 'remember your duty to your nation' and warned: 'The rifle in your hand should not be aimed against us. You should not guard our prisoners in the prison. You should not convey our heroes to the gallows.'[24] The seriousness of the threat was made clear when, on the same evening as the Rex cinema blast, a gunman opened fire on a Jewish CID detective, Arieh Polonski, and a male companion, Asher Nemdar, as they stood talking in a Jerusalem street. Polonski died two days later. The killing was described as a 'death sentence' on 'a trickster in the pay of the Jewish Agency and the C.I.D'.[25] Two more Jewish officers would be killed later that summer.

These operations were fairly straightforward to organize and carried limited risks. Defenceless Arabs were easy targets. Jewish policemen lived outside barracks within their own communities and were vulnerable once they left work. Taking on the British was a different proposition. Having declared their enmity to the Mandate, the Irgun trod carefully at first, restricting themselves to symbolic actions. Once again Levstein was at the forefront of the campaign. On 2 June teams posing as repair men levered up manhole covers in Jerusalem and blew up junction boxes, cutting off half the city's telephones. The exercise was repeated in Tel Aviv. The scale of the attacks required considerable manpower. Levstein claimed that 150 men were needed to manufacture, stand guard and plant the bombs.

Next he came up with a plan to blow up Jerusalem's central post office. The idea was appealing on several counts: 'Firstly it would mean a direct attack on a government institution. Second the building was next to the CID headquarters, hence an attack on that place would shake the secret police. Third, an explosion next door would attract the top CID investigators, including their bomb expert. This man had dismantled many of our bombs, and discovered our methods. It was extremely important to put him out of action.'[26]

Levstein made four letter bombs for posting in the large mailboxes set into the front of the building. Three were conventional time bombs. He claimed later that the fourth was designed not to go off but fitted with a booby trap to await the attentions of the police explosives expert, Constable Michael Clarke. On the evening of 10 June the bombs were posted and three duly exploded, tearing down the front wall of the post office. The following morning the fourth was discovered. Clarke went to work and the bomb exploded, killing him on the spot. Levstein would later describe the results with the same relish that he recounted all his bombing triumphs. 'His head was thrust in the air and stuck to the ceiling, with his eyes staring down. The explosion and the ghastly sight scared the CID personnel.'[27] Chief Secretary William Battershill visited the scene shortly afterwards and was made 'physically sick' by what he saw.[28] The 'beautiful hall … was now shattered' and there were body parts scattered about. He noted that 'discipline for the moment seemed to have vanished'.

Mandate officials worked on the assumption that they were under constant threat of assassination. Battershill had a 'sleuth' protecting him round the clock and carried a revolver and thirty-five rounds of ammunition at all times. These precautions, though, had been intended as protection from Arab terrorists. Now, it seemed, Jews posed an equal threat.

These exploits were publicized on Radio Liberated Zion. Blowing up the telephone network was presented as an attack on police and army communications, even though most of the lines knocked out belonged to Jewish subscribers. Listeners were invited to mock the discomfort of the British authorities. Reporting a bomb attack on the melon market at the Jaffa Gate entrance to the Old City, which killed five Arabs, the announcer 'regretted having disturbed' Sir Harold MacMichael who was at a meeting not far away in the King David Hotel at the time.[29]

The mockery had a vicious undertone. The Irgun style was to demonize its enemies. For some, hatred of the British was an article of faith. When, in 1938, fifteen-year-old, German-born Uri Avnery let it be known that he was eager to join the organization, he was summoned before an 'admissions committee'. The meeting took place one evening in a darkened schoolroom. He sat in front of a desk with a light shining directly into his eyes so that he could not see his questioners. 'They asked me, do you hate the English?' he remembered. Avnery loved English literature and particularly the novels of P. G. Wodehouse. When he said he did not, he 'really felt the consternation in the room'. He gave the same reply when asked if he hated the Arabs and sensed a similar response.[30] In the following years the anti-British animus would only deepen.

Stern did not start out disliking the British. He spoke English well and in his early writings there is no sign of any visceral anti-British or anti-imperial feeling. However, their havering policy – or lack of one – had earned his scorn and eventually his hatred. He admired strength and determination, almost regardless of the ideological source from which it sprang, and could thus find qualities to respect in a fascist like Mussolini, a Catholic reactionary like Franco and a communist like Stalin. They made no attempt to hide their natures – and in his eyes this made them easier to deal with. He had, after all, enjoyed a profitable and even warm relationship with the Poles, whose policies since 1935 had been openly anti-Semitic. The behaviour of the British in Palestine had shown them to be slippery and inconstant, betraying their commitments to the Jews while seesawing between appeasement and repression of the Arabs. To Stern that looked like weakness.

Like many in the Irgun he took heart from events in Ireland. The many dissimilarities between the circumstances of the Jews in Palestine and the Irish in Ireland were overlooked. Instead their eyes focused on one central fact. In Ireland in 1916 a small band of revolutionaries who enjoyed virtually no popular support had launched a sacrificial struggle against the world's greatest empire which only six years later had given birth to a free state. In an interview given to the *New York World Telegram* in July 1939 an Irgun representative purposely compared that organization to the IRA.[31]

The Irgun were delighted to find that their views had support from an unlikely quarter inside the enemy camp. Josiah Wedgwood, a descendant of the great potter, was a former soldier and Labour politician who had adopted Zionism as one of his causes. In a speech in the House of Commons he came out strongly in favour of armed opposition to the Mandate. 'We all respect people who are prepared to fight,' he said. 'The Irish people are revolting while the Jews are imploring favour … I heard that the Jews are intending to do things that are against the law. This is wonderful. The Jews are not helpless. Among them are organised persons and militarists. They are the people who want to remain free and independent. They believe that Palestine is theirs and they will not wait until it is handed over to the hands of the Mufti.' These sentiments naturally exasperated MacMichael and the Mandate authorities but delighted the Irgun, who aired them on Radio Liberated Zion.[32]

The police responded robustly to the Irgun provocations. Following the post office bombing they launched a manhunt across Jerusalem, raiding the addresses of suspected sympathizers and members. Levstein escaped from his lodgings in the Zichron Moshe quarter just before they arrived. The police discovered some explosives left behind by a previous tenant, Dov Tamari, as well as notes made by Levstein during his training in Poland. Tamari was tracked down and subsequently jailed for seven years.

On 5 August, Binyamin Zeroni, the twenty-five-year-old who had replaced Strelitz as Jerusalem commander, was driving his car through the city centre when he was stopped by an Arab policemen who then escorted him to the Russian Compound, a large stone complex, built as a hostel for Orthodox pilgrims in the previous century, which now housed the CID headquarters. According to the account he later gave to Yaacov Levstein, Zeroni was handcuffed and chained to a chair to await interrogation by Inspector Ralph Cairns. Cairns, from Preston in Lancashire, was thirty-one years old. He had joined the force eight years earlier and his quick wits and command of Hebrew had propelled him to the position of head of the Jewish affairs section of the CID and the scourge of the Irgun.

Cairns was presented by the Irgun as a sadist who took sick pleasure in abusing his Jewish prisoners. Zeroni in particular was to tell a harrowing story of the treatment he received at his hands. According to the account he gave Levstein, on walking into the room Cairns immediately struck him on the head and carried on beating him for fifteen minutes. The ordeal went on for four days as Cairns tried to extract information. 'I was stripped naked, my shoes and socks were taken off and I was made to lie flat on the table with my face up,' he claimed.[33] 'Cairns tried to make me talk, pinching and hitting me. My hands and legs were tied, my underpants stuffed into my mouth, as Cairns put a rubber glove on his right hand, and began to squeeze my testicles one at a time. A sharp pain shot through my body … he keeps squeezing.' Zeroni was allegedly subjected to an early form of waterboarding: 'Cairns wraps a bandage round my nose and fastens it with a clothes pin. I cannot breathe through my nose and I have to open my mouth. He goes out and comes back with a large kettle full of water and starts pouring the water into my mouth. I try to close my mouth but I can't breathe. I open my mouth and it fills with water. I try to breathe and the water goes into my lungs …' In between torture sessions Cairns played mind games with his victim, threatening to bring in his girlfriend and rape her in front of him.

Zeroni claimed that he was examined by the 'government physician' who checked that he was healthy enough to withstand further abuse. He also asserted that 'from time to time' Giles Bey and his deputy, Henry Bennett Shaw, 'came to witness the inquisition'. After four days of this, during which Zeroni says he revealed nothing, he was left alone for a day. That night, despite his sufferings, he managed to prise open the wire netting above his cell, squeeze through into the guardroom, creep past the sleeping Arab guard, turn the key conveniently lodged in the guardroom door and tiptoe into the police station's central courtyard, climb a high stone wall and a perimeter 'fence' and escape into the Jerusalem dawn.

How much of this is true? There is plenty of evidence from the Arab revolt to suggest that some Palestine Police officers were on occasion guilty of beating and even killing prisoners. These crimes, though, were committed out of sight of higher authority. Zeroni's claims are more sensational. He suggests that at the heart of the PPF, in its very headquarters, torture was routine and systematic and not only tolerated but observed by the force's top brass.

According to the PPF historian Edward Horne, who served in the force from 1941, 'torture as such was forbidden but it would be foolish to say that it didn't happen'. Arab officers in particular were likely to deliver 'a most terrific thump across the face or chest' if they suspected a prisoner was lying to them.[34] British officers, too, sometimes lost their temper and struck a prisoner. The fastidious Dick Catling admitted that when, in 1944, a man was brought in who was suspected of killing his friend John Scott, 'I thumped him. I thumped him hard. I was absolutely furious about this murder.'[35]

This was not the same as the extended, formalized brutality alleged by Zeroni. The claim that Giles was present at some of the torture sessions was, Horne said, 'in the realms of fantasy'.[36] As for Zeroni's account of his escape from the police station, a building Horne knew well, his verdict was: 'I can't see how it could happen.'

Whatever the truth of the matter, Zeroni was once again at liberty. According to Levstein he went into hiding in Jerusalem before being smuggled out to Tel Aviv by Stern and Efraim Ilin, the host of the lively Tel Aviv parties, who installed him at his sister's flat in the city.

Levstein went to see Zeroni shortly after his experience. 'The man was physically broken but his spirit was strong,' he said. To Levstein's approval, he was 'determined to seek revenge'.[37] However, he claimed that he had to push Strelitz and Stern to agree to move against Cairns. As a prelude, he planned to kill a Jewish officer called Gordon who, Zeroni said, had been present at the interrogations. Gordon was married to an English woman and 'was totally committed to the British cause'. He ran a wide network of informers and had gathered a mass of data on the Irgun. 'I was afraid that after we killed Cairns he might use his information against us and cause us a great deal of trouble.' The assassination was set up for Friday, 18 August. Gordon was waylaid as he returned to his home in

Zephaniah Street in the Kerem Avraham neighbourhood of Jerusalem for Sabbath supper. The would-be assassin stepped in front of him and pulled the trigger twice but the automatic pistol jammed. The attempt nonetheless had the desired effect. Shortly afterwards Gordon 'took his family and left the country without a trace'.[38]

Levstein then set about planning Cairns's death with his customary thoroughness. Official accommodation was scarce and, despite the growing risks, Cairns lived away from police premises. A team of watchers followed him to his home in a modern block in Rehavia, a residential district near the centre of new Jerusalem. They noted his routine. Cairns was in the habit of crossing a building site on his way to and from his apartment. During the night of 25/26 August a huge mine built by Levstein to a pattern he had learned in Poland was buried near a path that led across the site. The planters defecated around it to deter the curious. That Saturday afternoon Cairns was walking back to the flat with a friend, twenty-seven-year-old Inspector Ronald Barker from Reading, Berkshire, when the bomb, packed with thirty-three pounds of gelignite, was detonated by a command wire operated by one of the team watching from a workman's hut. Both men were killed instantly.

In the following day's *Palestine Post* this spectacular event appeared low down on the front page. Its columns were crowded with the dreadful news from Europe. All the reports pointed to war within days. German troops were deploying on the frontier with Poland. The German government was shifting from the centre of Berlin to the suburbs and the call-up of reservists was in full swing.[39]

The killings brought another appalled response from the Jewish Agency. This act of 'dastardly murder' had come at 'a fateful moment in the history of our people and of humanity at large ... when the lands of freedom and democracy must take their stand against tyrannical regimes'. It urged Jews to 'follow the ancient command' to 'eradicate the evil from thy midst'.[40]

The Irgun continued to watch the impending catastrophe through the narrow focus of their own obsessive struggle. Like the IRA, they regarded Britain's difficulty as their opportunity, and, with the Mandate's attention now deflected by the war, Stern's plan to bring in mass reinforcements from Poland gained acute urgency. On 31 August he asked Roni to pack his suitcase: he was leaving for Warsaw the following day. First, though, he had to attend a meeting of the Irgun command, due to take place at Efraim Ilin's sister's flat at 6 Aharonovich Street in the centre of Tel Aviv. That evening he joined Hanoch Strelitz and other commanders in the third-floor apartment. The meeting started with a report from Yaacov Levstein, who had arrived from Jerusalem, on the killings of Cairns and Barker. They then went on to discuss the liberation army plan. While they were talking they heard heavy footsteps in the hallway outside followed by the sound of fists drumming on the door. They ran to the windows. Armed police were swarming in the street below. There was no way out. Strelitz told someone to open the door. Tom Wilkin burst in, pistol in hand, at the head of a squad of detectives. The entire leadership of the Irgun Zvai Leumi was under arrest.

Young Avraham (right) – 'Mema' to his family – with his mother Liza and brother David.

Suwalki at the turn of the twentieth century.

By the time of this picture, the
adolescent Stern had already
experienced enough danger
and drama to last a lifetime.

Stern had a marked theatrical streak and liked performing. Photographed while in Suwalki, here he is in pierrot guise.

Stern (middle of the back row) with high school classmates in Jerusalem in the mid-1920s.

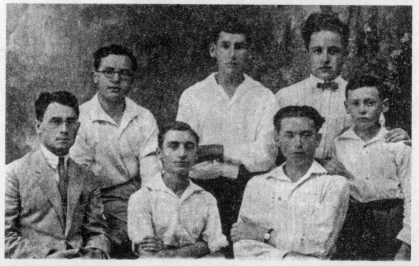

The 'delicate playboy'. Behind the dandyish appearance and courteous manner lay a ruthless will and a disregard for consequences.

Geoffrey Morton: 'some people seem to think that I was anti-Semitic, and others that I was anti-Arab. I wasn't. I was merely anti-terrorist, whether they were Arab or Jew.'

Avraham and Roni on their wedding day in 1936. He picked the flowers on the way to the ceremony.

Avraham Amper (right) in the late 1930s, fencing at a Betar military training camp he helped to set up with the assistance of the Polish authorities.

Ze'ev Jabotinsky pictured in August 1940 visiting Betar cadets at a camp in upstate New York. That evening he was dead.

Max Seligman (left), genial legal adversary of British rule.

The disciples. Schoolteacher Moshe Svorai and his wife Tova followed 'Yair' with unflagging loyalty and devotion.

Wealthy and well connected, Lily Strassman met Stern in 1937 and succumbed quickly to his charisma. With her husband Henryk she gave invaluable backing to Stern's Polish schemes.

FIVE

'And He is a Rebel, Eager for the Storm'

Three days after the raid, Europe was at war. Geoffrey Morton was on honeymoon in Britain when he heard the announcement. He broke it off to return to Palestine and a very different job. Until now, the activities of the Jewish underground had barely concerned him. He had spent the previous eighteen months on the front line of the struggle against the Arabs, as police commander of the town of Jenin, which made up one side of the 'triangle of terror' where the rebellion burned fiercest.

Morton had done very well there. His performance had been praised by General Bernard Montgomery, then serving in Palestine, and won him a gallantry award.[1] His new post presented completely different challenges. He was being given charge of the Criminal Investigation Department of Lydda District. The news came as a surprise. 'From my point of view there were three distinct drawbacks to this new appointment,' he wrote.[2] 'Firstly, that I was completely without experience in CID work; secondly, that during the last eighteen months I had been dealing exclusively with Arabs in rural areas, whereas much of my work would now be connected with Jews and urban areas; and thirdly, that apart from one or two one-day trips from Jerusalem, some years earlier, I had no personal knowledge or experience of the large and important areas concerned.'

Lydda* covered Tel Aviv, Rehovoth and Ramat Gan, all new Jewish towns that had sprung up in the preceding few decades. It

---

* Now Lod. I have stuck with the spellings of place names as they were used by the Mandate authorities.

also included the old Arab port of Jaffa. With the crushing of the
Arab revolt and the palliative effects of the White Paper, the Arabs
were quiet now, even if they were not satisfied. It was the Jews who
would present Morton with most of his problems.

While settling in he received a letter from his bride, Alice, which
'filled me with joy'. Morton had not expected to see her until the war
was over but she had somehow managed to get a passage out on an
Orient liner and would be arriving in a few weeks. This, he noted,
was 'no small achievement but it was typical of the resourcefulness
she ... displayed on many occasions'.[3] Alice Fowler was clever, musical, hard-working and adventurous. She had become best friends
with Morton's sister Marion when they were both training to be
teachers. She lodged with the family, now living in a spacious villa
in Calton Avenue, Dulwich Village, a green and prosperous south-
east London suburb. She had met Geoffrey when he arrived home
on leave in the winter of 1937 and 'began to go out in the evenings
to dance, theatres, dine etc with him'.[4] She was nonetheless taken
aback when, one evening, he proposed. 'I certainly liked him
immensely but had never once thought of him as a potential
husband,' she remembered. Geoffrey's certainty that they were made
for each other – and the prospect of an exciting life by his side –
persuaded her.

Neither was to regret the decision and Alice, born and brought
up in the tranquillity of Melksham in Wiltshire, where her father
was stationmaster, would prove more than capable of dealing with
the rough and tumble of life as the wife of a Palestine Police officer
while pursuing her teaching career. By marrying Alice, Geoffrey
wrote later, he 'acquired a loyal, devoted, long-suffering and coura-
geous wife and counsellor'.[5] The marriage was long and happy,
based on mutual respect and shared values. Above all, it was what
Avraham and Roni Stern's union was not – a partnership.

Morton set about finding them a home, renting a stone-built
bungalow in Sarona, a peaceful enclave shaded by eucalyptus trees
founded by German followers of the Knights Templar, which lay on

the eastern edge of Tel Aviv, just off the main road to Haifa. The bachelor life of mess and tennis court came to an end. Away from the dramas of the day the couple led a measured, middle-class existence, dining and playing bridge with friends and in the evenings tasting the pleasures of Tel Aviv. Despite the war, the latest films were showing at the city's cinemas and they enjoyed concerts by the world-class Palestine Orchestra. Geoffrey's musical tastes were broad, from Stéphane Grappelli to Stravinsky, while Alice, a trained musician, preferred more conventional fare. Tel Aviv was beautiful and boldly modern, built to a master plan drawn up by a Scotsman, Patrick Geddes, its houses, office and apartment blocks designed by young Jewish architects who had been inspired by the leading lights of the Bauhaus school. The result was a townscape of cool, curved balconies and blindingly white walls softened by the lush foliage flourishing in multiple squares and gardens. Beneath the stylish facades the many cafés lining Dizengoff and Ben Yehuda acted as informal trading floors, crowded with men and women buying and selling illegal gold and diamonds, forged papers and immigration certificates. They seethed with rumour and gossip as the patrons, drawn or driven there from every corner of Europe and beyond, devoured any scrap of news about their families and friends, now swallowed up by the 'night and fog' of Nazi occupation. Apprehension, uncertainty and a sick feeling of excitement hung in the air as each pondered his or her private fate and wondered where the riptides of war would sweep them.

In the broad, tree-lined boulevards, army lorries rumbled to and fro. The pavements and places of entertainment were crowded with men in uniform; airmen, sailors and soldiers, many of them Australian, Geoffrey Morton could have been among them. Just before the outbreak of war the officer commanding a battalion of the Argyll and Sutherland Highlanders whom he worked alongside in Jenin during the Arab revolt had offered him an immediate captaincy. He wrote afterwards: 'without pausing for thought I replied "thank you very much colonel but I think I'd better carry on where I am"'. Morton never expanded on why he turned down what was a flattering and unusual proposal. He was, however, well advanced on his career and had set his heart on reaching the top. If he left the police service there was no guarantee he could rejoin at the same level if he survived the war. Given that he seemed to relish danger and had already risked his life numerous times, it is unlikely his decision was based on safety calculations. For, as he later remarked, if he had accepted the Argylls' offer, 'I do not believe with hindsight that I should have been exposed to more personal danger than I was to experience in my next tour of duty.'[6]

Morton boned up on his new beat with his usual diligence, and 'every bit of information or gossip and every name which came to our notice for any reason was carefully sifted, assessed and indexed for future reference'. Ted Horne, who later served under him, remembered Morton as a surprisingly unobtrusive figure. 'If he came into a room, although he was a big man, you carried on what you were doing before you said "Hallo Geoff."'[7] He was a disciplinarian, but 'with a light touch' and 'a natural leader'. 'All his men said the same thing: "If Geoff wants it, it's good enough for us."' He relied heavily at first on his second in command – Tom Wilkin. 'Wilkie', as Morton called him, 'was a veritable tower of strength in every way, an excellent investigator and prosecutor, and a first-class Hebrew speaker; he knew more about Jewish politics and organizations than the rest of the Palestine Police put together'. He also had the gift of being able to express himself clearly and succinctly on paper. This, Morton judged, was 'a virtue possessed equally by his assistant in the Jewish affairs section Sergeant Stamp'. Bernard Stamp was brought up in a large family in Hull. He joined the Coldstream Guards when he was eighteen and transferred to the Palestine Police just after the 1929 riots. He left school at fourteen but had educated himself thoroughly and had an impressive knowledge of English literature. He also had a privileged insight into the life of the Yishuv. Like his friend and boss, Wilkin, he spoke Hebrew and had a Jewish girlfriend, Fay Schreiber. They had met one afternoon on Gordon Beach, a few hundred yards from the centre of Tel Aviv, and soon fell for each other. The match would create great problems for both of them. Fay's father, David, was strongly religious and patriotic. The thought of his daughter marrying both a non-Jew and a British policeman appalled him. When they broke the news of their engagement he disowned her and announced seven days' mourning in the family. According to Stamp's son, Dan, once it was known that his father was courting a Jewish girl he was taken aside by a superior and told that if they decided to marry, his career would hit a dead end and he could expect no further promotion. His father, 'a very honourable man',[8] ignored the warning. They were married in 1941 with Tom Wilkin as best man. This development would play an important part in subsequent events.

Morton was very impressed by his new deputy. 'I placed myself at Wilkie's feet to learn all I could of the Jewish political set up, which was so involved that many of the Jews themselves had but a hazy idea of the affiliations and functions of many of the groups,' he wrote. Although he was a newcomer to Jewish political affairs he did know some Hebrew, acquired while serving in Haifa, and while nowhere near as good as Wilkin's, 'it stood me in good stead after I had brushed it up a little'.[9]

With the coming of the war the Yishuv and Zionists everywhere had decided this was no time to let the bitterness caused by the White Paper to distort their view of the bigger picture. Britain had betrayed them, but in the long term it was still their natural ally in the struggle ahead. In the analysis of the Colonial Secretary Malcolm MacDonald 'it was vital for the Jewish national home that Britain should win the war. If Britain lost and Hitler won, there would be no national home. The Jews would be killed or expelled from Palestine, just as they had been 2,000 years earlier.' It was this understanding that led Weizmann to write to the Prime Minister Neville Chamberlain a few days before the outbreak of war, promising 'the Jews stand by Great Britain and will fight on the side of the democracies'. Jabotinsky, too, had pledged the New Zionist Organization's support for Britain and France and revived his idea of a Jewish Legion that would fight alongside the Allies against the Nazis. That did not mean that Britain could expect lamb-like docility from the Yishuv. The attitude there was summed up neatly by Ben-Gurion: 'We shall fight the war as if there were no White Paper, and the White Paper as if there were no war.'[10]

There would be many points of friction in the relationship. Britain's relief that the Arabs were subdued was considerable and the government was desperate to avoid doing anything to stir them up again and drive them into the arms of the Germans. Repeated offers to provide Jewish units to fight the Nazis were turned down on the grounds that they would provoke Arab anger and could be a pretext to create a force-in-waiting that might later turn against the Arabs and even the British.

At this delicate time, High Commissioner MacMichael wanted no private armies on his patch. That included the Haganah, which, no matter how keen it might be to fight the Nazis, ultimately took its orders from the Jewish Agency. When, on 5 October, a British Army patrol came across a forty-two-strong band of Haganah men drilling close to Yavniel, near Lake Tiberias, they were arrested and later given long prison sentences.

The outbreak of war brought no relaxation of the campaign against illegal immigration. In occupied Poland the worst fears of the Zionist prophets were starting to be realized as Jews were herded into ghettoes or transported to forced labour camps. The lucky few who had escaped or bought their way out of Hitler's expanding empire were crowding the Black Sea ports seeking passage to Palestine. Britain exerted maximum diplomatic pressure to prevent the refugee ships sailing. When boats did land the passengers were arrested and taken to the camp for illegals at Athlit, near Haifa, with a view to shipping them out again, using force if necessary, to the British colony of Mauritius. Winston Churchill had opposed the White Paper and deplored the treatment of refugees. On becoming

Prime Minister in May 1940 he discovered that Foreign and Colonial Office resistance to lifting the immigration barrier was fierce.

According to their chilly mandarin logic it made no sense to soften the official line. The prison door had slammed behind the Jews of conquered Europe. Letting in twenty or thirty thousand refugees would make no real difference and could only serve to spark another Arab uprising and a possible alliance with Nazi Germany, which might well lead to the expulsion of the British from Palestine. MacMichael set the tone of fierce opposition to any relaxation. 'Has every Jew the right to come to Palestine?' he demanded rhetorically of the new Colonial Secretary Lord Moyne early in 1941. 'Has every Jew who can reach Palestine the right to remain there?'[11] This attitude would lead to a string of tragic episodes that would burn into the psyche of the Yishuv and increase the store of bitterness towards the British.

One way of blocking the growth of Jewish private armies was raiding their armouries. The Irgun and the Haganah had begun breaking into military installations and bribing soldiers to add to their stocks of weapons and ammunition. Geoffrey Morton was soon reapplying the methods he had used so successfully on the Arabs of the 'triangle of terror'. He spread the word that he would pay well for information leading to weapons seizures. He was soon contacted by a recent immigrant whom he called 'Jacques' who tipped him off about an arms cache in the colony of Mishmar Shalosh in the Galilee. On 16 January, Morton led a raid on the place and found fifteen rifles, two pistols, forty-five Polish-made bombs, ammunition and detonators where he was told they would be – hidden under the tiled floor of the post of the official Jewish Supernumerary Police which guarded kibbutzim and agricultural settlements. A week later another tip from Jacques led him to the settlement of Ben Shemen, near Lydda. Once again arms were found under the police station floor.

Morton prided himself on his straightforward application of the law. Late in life he wrote, 'some people seem to think that I was anti-semitic, and others that I was anti-Arab. I wasn't. I was merely anti-terrorist, whether they were Arab or Jew.'[12]

In his new job he soon discovered that, although he might favour such an approach, the authorities were more circumspect. The Yishuv was far more politically sophisticated than the Arab community of Palestine. Jews in Britain and America wielded real power when it came to shaping policy and forming public opinion. British imperialists did not shrink from harsh, even brutal measures when faced with challenges to their rule. In the Jews of Palestine, though, they were facing a subtler and more sophisticated opposition than they were used to. For this reason British policy – even if apparently set in stone – had a habit of crumbling when it collided with the flinty resistance that local and international Zionists were adept at mounting. At the basic operational level, this meant that the signals emanating from headquarters had to be listened to carefully for shifts of tone and emphasis.

Decisions taken from on high did not always filter down to those on the ground. In London the War Cabinet had decided in February 1940 that in order not to provoke Zionists and thus hamper the war effort, there would be no 'drastic measures to obtain possession' of illegal Jewish armouries.[13] At exactly that time, Morton received information that a large arsenal was hidden in a synagogue in Tel Aviv's Ben Yehuda Street. Against his natural instincts, he hesitated to race off and raid it. There were obvious religious and political sensitivities involved. Instead he reported the tip-off and asked Jerusalem for authority to conduct a search. 'I never got it,' he remembered, 'nor indeed any reply to my report.'[14] Cases like this confirmed his view that political considerations determined how the law in Palestine was applied. It grated on his most firmly held convictions. For Morton the law was not a malleable concept to be pulled and twisted by the dictates of expediency. It was a majestic construct, towering over the conduct of ordinary mortals. Whatever accusations might be made against him later, Morton truly believed in the virtue of his calling, something he shared with the man who was to become his great adversary.

For the time being things were quiet. In Europe, Germany was still digesting the new territories swallowed by its victorious armies. No one expected the lull to last. The question of how to cope with a renewed Nazi onslaught preoccupied everyone in Palestine, including the remnants of the Irgun Zvai Leumi. As a result of the CID raid on the flat in Aharonovich Street on 31 August 1939, all the top commanders were now banged up. Avraham Stern, Hanoch Strelitz and Yaacov Levstein, along with two other Irgun men captured in the operation, had been interrogated by a team led by Tom Wilkin for ten days in an attempt to get them to confess to the killing of Cairns and Barker. Writing later of his experiences, Levstein made no claims of torture or beatings – though he attributed this restraint to his interrogators' fear that they might suffer the same fate as Cairns and Barker. The captives lied and stone-walled. With no hard evidence to link them to the assassinations, they could only be detained under the emergency regulations brought in to combat the Arab rebellion, which allowed for their open-ended detention.

The five were sent to the camp at Sarafand, a compound of huts set inside a large British military base close to Ramleh. There they were reunited with their former commander David Raziel, who had been arrested six months earlier. It soon became clear that his views now diverged sharply from those of the new arrivals. Raziel endorsed Jabotinsky's view that in the current dire circumstances the Irgun should not be fighting the British but helping them. The Mandate authorities had already identified him as a man they might do business with and he received at least one visit from Giles Bey, to whom he had addressed the conciliatory letter at the end of 1938. All this was disturbing to the new arrivals. 'Occasionally I would hear bits of conversation among the Irgun commanders which alluded to a disagreement between them and Raziel,' wrote Levstein.[15] This was putting it mildly. Relations between the command – and particularly Stern and Raziel – would deteriorate sharply, first into hostility and suspicion and then into something close to hatred.

The inmates were treated as political prisoners and the regime was fairly relaxed. Stern spent his time in endless discussions and writing poems. Levstein the bomb-maker now took on the role of amanuensis to 'Yair'. 'I helped him copy the poems and look up words in his Bible Concordance and his dictionaries as he searched for rhymes,' he remembered. It was in Sarafand camp that Stern wrote one of his best-known poems, 'To Our Mothers', which typifies the blend of grandiosity, triumphalism and romanticized violence that imbues much of his work.

> A mother's tear, wailing for her Isaac
> God in his fury will avenge, in His mercy redeem;
> And Jacob will wrestle with man and God,
> And Israel will rise over Edom and Arabia
> His foot on their neck – kings and rulers
> Between the three seas and the two rivers
> Egypt the foundation and Assyria the roof;
> David's kingdom will be established in blood
> And the entire nation will be saying as one, Amen,
> Amen![16]

Stern frequently used biblical images in his poetry. His upbringing had not been particularly religious but in adulthood he had come to observe the Sabbath and the High Holy Days and Roni had been instructed to keep a kosher kitchen. His Judaism, though, seems primarily to have been not a guide to how life should be lived but a source of political revelation offering the example of divinely inspired warriors who slaughtered their enemies and carved out kingdoms.

Towards the end of October, Raziel was taken away from the camp. The Irgun contingent were alarmed. According to Levstein they 'thought they were taking him to the CID headquarters in

Jerusalem to question him and perhaps even torture him and put him on trial'. There was talk of a hunger strike. It was not necessary. The following day Raziel was back. He was not being put on trial. He was being set free. Before he left, the British allowed him to meet Stern and the rest of the Irgun command in a special room, under their surveillance. 'The discussion was long,' wrote Levstein, 'and apparently very heated.'[17]

The heat was surely generated by Raziel's revelation of the terms of his release. On leaving Sarafand he had been taken to Jerusalem to meet Pinhas Rutenberg, one of the founders of the Haganah and the man he had been on his way to see when he was arrested in May. Rutenberg carried a proposal from the British. If Raziel – who was still officially the Irgun commander – ordered his men to cease operations against them and assisted the war effort, they would let him go. There were further inducements, in the form of cash payments to the Irgun and a promise not to interfere with its propaganda activities. In addition, they would be granted a quarter of the immigration certificates to bring in whom they wished. Raziel accepted knowing very well that this would put him on a collision course with Stern. Although just as dedicated as Stern to the Irgun's ultimate aims, he had always shown greater tactical flexibility, staying loyal to Jabotinsky's overall leadership and retaining the hope that some sort of *modus vivendi* could be established with Palestine's rulers. Stern was convinced that this was a delusion. While Raziel was talking about joining forces with the empire, Stern was adamantly opposed to any Jews putting on British uniform.

Raziel left prison on 24 October. The stage was now set for another split. In time the Irgun's 2000 or so members would have to make up their minds on a crucial question that had both a strategic and a moral dimension. Did they lay aside their quarrel with the British and, with Raziel, link up with them to fight the bigger enemy of Nazi Germany? Or did they stick to the course set by Stern and Strelitz and concentrate on driving the imperial occupiers from Palestine?

Three months after Raziel's departure, the remaining Irgun leaders were moved to a new prison at Mazra'a (Mizra, to the Jewish inmates), near Acre. There, pro-Nazi Arabs and Jewish undesirables were locked up in separate camps. The detainees included Jabotinsky's son Eri, captured aboard an immigrant ship he was bringing in from Romania which was intercepted by a Royal Navy destroyer on the high seas. Life in Mazra'a was good. There were no squalid dungeons where light never penetrated of the sort that featured in Stern's poetry. 'We must once again thank God for our living conditions,' he wrote to Roni.[18] 'Every day meat, milk, tasty bread. Once a week we go to the sea. Hot water twenty-four hours a day, six days a week. It's almost paradise. Only the basic by-the-way thing is missing: a bit of freedom. But, like we say, this too is "a question of time".' Roni was able to visit him regularly. Even in jail he was preoccupied with his appearance and there were several requests for a favourite blue shirt, a pin-stripe suit and stiffeners for his shirt collars.

In between the games of dominoes and the painting and gardening sessions there was plenty of time to think. The soothing rhythms of prison life had not subdued him. On the eve of their sixth wedding anniversary he wrote Roni a strange letter in which, while declaring his love, he gave her the option of cutting her losses and leaving him. It was the old problem. She sought only peace and normality as the wife of Avraham Stern. But Stern was now 'Yair' and had consciously rejected domestic calm for a life of perpetual struggle and risk. For her 'silence is happiness'.[19] He, however (borrowing the lines from the Russian Romantic writer and poet Mikhail Lermontov), was 'a rebel eager for the storm/as if in it prevails tranquillity'.

He went on: 'My gentle one, know that if you feel it is all too much, that you must leave me, I will understand you and love you as I love you now: with gentleness, sincerity and faithfulness. I was happy with you, you are my joy, my tranquillity, my rest. With you I am secure, it is warm, light.'

Beyond the barbed wire, Europe was in the grip of a mighty convulsion as transformative as a new geological epoch. Stern's imagination was fired with grandiose visions that self-consciously defied the commonsense judgements of Raziel, Jabotinsky and the Revisionist mainstream. He was edging towards a conclusion that even he was reluctant to acknowledge in public. His new concept, which he cautiously tested on his fellow inmates, was that the Irgun should take their hostility to Britain to its logical conclusion. Instead of joining forces with the empire, as Raziel argued, they should team up with its enemies. It was true that Nazi Germany embodied anti-Semitism, but the Polish government had been anti-Semitic and he had successfully done business with it. Why not try the same approach with the Axis powers and forge a deal whereby they would send the Irgun their unwanted Jews and the Irgun would fight on their behalf in Palestine?

These views were not known to the Revisionist chief in Palestine, Dr Aryeh Altman, much less to the British, when he persuaded the authorities to let Stern and his companions go with an undertaking that the movement would ensure they stayed out of trouble. They were released on 18 June 1940. The war had just entered a new and terrible phase. The Germans had smashed through France's defences and the country had surrendered. The Italians, who had hovered, jackal-like, at the edges until the kill was assured, declared war on Hitler's remaining enemy, Britain. Palestine was now directly threatened from two sides. In the north, Vichy collaborationist forces were in possession of Lebanon and Syria. To the south and west, Italian troops would soon be advancing on Egypt as Italian warplanes launched raids on Haifa and Tel Aviv.

These developments only strengthened Stern's belief that the British were heading for defeat and the interests of the Jews were best served by a deal with the devil. The day after their release, Stern and Strelitz met Raziel with some others of the command. Inevitably it was a rough encounter. Stern and Raziel disagreed about everything. Raziel had known for some time that he had lost the confidence of the Irgun leaders inside and outside prison and since his release he had failed to reimpose his authority on the rank and file. At the meeting he repeated the decision he had already taken to resign as commander-in-chief. This triggered some form of election that resulted in Stern being installed in his place.

The matter did not end there. Stern's elevation was not welcomed by Jabotinsky, who persuaded Raziel that he must fight back. In the power struggle that followed, both Stern and Raziel sought the endorsement of Jabotinsky, now living in New York. Stern might have long since parted ideological company with the patriarch, but Jabotinsky was still the Irgun's 'supreme commander'. In order to cling on to his new position, Stern needed his support, and he fired off a long letter accusing Raziel of numerous abuses of authority. Raziel in turn made his own appeal to the chief. It consisted of a viciously eloquent dissection of his old friend's character.

'Concerning [Stern], this delicate playboy, hovering over this base, earthly world in holy piety, almost not touching the impurity of this world with his angel's wings, careful not to speak against a person so as not to dirty this overspreading sanctity – this charming boy has been revealed as an expert in intrigue.' Stern was a master of dissimulation with a fine appreciation of timing. 'One sees nothing before the decisive hour. When the time comes to show one's cards, the job is nice and clean, a delicate ivory statue wearing a tie in good taste and smart suit with the trousers precisely creased. In short, an unscrupulous intelligent person, who so distorts the facts that the borders of reality mean nothing to him ... Where did he learn this pleasant skill? The devil only knows. Actually, I think it's not new to him. This is the way he has been from the start ...'[20]

The tussle would go back and forth for several weeks. In that time both men vied for the loyalty of the organization, making their case in person or through their supporters in numerous clandestine meetings in flats and schools under cover of darkness. Among the listeners was Uri Avnery, the young German immigrant whose assertion on joining that he did not hate the 'English' had caused consternation among his superiors. To the rank and file like him the schism came as a surprise and a shock. 'When you live in the underground it completely absorbs you,' he said many years later. 'The organization was everything, and then suddenly there is this rift. It's terrible! The whole world is breaking apart. Everything you believed in suddenly becomes doubtful ... Stern says of Raziel that he's a British agent. Raziel says of Stern that he's a Nazi collaborator.' Avnery recalls that the pro-Stern advocates were quite open about the proposal for some sort of alliance with the Axis. As someone who knew the realities of Nazi oppression first hand, he 'refused to accept the idea' and eventually went with the Irgun.[21] The power struggle ended in defeat for the 'delicate playboy'. Raziel was reappointed as commander-in-chief and he ordered Stern to knuckle under. The bad blood between the two men made the idea of submission impossible. On 17 July 1940, Stern announced the formation of a new body, the Irgun Zvai Leumi B'Yisrael (the National Military Organization in Israel). His beliefs had now crystallized into a creed in which might and will determined everything, the weak overcame the strong and the life of one nation was built on the debris of another.[22]

Stern set out his aims in an inaugural proclamation. 'We take upon ourselves three tasks: To unite all those loyal, proud and fighting ... in the ranks of the Hebrew liberation movement; to appear before the world as the single representative of the Jewish fighters and institute a policy of eliminating the Diaspora; to become as quickly as possible a force capable of taking control of the country by force of arms.'[23]

In the desperate circumstances of the time it seemed a wild dream. No more than a hundred Irgun members followed Stern into the wilderness. The split was overshadowed by a completely unforeseen event. On 4 August, while visiting a Betar camp at Hunter, a village in the Catskill Mountains in New York State, Ze'ev Jabotinsky suffered a heart attack and died. He was fifty-nine. His death removed from the Revisionist movement its inspiration and its prophet. With his passing, Stern lost a father figure but one whose authority he had come to resent and to challenge. His sorrow was therefore mingled with a sense of liberation. Despite their differences, Jabotinsky could not be ignored and even from afar he was capable of exercising some moderating influence on Stern's thoughts and deeds. Now he was gone there was nothing to restrain him.

SIX

'In the Underground'

Stern's stand had left him high and dry. He could take some comfort from the fact that he was now undisputed boss of a band of dedicated followers – albeit a very small one. On the other hand, his defection had cut him off from the Revisionist movement's considerable resources. He and his followers were virtually friendless and without money. Before he went to jail, Stern had lived a comfortable life, travelling widely and mixing often with rich and powerful people who were impressed by his intelligence, his charm and the romantic aura generated by his burning sense of purpose. His prison stint had been no great ordeal. Indeed his experience of hardship was almost entirely imaginary, distilled in his concept of the 'anonymous soldier' – alone, hunted, certain only of the inevitable rendezvous with death. From now on, these fantasies would become increasingly real.

A glimpse of the dismal circumstances in which the Stern faithful lived was provided by Yaacov Polani. Polani was born in Slonim in Poland and from childhood 'had adventurous inclinations'.[1] The Jews of the town were assimilationists who 'put my back up and I always wanted to annoy them'. He emigrated with his family to Palestine in 1922. His father bought a farm in Herzliya, just north of Tel Aviv. Yaacov got a job packing oranges. Some fellow workers were in the Irgun and talked him into joining. He attended a basic training course at nearby Kfar Saba, run by Hanoch Strelitz, and was later sent to Poland to one of the training camps overseen by Stern.

When the split came, Polani was acting commander of the Irgun in Herzliya. While most stayed with the Irgun, he and a few others joined up with Stern. 'We had no money or means of existence,' he told the police after being arrested in 1942. 'I was in a difficult position as I was regarded as responsible in the eyes of my men. I demanded help from Stern but got nothing from him.' Strelitz, who along with Binyamin Zeroni, the Jerusalem jailbreaker, had sided with Stern, was not much more use. When Polani met him in the street and told him of his troubles, Strelitz replied 'don't worry me with such matters. Let those who complain go to hell. There are more important things to worry about.' Polani and his men 'led the life of dogs'. The coffers were empty. He was paid only one pound a week to live on and could eat only once a day. It was no better for the leaders. Stern himself 'received a very small salary, no more than that of a ghaffir (watchman)'.

Nelly Langsfelder, who had arrived in Palestine from Vienna two years before, joined the Irgun then sided with Stern in the split, remembered living on a diet of falafel, oranges and bananas. One of her duties was to stick up posters denouncing the government and urging young Jewish men not to join the British forces. The posters were immediately torn down by the police or the Haganah, whose men were now filling the ranks of the military. She and her companions took to handing out leaflets in the streets. They thought of distributing them inside cinemas but had to give up the idea 'because we didn't have the money to buy tickets'.[2]

Since releasing Stern from captivity, the police had been keeping half an eye on him. They were aware of the schism with Raziel and the subsequent formation of what they were beginning to call the 'Stern group'. The Chief Secretary was starting to take an interest. Battershill had moved on to govern Cyprus, and not a moment too soon. His job was getting him down. 'One works all day and half the night and gets nowhere in the long run,' he reflected. 'One is tempted to say, How long O Lord how long?'[3] The new man was John Stuart Macpherson, who had previously served in Nigeria and came to the multiple problems of Palestine with new eyes. In September 1940 he wrote to the Inspector General of the Palestine

Police, Alan Saunders, asking whether he intended to rearrest Stern and the four other Irgun men who had gone to prison with him.[4] Saunders joined the force at its birth in 1920 and, apart from a twenty-month stint in Nigeria, had served with it ever since. He had been given command in 1937 and was respected by his peers in the administration and the men under him for his shrewd grasp of Palestine's affairs. The police chief gave a relaxed reply. 'There is no doubt that the responsible leaders of the Revisionist Party have been genuinely exercised over the formation of this group and are making every effort to suppress it,' he wrote. 'They claim that its influence is now practically negligible and that it will shortly dissolve altogether.' In the circumstances he took the view that 'the arrest of the five persons referred to … is not desirable at present'.[5]

Three days after writing this, Saunders was forced to change his mind. Stern's dire financial situation had driven him to desperate measures. He had decided to start robbing banks. Even for someone so adept at finding pure justifications for dubious acts, the decision was an uncomfortable one. Yaacov Levstein recorded 'Yair' telling him, 'I know that a bank robbery, even for a good cause, is something our men find very difficult to bring themselves to do. It is not our usual way of operating … but we have no choice.'

Levstein was authorized to set up two bank jobs in Jerusalem, where he was now the group's commander. One failed – for reasons not disclosed. The other, at the Japhet Bank, succeeded but the haul, Stern informed him, was 'just not enough'. They had to 'go after the big money'.[6]

The next target was a large branch of one of the Mandate's main banks, the Anglo-Palestine, on Tel Aviv's busy Ben Yehuda Street. The heist was to go ahead on Monday, 16 September 1940, but before it did the war made a sudden and shocking appearance. The Italian air force had already launched raids on the oil facilities and port at Haifa. There was nothing of strategic interest in Tel Aviv and the expectation had been that its inhabitants were in no great danger. At four o'clock on the afternoon of Monday, 9 September, air raid sirens sounded. Moments later bombs exploded in the city centre and an Arab village to the north-east, dropped by aircraft flying from bases on the islands of Rhodes and Leros. The raid lasted only a few minutes but the death toll would reach 137. Geoffrey Morton was in his office at the time and 'had a good view of the whole show'. He went immediately to the scene and 'found the ARP personnel and Fire Brigade already on the job and doing excellent work'. Australian soldiers also 'got down to it with a will' and Morton was impressed by the calm of the victims. 'The injured bore their hurts with great fortitude and waited quietly to be evacuated,' he noted in his weekly report.[7]

Avraham Stern was with Roni at the latest of their endless succession of digs, a one-room flat in a block of flats at 57 Pinsker Street near the city centre, when the alarm sounded. They ran to the stairwell just as a bomb landed in the yard outside, blowing in the entrance. Stern crouched over his wife to shield her from the blast. She was hit in the head by a piece of metal and he was peppered with flying debris which was later picked out by a doctor friend from Warsaw. The experience would do nothing to dent his enthusiasm for cutting a deal with the Italians.

If anything, the raid was further proof that Britain was on its last legs. Two days before, London had come under intense bombardment from the Luftwaffe for the first time since the start of the Battle of Britain. Even to the empire's friends, it seemed that the end might not be far off. On the same day as Tel Aviv was attacked, a strange ceremony took place at Rachel's Tomb, a Jewish holy site in Bethlehem. A procession led by the Chief Rabbi and including the Jerusalem District Commissioner Edward Keith-Roach walked seven times around the shrine, uttering prayers for British victory and the health of the King, the Queen, Sir Harold MacMichael and Mr Keith-Roach himself.[8]

Britain's difficulties were encouraging. Without the wherewithal to sustain his men, though, he was unable to exploit the situation. As the citizens of Tel Aviv resumed normal life, preparations for the robbery began. Stern kept aloof from the practicalities and would certainly not be coshing any cashiers. Yehoshua Zettler, a twenty-four-year-old whose family home in Kfar Saba had been destroyed by Arabs in rioting in 1921 and who had taken part in the attatck on Bir Adas in which five innocent Arabs were killed, was put in charge of the operation. He was nicknamed 'the Farmer' and in Polani's opinion a 'rough and uneducated' character, and 'like an Arab'. Binyamin Zeroni was responsible for the planning. Somewhat to his annoyance, Yaacov Levstein was hauled in from Jerusalem to act as Zettler's deputy, even though his area of expertise was explosives rather than armed robbery. They would be joined in the 'assault group' by Eliyahu Giladi; bold and energetic, he was considered too wild even for his comrades who would eventually kill him for putting the organization in danger. Moshe Moldovsky, leader of the Bir Adas raid, was charged with guarding the bank door once the raid began. Avraham Amper, the originator of the military training camps in Poland, and Zelig Zak, a recently arrived Polish émigré currently working in a British Army canteen, would be stationed on a nearby rooftop, armed with 'noise bombs' to divert attention from the robbery when the action started. Shmuel Kaplan, who earned his living as a driver, was designated wheelman of the getaway car. Another team member, Max Goldman, would follow on a motorbike. In order to confuse pursuers, the car would stop at an opportune moment, and one of the team would alight with the loot, climb onto the back of the bike and zoom off in a different direction.

The morning of 16 September was another of those long, hot days of flawless blue skies and harsh, flat sunlight that stretch from March to November in the Holy Land. At 12.20 p.m., the staff of the Anglo-Palestine Bank on Ben Yehuda Street were preparing to pull down the shutters and head for home or the cool and shade of one of the little cafés in the streets nearby that slope westwards down to the sea. They scarcely noticed three young men who walked in separately, to join a handful of other customers standing at the counters. According to Levstein's account, 'we tipped our hats as we entered, as if we were greeting those inside'. This action released hidden masks, pulled down over their faces by small lead weights. They drew their guns and 'the Farmer' stepped forward 'and announced in a deep, steady voice: "We are confiscating funds for the Hebrew Underground, to fight for national liberation. Stand up quietly and raise your hands, turn to the wall and lean against it and follow my orders. Anyone who interferes with the Hebrew underground is risking his life."'

To reinforce the point, Amper and Zak's 'noise bombs' now began to explode outside. The safe door was open. Levstein then 'jumped on the counter. The cashier bent down, and I skipped over him toward the safe … I took a thin cloth bag out of my pocket and began to throw in the money.' There was lots of it, large, white bank-notes covered in seals and crests and copperplate script which crackled agreeably in his eager hands. When the bag was full he vaulted back over the counter and the team retreated through a side door and into the alleyway which led out the back to a side street, where Kaplan was waiting in a Mercedes saloon. Zettler was the last one out. Levstein said that, as 'the Farmer' left, he hung a package on the doorknob and told the cowering clerks that it was a bomb which would explode if anyone tried to open the door. His account gives the impression that the operation was carried out as considerately as the circumstances allowed. The victims told a different story. Once inside the bank the 'assault team' had loosed off a volley of shots into the ceiling, leaving the staff in no doubt that they were dealing with desperate men.

The getaway was similarly noisy. As they drove away, Moldovsky 'suddenly took out his gun and started shooting at a youth walking outside'. The boy dropped to the pavement, unharmed, but the racket alerted a taxi driver who bravely gave chase. Zettler leaned out of the window and opened fire, smashing a hole in the pursuer's windscreen. The have-a-go hero veered away and, once they reached a quiet stretch of road, Kaplan pulled up. Levstein, clutching the money, hopped out and onto the pillion of Goldman's motorbike, which had pulled up behind. In his haste, he spilled some notes from the satchel but Goldman yelled at him to leave them and they sped away.

They took a roundabout route to the rendezvous, a room in an apartment block at 36 Bilu Street, just off Rothschild Boulevard. There a man and a young woman were waiting for them. They took the cash and packed it into the back of a large, framed picture. It was big money, just as Stern had hoped: 4300 pounds in used notes. Then they set off to deliver it to him. Everything, it seemed, had gone remarkably well.[9]

The Anglo-Palestine Bank robbery was to be a turning point in Avraham Stern's story. He now had the cash to pay followers, fund further operations and buy weapons. There was even enough left over to finance a clandestine newspaper, Bamachteret (In the Underground). But the scale and daring of the operation had transformed the status of the Stern band in the eyes of the Mandate authorities. They were no longer a nuisance the Revisionists could be left to deal with in their own fashion. They were a menace to law and order. As Stern's ambitions became clearer, they would soon also be seen as a threat to the British war effort.

The sense of satisfaction at the way the raid had gone did not last long. The planning had been quite thorough but there were several amateurish loose ends that the police were quick to pounce upon. As Max Goldman weaved the bike through the backstreets, someone had made a note of its number plate. When the police checked they found it was registered in the name of one Yehoshua Zettler. By the end of the day he was in police custody.[10] The team members did not linger long at the rendezvous and quickly went their separate ways. Even so, it seems someone tipped off the police for the Tel Aviv police raided the Bilu Street apartment block that afternoon. Geoffrey Morton was with them. 'We visited a house in which a pistol was found and also a black mask and a quantity of clothing soaked in perspiration,' he noted. It did not take long to discover that the room was rented in the name of Shmuel Kaplan ('a known

Revisionist terrorist') and by the end of the day he, too, was in a police cell.

The robbery had taken place on Morton's patch. He was not, however, given charge of the investigation. Instead, Assistant Superintendent Solomon Soffer was brought in from Jerusalem to head the inquiry. Soffer was one of the longest-serving Jewish officers in the Palestine Police CID and since the early 1930s had built up a reputation for zeal and efficiency combating drug smuggling, counterfeiting and fraud. He had proved equally effective fighting political subversion.

His arrival did not seem to bother Morton who recorded that he 'discussed all aspects with him' and 'decided to strike off Wilkin to work on the case with him'.[11] This can hardly have been welcome news to Tom Wilkin who had already had to suffer Soffer horning in on his turf and co-opting some of his most valuable contacts. His antipathy to him was by now obvious. 'The Wilkin–Soffer hate is well known,' noted Giles Bey in a report.

The story of their rivalry was revealed by Soffer in a lengthy memo to Giles that gives an idea of the complexity of the relationships between police and the underground. No one was precisely who they seemed to be, all loyalties were elastic and nothing was to be taken for granted. In May, Soffer had gone to Tel Aviv to investigate undisclosed crimes. On his travels round the cafés, bars and restaurants where servants of the Mandate mixed with the local population his curiosity had been piqued by a man called David Rosenthal whom he noticed 'associating with several police officers'. Rosenthal, a Polish Jew, 'was only too glad to offer them drinks etc. He was always dressed well and frequented all the notorious cafés. I made inquiries as to the source of his income but no one could satisfy me with the correct information.'[12]

Soffer 'decided to make friends with him, which advantage he seized immediately'. Very soon the amiable Mr Rosenthal offered to introduce him to someone very special, 'a person who is (in his words) – the almighty'. This man could 'abduct, detain persons, get rid of them etc. I elucidated that from him that the person is one of the heads of the IZL (Irgun Zvai Leumi).'

When the introduction took place a few days later, Soffer learned the identity of the mystery man. It was none other than Ephraim Ilin, host of Tel Aviv's most interesting parties and, although not a commander, a very good friend of the Irgun. The first meeting was rather an anti-climax. Ilin* was 'not very talkative' and both men took 'care not to divulge names of persons responsible for detailed activities'.

One thing the pair did let slip was that they were 'very close friends of Inspector Wilkins [sic] and that they assist him [in] his work, especially against Nazis and communists'. Soffer quizzed Wilkin about them, who admitted he 'knows their affiliation with the IZL and benefits [from] the most important information from them'.

Ilin's initial caution did not last. Before long he was in touch with Soffer, suggesting they might be able to help each other out. He had a friend, currently detained by the authorities under the emergency regulations, who was a 'very important figure in the IZL'. If Soffer would arrange his early release Ilin could organize all sorts of favours. He could supply any number of young men to tail suspected criminals. Furthermore, he could 'arrange for the kidnapping of criminals and force confessions from them'. If this was not enough, the Irgun was prepared to pay up to six hundred pounds for his freedom. The name of the man was Avraham Stern.

The approach came to nothing. Soffer returned to Jerusalem and, at the end of June, Stern was released. Soffer saw no more of the shady pair until the late summer, when he ran into David Rosenthal in Jerusalem. They went for a coffee and Rosenthal could not resist telling him that more robberies were planned to get money 'to purchase arms for the defence of the country on the occasion of any

* Soffer spells it 'Eylan' in his report. Hebrew and Arabic names were phonetically transcribed and often appear in different forms in official documents.

outbreak by the Arabs or the Jews, in case the British forces are defeated by the enemies, or in case the British Government will favour the Arabs politically after the end of the war'.

Soffer reported the conversation to Giles. It may be that, having delivered the warning about the likelihood of future robberies, he was the obvious choice to lead the investigation when Rosenthal's tip turned out to be true. When he arrived in Jerusalem to begin the search for the perpetrators of the Anglo-Palestine job his first act was to try to get in touch with Ilin and Rosenthal. If anyone knew where to reach them it was Tom Wilkin. He turned out to be most unhelpful. Soffer described how he 'asked Inspector Wilkins [sic] among other things to get in touch with these two gentlemen and see what information they may have about this case. The said Inspector Wilkins brought me no results ...'

Soffer, though, was quite capable of making progress on his own. Under his questioning, Shmuel Kaplan, in whose room Zettler, Zeroni and co. had gathered after the Anglo-Palestine heist and who had since been arrested, had come up with an extraordinary proposal. If Soffer freed him for a day, he would contact the perpetrators and try to persuade them to surrender. Surprisingly, Soffer agreed. 'On 26 September I let Kaplan go before noon,' he informed Giles. 'Between 1800 and 1900 hours he phoned me that he wants an extension of time as he arranged an appointment of those concerned at a late hour.' Soffer consented once again, and also promised Kaplan that he would not be followed. They agreed to meet up at midnight. For a bank robber, Kaplan seems to have been a man of unusual probity for instead of disappearing he kept his word and turned up at the rendezvous. He appeared rather crestfallen. His contacts had now changed their minds and had refused to meet him. No reason was given, but their attitude was hardly surprising given the likelihood that they would be walking into a police trap. 'Kaplan felt very much upset about it believing that the party will probably consider him a traitor,' Soffer reported. The detective 'formed the impression' that one of the people Kaplan had hoped to meet was Stern.

After Zettler and Kaplan there were no more arrests.[13] Stern's trail was cooling fast. On 18 October, Giles ordered one of his senior officers to approach David Raziel to see if he could help them track down his former friend. The meeting took place in the Arab National restaurant in East Jerusalem. The unnamed officer described how he started off talking about the government's concern at the recent activities of the Stern group. As well as robbing banks they were 'also said to have attempted to establish contact with the Italians', though he admitted that 'how true this latter point was I could not tell'.[14] However, the government had decided that 'the continued existence of this group was not in its interests, and we are anxious to trace Stern and certain of his followers'. The officer pointed out that the Revisionist movement and the Irgun were now supposed to be on Britain's side and should therefore be morally obliged to oppose Stern and his men. However, their leaders had 'not openly denounced them as traitors to the Revisionist movement'.

Raziel accepted that the Stern group was operating against both the Revisionists' and the government's interests. However, he 'regretted he could not help us to find Stern. Even if I produced evidence of the alleged Italian connection ... he could not denounce a member or an ex-member of the Irgun.' Raziel seemed eager not to appear too unhelpful and threw the policeman a comforting rumour. It appeared that Eliahu Golomb, the leader of the Haganah in Tel Aviv, 'had planned to arrest Stern and a few others and keep them in some remote ... colony to cool their heels for a spell. He thought something of the kind might have happened already.'

Whether or not Golomb, a tough pragmatist and a founder of the Haganah who had tried to build better relations with the Irgun, ever contemplated such a plan, it did not come to fruition. Anyway, it would no longer be enough to satisfy the British. All the Mandate security services now had the Stern group in their sights. On 25 October, Giles Bey received a handwritten letter from a senior officer at British Forces headquarters in Palestine. The writer – whose signature is indecipherable – said that, as it now seemed unlikely that the group would be put away on criminal charges, the emergency regulations should be used to round them up.[15] According to an internal CID memo, the Jewish Agency and 'a responsible Revisionist leader' were of the same opinion. A wanted list was drawn up with thirty-seven names on it; at the head of it was Stern, who was said to have 'disappeared' and was last reported to be in Metula, a village on the Lebanese border. On 6 November the police swooped, raiding a number of addresses and capturing fourteen of those on the wanted list. The accuracy of the intelligence suggested that someone inside the organization had supplied the information.[16]

The round-up was prompted in part by the fact that intelligence reports were starting to put flesh on the bones of the rumours of Stern's pro-Italian activities. 'Information from a very large number of reliable sources has consistently affirmed that the Stern group's policy was to ingratiate themselves with the Italians with the idea that should the Italians invade the country they would be backed as the dominant Jewish party,' reported Harry Rice, Giles's deputy at the CID, on 8 November 1940.[17] This was a sensational claim. The full story of Stern's international intrigues would turn out to be even more extraordinary.

SEVEN

'They Will Cover Your Memory with Spittle and Disgrace'

The idea of an Italian alliance had been floating around since the early days of the war. It was planted by a man called Moshe Rothstein, a mysterious figure in a very murky story. Rothstein said that he was in contact with Italian secret agents and approached the Irgun with an interesting offer. He claimed that the Italians were keen on a partnership with some anti-British force in Palestine. The Irgun, with their nationalist and militaristic ideology and record of antipathy to the empire, seemed the perfect fit.

It is unclear exactly when the initial approach was made. Irgun veterans would later say that the first overture was to David Raziel shortly after he emerged from Mazra'a in October 1939. Raziel treated it with extreme caution. He had, after all, agreed to cooperate with the British and although Mussolini had not yet signed up to Hitler's war, cosying up to the Fascists could only be interpreted as a hostile act. There were also real doubts as to Rothstein's bona fides. He had been hanging around the fringes of the Irgun since the early thirties when he lived in the Revisionist stronghold of Rosh Pinna. He had played little or no part in operations and how he came to be in touch with the Italian secret service was a mystery.

Rothstein was lying about his Italian connection. He did, however, have a clandestine relationship with another intelligence service. He was closely involved with the Haganah's Shai. The Haganah saw themselves as the legitimate defenders of the Yishuv and the Irgun as dangerous usurpers. They therefore had a strong interest in doing them down. The initial approach to Raziel seems to have been a provocation designed to generate black propaganda to be used, when appropriate, against their rivals.

With Raziel's decision to back the British and the subsequent improvement in relations between the Revisionists and the Yishuv's leftist establishment, the Irgun appear to have taken over Rothstein and his plot and proceeded to run it against Stern. This was certainly how the CID interpreted events. 'It has been known for some time that following the split which occurred in the IZL (Irgun) in the summer of 1940 and the subsequent formation of the Stern Group, the policy decided upon by the former organization to prevent further members from being enticed away to Stern's programme ... was to expose and emphasize his relations with a foreign power – ie Italy,' wrote Alan Saunders to Chief Secretary Macpherson when summing up events at the end of 1941.

'With this end in view certain Irgun leaders engineered a meeting between Stern and a person [i.e. Rothstein] ... who introduced himself as being in touch with the Italians and able to negotiate on their behalf. Through this person the trick prospered for some time and served the double purpose of keeping the Irgun informed of Stern's intentions regarding collaboration with the enemy and at the same time actually preventing the group from getting into touch with the Italians.'[1]

The man manipulating the plot was probably Israel Pritzker, a senior figure in Irgun intelligence. Pritzker was on close terms with the CID and a copy of the proposed agreement between Stern and the Italians was soon in their hands.

For all his academic brilliance, Stern could be remarkably gullible. He had been in prison at the time of Rothstein's first appearance, which could explain his willingness to at least examine the bait that had been rejected by Raziel. His eagerness to bite on it, though, alarmed his lieutenants who warned that it could be a trap. Stern was unconcerned. He argued that, at worst, Rothstein was an *agent provocateur*, in which case the knowledge that the group was prepared to do a deal with the enemy might wring some concessions from the British. At best, he might be genuine.

Italy was now on Palestine's doorstep. A few days after the Italian air force bombed Tel Aviv on 9 September 1940, a large Italian army entered British-held Egypt, advancing sixty miles to construct a forward base. These developments appear to have encouraged Stern to believe that it might not be long before Fascist troops were marching into Palestine. If an Axis victory was imminent, it was a matter of urgency to have arrangements in place before Britain fell.

Rothstein was in possession of what purported to be some draft proposals from the Italians. According to some Stern group survivors the document went back and forth with additions and amendments before being agreed. The result was the so-called 'Jerusalem Agreement'. It was a very damaging document. For all his talk of a proud 'Kingdom of Israel', Stern seemed prepared to sacrifice sovereignty to the Fascists on several key matters. Under its terms, Italy would organize the transfer of Jews under Axis control to their homeland and provide the wherewithal for a Hebrew army. The Jews would get a state – but it would be modelled on Mussolini's Italy and built along corporatist, Fascist lines. Its foreign policy was to be identical to that of Rome, making the new Israel an Axis satellite. The Italian navy would be given Haifa as a base. The Old City of Jerusalem, the longed for, mystical heart of Judaism, would be, with the exception of the Jewish holy places, placed under Vatican control. There is no evidence that these proposals ever reached the Italians and their circulation was limited to the intelligence departments of the Irgun, the Haganah and the CID. Rothstein was eventually rumbled and Yaacov Levstein given the job of killing him. The career double-crosser was understandably prudent and moved lodgings constantly. When Levstein finally tracked him down the house was full of Rothstein's relatives and 'since we did not wish harm to innocent people we cancelled the operation'. Rothstein disappeared thereafter 'and we never heard from him again'.[2]

In attempting to strike a deal with the Fascists, Stern at least had the excuse of entrapment. But at the same time as the Rothstein affair was playing out he was engaged in another overture to a foreign power, one that was even more ruinous to his reputation and which was not prompted by the manipulations of an *agent provocateur*. The Italians were the junior partners in the Axis. The real masters of Europe were the Germans. It was they who held the fate of Europe's Jews in their hands and it was they who had the means to deal Britain the death blow.

Stern's idea was a logical continuation of the process that he had begun so successfully with the Poles. If Poland could become a partner in the Irgun project, why not Germany? The principle was the same. They wanted rid of their Jews. Those struggling to bring about the rebirth of Israel needed them – to oppose the British and to populate the land. It was an equation that, in his eyes at least, seemed ripe with the possibilities of mutual benefit.

At the end of September, a few weeks after the Anglo-Palestine Bank robbery, he sent an envoy to Beirut to make contact with the Germans. Since the fall of France, Lebanon had gone from being a friendly territory to an outpost of Vichy loyalists who were collaborating enthusiastically with the Italians and Germans. Both had diplomatic missions in Beirut. The man chosen for the mission was Naftali Lubentchik, a sophisticated Moscow-born polyglot (he spoke seven European languages) who was in charge of the Stern group's finances. His job was to open lines of communication with the Nazis, but also to contact Italian officials to find out whether or not there was any substance to the Jerusalem Agreement pantomime.

Levstein, who had been moved to Haifa to escape police heat following the Anglo-Palestine affair, was in charge of Lubentchik's arrangements. He had dealings with Jewish and Arab smugglers who moved people and weapons between Haifa and Beirut. He had also found an ally in the French. Under the 'confused conditions it was easy to obtain arms, even from the official French sources who wanted to be paid in hard currency,' he wrote. 'Those sources gladly supplied us with arms of all kinds, knowing that they were intended to attack their British enemy, thus combining French patriotism with profit making.'[3] Lubentchik assumed the identity of a Maronite businessman who had been in Haifa to buy merchandise. He reached Beirut without trouble and soon made an appointment to see a visiting German diplomat, Werner Otto von Hentig.

Von Hentig was head of the Foreign Ministry's Levant section. He was a survivor from the pre-Nazi era who had served the Kaiser and the Weimar Republic and regarded himself as an honourable man untainted by anti-Semitism. He had been sent to Lebanon and Syria on a month-long fact-finding mission. His task was to check out reports that the French were treating German citizens in the area badly and also locking up pro-German Arabs. On arrival he chose to install himself in the unobtrusive Monopole Hotel rather than the swanky St George and was soon receiving a throng of supplicants seeking the Reich's favour.

'The most remarkable delegation came from Palestine itself,' he wrote in his autobiography. It was led by 'an exceptionally good-looking young officer type'.[4] Von Hentig's memory is faulty on this point and in fact Lubentchik was on his own. Many years later, at the age of ninety-seven, the diplomat gave a fuller version of the encounter to an Israeli journalist. 'The Jewish young man made a fine impression,' he told Shlomo Shamgar of *Yedioth Ahronoth*.[5] 'He was well dressed and had a gift for political persuasion. He told me of his anti-British organization and his willingness to join with the Reich to continue the war against the British. In exchange for participation in the war against the British, he proposed that the Reich help his organization establish a Jewish state in Eretz Yisrael and allow the Jews from the occupied lands to make aliyah [immigrate] and settle in it.'

The proposals drawn up by Stern were set out in a memorandum which carried the stamp of the 'IZL in Israel', which von Hentig passed to the Foreign Ministry.[6] They were repeated in another document, dated 11 January 1941, drawn up by the German naval attaché in Ankara, Admiral Ralf von der Marwitz, and given to the German ambassador in Turkey who transmitted them to Berlin. How he came to hear of them is a mystery, though French intelligence may have tipped him off. In setting out his offer Stern was being economical with the truth. He left out the fact that 'IZL in Israel' was only a fragment of the original Irgun. This made his offer of help slightly more impressive. He was offering 'active participation in the war on the German side'. The Nazis would have the use of his men, in the Middle East and Europe, to carry out sabotage and espionage operations against the British. His condition was that the 'aspirations of the Israeli freedom movement are recognised'. These were the establishment of an independent Jewish state in Palestine, populated by the Jews of German-occupied Europe who should be allowed free passage to emigrate there.[7]

Von Hentig said he received no reply to the proposals before he left Beirut. On returning to Germany he asked Ernst von Weizsäcker, the deputy head of the Foreign Ministry, whether he had seen the memorandum. Von Weizsäcker 'sharpened his gaze. "Do you really think the Reich could be interested in a Jewish state in [Palestine] when we are trying to win over the Arabs and Muslims to further our war aims?"' he asked.

It was a good question. The Germans had already made it clear that their strategy favoured the Arabs. German intelligence and military officials were at that moment working with Iraqi generals and the Mufti, who was now conducting his anti-British and anti-Jewish activities from Baghdad, involved in a conspiracy that would result a few months later in the overthrow of the British-installed Iraqi monarchy. More fundamentally, why did Stern think Hitler would be interested in anything that might bring long-term benefits to the Jews?

Stern's belief that a deal with the Germans was both desirable and possible was not a momentary aberration. He clung to it even when it was clear that it would not and could not lead anywhere. In the endless discussions that were an inescapable part of life in the underground, he drove home the distinction between an 'enemy' and an 'oppressor'. The Jews' enemy was the British who occupied their land and, as the White Paper proved, were now bent on blocking the establishment of a Jewish state. The Germans, for all their hatred and persecution of the Jews, were mere oppressors. Only by fighting the British could you hope to change their minds. Stern was not opposed to an understanding with them. But they would first have to recognize the leadership of the Yishuv as a temporary government that would establish an independent state at the end of the war, recognized by Britain. Until that happened, any collaboration was an act of treason.[8]

It was some time before Lubentchik's account of the episode reached Stern. It described how von Hentig had explained to him that there were two schools of thought among the German leadership regarding the Jewish question. Some took a *realpolitik* approach and proposed the expulsion of the Jews to some far-flung territory Madagascar perhaps The *idealpolitik* faction was committed to the total annihilation of European Jewry.[9]

Despite the failure of Lubentchik's mission, Stern continued to harbour hopes of an alliance, spinning fantasies of how collaboration might work. Some were so wild that he shared them with only a chosen few. He confided to them a plan whereby he would offer 'help divisions' made up of tens of thousands of young European Jews to the Wehrmacht to fight with them against the British in North Africa. If the Germans never made it to Palestine, the 'help divisions' would then desert and head for the Holy Land. Such was his devotion to a deal with the devil that he was prepared to stand at the head of a quisling government, willingly accepting his inevitable assassination by Jewish patriots. This, he told a friend, 'will be my sacrifice to the resurrection of the kingdom of Israel and the rescue of the Jewish nation'.[10] Such suicidal visions may have seemed plausible to Stern himself but to most they were incomprehensible.

Apologists would later claim that his policy was driven solely by the burning urge to pursue all means possible to rescue Europe's Jews. But Stern's own words suggest that his main motive was to obtain the manpower for the conquest of Palestine. 'All we want of the Germans is to enable us to transfer this army to the coasts of Eretz Yisrael [the Land of Israel], and the war against the British to liberate the homeland will begin here,' he declared to an old comrade, Yaacov Orenstein. 'The Jews will attain a state, and the Germans will, incidentally, be rid of an important British base in the Middle East, and also solve the Jewish question in Europe.'[11]

But as Orenstein vainly attempted to point out, this was never going to happen. German hatred of the Jews precluded them from agreeing to any proposal, no matter how logical. Stern's admirers would also try to justify his actions by explaining that at the time of these machinations, no one knew of the Final Solution to exterminate all Jews within Germany's reach. It was true that the Wannsee Conference which formalized the murder programme did not take place until the end of January 1942, but it was already appallingly clear that German intentions towards the Jews were evil and that no accommodation was conceivable. The newspapers were full of dreadful stories. Stern had the evidence of his own family as to what the Jews of Europe could expect.

The war arrived in Suwalki on 1 September 1939 when Luftwaffe aircraft bombed the barracks around the town. A few days later the Polish army and police fled. The town was briefly occupied by the Soviets before they ceded it to the German army, who marched in trailing the Gestapo in their wake. On Saturday, 21 October, the Jews of Suwalki were told they had a fortnight to clear out. The Lithuanian border, fifteen miles away, was closed. The Germans' new friends, the Soviets, were also denying entry to Jews. Family groups trudged over the fields trying to find an unguarded spot. Some were caught and turned back; others were shot. Among the refugees were Mordechai and Liza Stern. 'They took some money and some coats and they ran away to the forest, towards the Lithuanian border,' said their grandson Yair. 'It was as cold as hell. During the stay in the forest my grandfather got paralysed in half his body. My grandmother carried him – I don't know how as she was a very small woman.'[12]

Somehow she struggled across the frontier and paid a farmer to take Mordechai by horse and buggy to a hospital, where he died, apparently of a lung infection. About 3000 Jews from the Suwalki area made it to the temporary safety of Kaunas in Lithuania. The same number were left behind. On 2 December they were ordered not to leave their homes. The Jewish part of town was surrounded by SS troops and police and the inhabitants driven into the synagogue, jail and hospital. Everything of value was taken from them. Herded by vicious, snapping guard dogs, they were then marched to the railway station and loaded into sealed wagons for a two-day journey to Lublin. According to Dr Kasriel Eilender, a historian of the Jews of Suwalki, 'most of them were shot in a forest near a locality called Łomazy' (eastern Poland).[13] Liza Stern stayed on in Kaunas where she managed to obtain a visa for Palestine from the British consul, who issued 700 certificates for Palestine in 1940 before the Soviets marched into Lithuania.[14] She arrived via ship from Odessa sometime in the latter part of 1940.[15]

Stern would have heard her story and hundreds like it, yet nothing it seemed would deter him from the notion that the Germans were open to reason or that the British – to whom he owed the deliverance of his mother – were the real enemy.

When Yehoshua Yeivin, a Revisionist pioneer who had once declared an enthusiasm for fascism, told him, 'they will say of you that you assisted Hitler … they will cover your memory with spittle and disgrace', he simply replied: 'I know that …'[16]

With no outside help forthcoming, the group was effectively moribund. The Anglo-Palestine Bank robbery had been followed in December by the blowing up of the Mandate's immigration office in Haifa. For most of the following year, though, operations were severely limited and the 'anonymous soldiers' mainly stayed indoors. It was not just the lack of resources that inhibited them. Their names were now all too well known to the police. Their relative inactivity did nothing to diminish the efforts of the CID to nail them.

The Mandate's intelligence agencies soon got to know about Lubentchik's mission to Beirut from a 'hundred per cent reliable' source, though they believed he had gone to see the Italians rather than the Germans. For a while, there was nothing to suggest that these overtures had got very far or presented any real threat to Palestine. In the spring of 1941 came hard evidence that the Stern group presented a genuine menace to security. On 17 March, following a tip-off, the police raided the home of a Stern loyalist named Itamar Ben Haroch, who had slipped into Palestine illegally. According to the CID report 'a search of his room produced a sketch indicating the position of Military camps in the Rehovoth area, including those at Jul-us, Qastina, Gadera and Nesa Taiyona and the aerodromes at Tel Nof and Aqir'.[17] In addition, they found records of the movement of British forces between Palestine, Britain and Greece. Here, surely, was active treason.

Stern and his men had moved to the top of the CID's target list. In a letter written on 18 June 1941 to a veteran officer called Raymond Cafferata ordering the arrest of two suspects, Giles Bey described the group as a 'collection of Jewish Quislings'. They were 'a danger to the war effort in this country ... accordingly we must not be squeamish in combatting them'.[18] In later reports they are referred to as a 'Fifth Column' whose object was 'to build up a vast organisation so that in the event of an enemy attack on this country they can assist that enemy by destroying communications, bridges, railways and any other object that will disorganise the internal security of this country'.[19]

The tone was set for a vigorous campaign. Police operations in Palestine were almost always conducted with an eye on the political implications of the action. Stern and his men, though, had crossed a line and the toughest measures were now considered justified. Giles Bey's letter stressed 'the group is dangerous and we cannot afford to take chances'.

The CID were already getting some important results. On 21 May, detectives led by Tom Wilkin swooped on a flat in a house at 48 Keren Kayemet Boulevard in Tel Aviv. It was the home of a teacher called Moshe Svorai and his wife Tova. They had a lodger, none other than Yaacov Polani, the boy from the Herzliya orange groves who had received military training in Poland. On the night of the raid two other men were present – Yehoshua Zettler, 'the Farmer', who had led the Anglo-Palestine Bank robbery, and Yaacov Orenstein. A search turned up more documents 'which again proved the activities of the Group in the collection of information of a military character'[20] and which Wilkin believed provided sufficient proof to charge them all under the Official Secrets Ordinance and the Defence Regulations. They were taken to the Northern Police Station in Tel Aviv. Security seems to have been extraordinarily lax. Polani and Zettler, the latter of whom had given the police a false name and whose true identity remained undiscovered, decided to try to escape. 'In the morning,' Polani told the police some months later, 'when the door of the Station opened we dashed out and jumped over a fence.'[21] Both got clean away.

By this time Polani had all but ceased his underground activities. Svorai, however, was a significant catch. He was a teacher from a village near Haifa, an Irgun man from the outset who had done six months behind the wire. He had been persuaded by Stern to give up his job and move to Tel Aviv as the group's intelligence chief. Moshe and Tova were among Stern's most dedicated disciples and would remain so for the rest of their long lives. 'Yair was a special person, completely different from all around him,' Svorai said not long before his death in 2011.[22] His conversion to Yair's world view was a testament to Stern's remarkable eloquence. Moshe Svorai might be expected to have been repelled by Stern's overtures to the Axis. After all, one of his first acts as a young activist had been to tear down the swastika flag flying over the German diplomatic mission in Jerusalem, a feat that won him the heart of Tova. Stern's words dissolved all doubt. Svorai later described how Yair talked 'in a monotone, without pathos, as if he was speaking in a straight line. There was something hypnotic in the way he looked at you – it was penetrating, unique and it was hard to look back at him if he caught your eye. His eyes were steel grey. They flashed with lightning. His face was full of nobility and impressively delicate.'[23]

Polani, too, bore witness to Stern's mesmerizing persuasiveness: 'As a speaker [he] held us all in a trance. His clever, deep set eyes, his even manner of speech, his ability to express himself in short, clear sentences – all captivated us.'[24]

CID records show the raid on the Svorai's flat had been based on information from a source in the seaside town of Netanya, just up the coast from Tel Aviv. The informant was referred to in Giles Bey's letter to Cafferata: 'So far what has come to us has been from one source only, but a source which has proved *most* reliable.'[25]

This source might possibly be the same person who, in the autumn of 1940, had supplied the head of the CID's political department, District Deputy Superintendent Roderick Musgrave, with precise details about the Stern organization. A document in Hebrew in the Haganah files lists the names, functions, addresses, workplaces and meeting points of all key members of the group from Stern down, and singles out those responsible for the Anglo-Palestine Bank job. The informant reveals that his name is among those on the list. In the event of his arrest, he would identify himself as 'Mr Levine' so that the police would then be able to return the favour and let him go.[26] Though clearly intended primarily as an insurance policy, the approach might well have led to a more regular arrangement. The continuing references in police reports to solid inside information suggest there was at least one energetic traitor in Stern's inner circle at the time.

The list provided a solid foundation of fact on which the CID could build up a clear intelligence picture. The arrests that followed from it also gave opportunities for broadening their range of sources. One of the men whom Giles Bey wanted Cafferata to arrest was Arieh Menachem, a labourer of Yugoslav origin from Netanya.

Two months after the request he was finally picked up. Menachem was questioned by Assistant Superintendent Barham, who was based at Tulkarm police station. Barham did not have to lean very hard on Menachem to win his cooperation. He seems to have told the superintendent what he wanted to hear, confirming Stern's status as a fifth columnist. He later provided more information, claiming that Germany and Italy had 'promised him full help in arms and money and the formation of an independent Jewish state in Palestine'.[27] In return they 'asked for maps and plans of military strategic points in Palestine'.

At some point Menachem decided to atone for his earlier allegiance. In a letter written in Croatian to an unnamed policeman he describes how he decided to turn against his former comrades: 'I came to the conclusion that if I continued in this way I should never become a man, and besides this Stern's fight is against England and this is the greatest crime a Jew can commit.' He was now willing to work against the group in Tel Aviv. 'It only depends on you,' he concluded. 'If you will give me the chance to become a man.' Menachem was given his chance. His success, if any, was short-lived. A few months later Stern's men discovered he was a British spy and shot him dead in Netanya in the early hours of 6 September 1941.

The British penetration deepened the atmosphere of fear and distrust inside the organization. When Moshe Svorai was arrested, Stern was living with a friendly family but moved out as soon as he heard the news. In June, Roni managed to find a room for him in a house in Balfour Street, belonging to an elderly couple. It had a separate entrance so comings and goings were less easy to monitor. By now Stern rarely appeared in daylight hours, only slipping out when darkness fell to see friends. Lily Strassman was in town. The war had smashed her gilded world to pieces. She had managed to reach Palestine in June 1940 via Italy. Her husband, Henryk, who had been an officer in the military reserve, was dead, murdered not by the Germans but by the Soviets in Katyn Forest, in one of the massacres of the elite that followed their invasion of Poland. At nostalgic evenings at Lily's Tel Aviv house Polish émigrés gathered to remember the old days.

Stern's contacts with those nearest to him were tenuous. He lived alone in the new flat. Roni would visit on Shabbat and they would stay closeted together, seeing no one. He rarely met his mother. He had no money to support her and Liza was reduced to working as a live-in nurse and au pair to an elderly invalid in Tel Aviv.

His most constant companions were Avraham Amper and Zelig Zak, both of whom acted as his bodyguards. One of Amper's duties was to keep an eye on legal immigrants disembarking at the ports and identify potential recruits. There were few takers. One who did join the ranks was Israel Eldad, a right-wing former philosophy student. Eldad shared Stern's intensely ideological mindset. When Stern revealed his latest strategic blueprint, a statement of eighteen 'principles' for the rebirth of Israel, Eldad responded with a commentary that covered forty-six pages of a notebook.[28]

At least someone was taking his ideas seriously. Outside the claustrophobic world of the group the Yishuv was backing Britain. In May the 'National Institutions' had urged all men aged between twenty and thirty to join the services. By then 8000 Jewish Palestinians were already serving.[29] Their attitude was summed up in a police report, written by one of Geoffrey Morton's men, Sergeant Alec Stuart, describing an incident he had witnessed in a Tel Aviv café when a party of about fifteen Jewish soldiers marched in. 'One of this press gang took over the microphone whilst the remainder "sorted out" the patrons, two of whom were finally ejected in a quiet but forceful manner.' The man at the mic 'made an impassioned speech in Hebrew' stating that the best way of combating 'the Nazi atrocities [against] their brethren is to enlist in HM Forces and finally come to grips with the hated enemy and the persecutors of their race ...' The speech was 'received quite enthusiastically by members of the audience'.[30]

David Raziel had himself put on British uniform. Relations between the official Irgun and the authorities had improved to the point where plans were hatched to use Irgun men in special operations in the area. In the early summer of 1941, Palestine's situation was looking increasingly precarious. British forces had been driven out of Greece and then humiliated in Crete. In the Western Desert, Rommel had arrived to halt an Italian collapse and was now pushing Wavell's army back to the frontiers of Egypt. In Iraq, the April coup engineered by the Germans had installed a pro-Nazi junta in power in Baghdad with General Rashid Ali at its head. In May, Luftwaffe aircraft began to arrive. With Vichy troops occupying Lebanon and Syria, Palestine was starting to feel hemmed in.

When, on 29 April, Rashid Ali began besieging the British base at Habbaniya, fifty miles west of Baghdad, Britain sent a relief force from Transjordan which marched up the Euphrates plain towards the capital. Meanwhile, a four-man Irgun team led by David Raziel flew into Habbaniya. It was tasked with sabotage and its first job was a diversionary raid on an oil installation near Baghdad. The squad had another unofficial target in mind. They planned, if the opportunity presented itself, to kill the Mufti, now enjoying the hospitality of Rashid Ali. When the raid was called off, they were sent instead on a recce mission to discover the strength of Iraqi forces near Fallujah. On 17 May, the jeep carrying the party, accompanied by a British major, had paused by a flooded area when a German light aeroplane appeared and dropped a single bomb. Raziel was struck in the head by a splinter and killed and the major was decapitated.

It was Roni who brought Stern the news of Raziel's death. Despite their estrangement and the angry words that had flown between them, 'the shock was very great,' she recalled. 'Yair's head slumped and he held it in his two hands. I saw his shoulders were shaking with sobs. After a moment he recovered and regained his composure.'[31]

Raziel's death must have intensified an already acute sense of isolation. They had once been David and Jonathan. Stern began to think that his own end – imagined so often in his poetry – might not be far off. Yitzhak Yezernitzky, better known later as Israel's Prime Minister Yitzhak Shamir, who had arrived from Poland aged twenty in 1935, joined the Irgun four years later, carried out his share of shootings and bombings and followed Stern in the split with Raziel, recorded a conversation as the pair walked one evening through Tel Aviv's dark backstreets. Stern told him that it was 'as clear as day that [the] police wouldn't be satisfied with arresting him but would kill him on the spot. He said this in a quiet voice, with no emotion, and added that he was sure his murder wouldn't be the end … On the contrary the murder would increase the movement's strength and many would join the ranks.'[32]

Stern took premonitions seriously. He was superstitious. He read horoscopes and touched wood. Binyamin Zeroni remembered how once during a meeting a spider fell from the ceiling and onto Stern. Zeroni went to kill it but Stern stopped him. 'It's forbidden to kill a spider at night,' he said. 'If we do a catastrophe will befall us.'[33]

With the dearth of money, the skulking, fugitive existence, where every knock at the door might herald the arrival of the CID, the organization was slowly dying. What was needed was action. But action required money. The extortion that the group practised against wealthy Jews yielded limited returns. In Netanya, local businessmen who were leaned on had had enough. A police report noted that 'demands have become excessive and one or two persons have refused to pay'.[34] When one man refused to cough up fifty pounds a 'gang of thugs' raided his residence and 'his home and furniture were liberally daubed with human excrement'. It was time for another bank robbery. On the night of 13/14 July, a team tried to break into the Arab National Bank in Jerusalem. The operation was a total failure. Once again Stern did not take part, confining himself to reciting psalms while the attempted robbery was in progress.

The failure prompted a crisis meeting at which frustration over the record of failure and deep misgivings about Stern's German policy combined to spark a vicious quarrel. The revolt came from the top. Hanoch Strelitz, for several years an intimate and ally of Stern, and Binyamin Zeroni, who had shown his resolution and boldness in numerous actions, had had enough. According to

Yaacov Levstein, the two now 'saw no point in fighting the British while World War Two was at its peak.'[35] Indeed, like the Irgun they were now 'in favour of helping the British war effort'. Zeroni, with Strelitz's approval, had already contacted Yaacov Meridor, an Irgun commander who had been with Raziel when he died, to see if they would be interested in allowing the Stern group back into the fold on equal terms. Knowing that Stern was unlikely to agree to the move, a contingency plan was in place to deal with him. He would be seized and kept under house arrest and confined to harmless activities such as writing poetry. As it was, the initiative came to nothing, but the scheme was a measure of how estranged Stern had become from his old comrades.

The emergency council brought together Stern and his two deputies and six or seven area commanders. It lasted more than a week and took place in a succession of hideaways in Tel Aviv. Stern spoke first, reiterating his determination to carry on trying to cut a deal with the Germans while at the same time launching a wave of actions that would boost the group's standing in the eyes of the Yishuv. After Stern, it was Strelitz's turn.

He rejected everything that Stern said. It was pointless to talk of operations when they had no resources to sustain them. The correct course was to reunite with the Irgun and seek 'rehabilitation' with the rest of Jewish Palestine. The measured tone of the opening exchanges soon broke down into quarrels and threats. Yaacov Levstein, whose loyalty to Yair would never waver, rounded on Strelitz for his perceived treachery and barked that he deserved 'to be shot in the head'.

Stern retained his habitual, dreamy calm but it was no protection against the verbal lashing that ensued when Zeroni unloaded months of harboured resentment. He insisted that Stern should abandon all ideas of an alliance with the Axis. Furthermore, he declared that if there were to be any more operations, he would be in overall charge of them. 'I told Yair that since you were never a fighter and you have no idea about actions, you can't order me about when I lead them,' he remembered.[36] Stern would not agree. In Zeroni's opinion, he was 'jealous of Raziel' and wanted to appear a man of action and not a mere thinker. Stern's failure to pull a trigger or plant a bomb also rankled with Strelitz, who threw at him the charge that he had 'never been out on an operation'. To a man who styled himself Yair after a great Hebrew warrior, the accusation must have burned like acid.

For the rest of those present, though, Stern's authority held firm. After three days it was clear that Strelitz and Zeroni had failed to win over the area commanders and the pair left, eventually to rejoin the Irgun. The final parting was ugly. As Zeroni flounced out he offered a prophetic warning to Stern: 'You won't hold your own for long. The British will get you.'

Stern was now commanding a rump of a rump. They had no money and no friends. The might of the British Empire, the sentiments of the Yishuv and their former comrades in the Revisionist movement were now ranged against them. Their numbers were pathetically small: Haifa and Jerusalem had about twenty to thirty members, Tel Aviv thirty to fifty and the surrounding area perhaps another thirty. The founder members of this tiny club nonetheless felt the warm glow of exclusivity. The showdown, said Levstein, had 'raised our morale, deepened our conviction that we had chosen the right way in our struggle for national liberation, and restored our faith in the leadership'.[37]

It was time to resume the fight. Stern's determination to seal a pact with the Nazis was undiminished and in December Nathan Yellin-Mor, his old journalist colleague from Warsaw days, was dispatched on what was to prove another doomed mission. At home, there were two urgent goals. One was to raise money through another major bank raid. The second, according to Levstein, was to liquidate their enemies in the CID. Geoffrey Morton's name was at the top of the list.

EIGHT

A 'Trap for the British Brutes'

Just after 8.30 on the morning of Friday, 9 January 1942, a middle-aged accountant called Zvi Kopstein was waiting at a bus stop on Ahad Ha'am Street in the centre of Tel Aviv. Tucked under his arm was a brown leather satchel containing nearly eleven hundred pounds in notes and silver coin. Kopstein had picked up the money a few minutes before from the nearby Hapoalim Bank. It was the week's wages for the staff of the Hamashbir Hamerkazi cooperative store where he was chief cashier.

The streets were full of people and there were plenty of witnesses to what happened next. Two men closed in on Kopstein and clubbed him over the head with a length of rubber-covered piping. They snatched the satchel and ran off in the direction of Rothschild Boulevard. Kopstein was only dazed. He staggered to his feet and ran after his attackers, shouting at passers-by to stop them. The response was impressive. 'Many people joined in the chase,' he said in evidence later. 'There was a hue and cry.'[1]

As they fled the robbers were joined by a third man to whom they passed the loot. He broke away and disappeared. The crowd were hard on the heels of the other two, who turned and fired at least one pistol shot over their pursuers' heads. The chase continued along Lilienblum Street, parallel to Rothschild Boulevard. Outside the Eden cinema, the pair split up. One of them, a nineteen-year-old called Nissim Reuven, made off in the direction of Jaffa. He was headed off by two Jewish policemen from a nearby station who fired a shot at him. Reuven threw down his revolver and, calling out 'Enough', surrendered.

The other robber, Yehoshua Becker, ducked into a store room at the side of the Eden cinema. Two policemen who had joined the hunt, a Jewish constable called Schleimer and a British constable named Stoodley, saw him and followed him in. Stoodley was armed with a Smith & Wesson .45 revolver. Becker was crouching behind a packing case. There was an exchange of shots and Stoodley withdrew and took cover by a bomb shelter. Becker ran out, fired several times in his direction and made off again, pursued by a crowd. A quarter of a mile further on he turned into an alleyway. The soft sand underfoot slowed him down and his pursuers caught up with him. They were laying into him when the police arrived, saving him from further punishment.[2] Becker's wild firing had failed to hit any policemen, but he succeeded in killing two passers-by. Abraham Ben Abraham, forty, a porter at the nearby bus terminus, died instantly from a shot to the head. Eighteen-year-old Matitiahu Federman, a railway worker, expired shortly after being brought in to the Hadassah Hospital with a bullet in his chest.

The wages snatch was dramatic proof that, despite numerous setbacks, Avraham Stern's new organization meant business. Immediately after the defections of Strelitz and Zeroni, Stern had announced a plan of action. According to Yaacov Levstein, the first priority was to raise funds 'to finance our arms purchases, caches, hiding places and general operation'. With the proceeds of the robbery, that first aim had been achieved. Stern decided it was now time 'to move on to the second stage', namely to 'liquidate our direct enemy, the CID'.[3]

That meant Geoffrey Morton and Tom Wilkin. The task of killing them was put in Levstein's capable hands. Both men had known for some time that they were high on the Stern group's hit list. The proposal to assassinate them appears to have originated with Moshe Moldovsky during one of the eternal discussions about tactics and plans that took place in Mazra'a.[4] Since the spring of 1941 the two detectives had formed the spearhead of the drive against the Jewish underground. The raid on the Svorai apartment in May was led by

Wilkin and directed by Morton. In December they followed up this coup with another successful operation which was obviously based on inside intelligence. On 2 December, detectives raided a flat in Tel Aviv where Yehoshua Zettler, who had been on the run since escaping from the early round-up, was holed up. As well as capturing 'the Farmer', they also scooped up another five of Stern's men, including Yitzhak Yezernitzky, soon to be Yitzhak Shamir (and hereafter referred to by that name).

The decision to kill prominent police officers required some justification. To avoid further alienating the Yishuv, Stern needed to be able to present the deed as an act of retribution. That was how the killing of Cairns was explained. The victim had been portrayed as a torturer (though no such claim was made against Barker who died with him) and his assassination therefore an act of revolutionary justice. The Stern group would subsequently try to present Morton and Wilkin in a similarly lurid light. The pair were depicted as a diabolical partnership, with Wilkin's guile and knowledge complementing Morton's ruthlessness and energy. Shamir, a hard man to impress, underwent interrogation by Wilkin and marvelled at his 'awesome fund of information ... about the network of the Jewish undergrounds'.[5] Levstein was equally respectful of his enemy. Wilkin was 'the most cunning of the lot'. He was 'extremely cautious' and 'preferred to resort to deception'. He 'told people he was sympathetic to our national aspirations ... in reality he was Morton's right-arm man, his brain and his memory without whom the damage done by Morton might not have been so great'. Morton, he claimed, had won his numerous decorations 'because of his cold-blooded murderous traits of character. He used to murder his victims without bringing them to trial. He had killed several Arabs in this manner, and more than once during his searches for arms in the kibbutzim, some kibbutz members were murdered'.[6] No evidence was produced for these allegations, because there was none to offer. In Morton's career to date he had shot only one man dead, an Arab multiple murderer called Ali Husni Siksik. He had been in a party of three policemen who tracked him down to a village near Tel Aviv in February 1941. Siksik had been discovered in a grain store and tried to open fire with an automatic pistol but his gun jammed. So, too, did Morton's .32 Mauser. Fortunately, he managed to clear the blockage, before Siksik did the same, and put two bullets in him. Morton did mount weapons searches at kibbutzim, but there is nothing to suggest that any of these ever resulted in bloodshed.

Morton and Wilkin's real offence was that they were extremely good at their jobs. Wilkin had a deep and subtle knowledge of the workings not just of the Stern group but also the Irgun and Haganah, with whom he cooperated closely. He was notorious for his reluctance to share this intelligence too widely. He seems to have made an exception with Morton, however, who had also cultivated his own sources, and this joint fund of knowledge underpinned their campaign. Unless these two were removed, the group was in danger of being whittled away to nothing by their relentless sleuthing. There were now only a handful of men left on whom Stern could rely. Among them was Moshe Svorai who had made a dramatic reappearance in Tel Aviv. At the end of November he had been taken from Mazra'a to Tel Aviv for dental treatment. When his guards stopped for coffee he asked to go to the toilet and promptly disappeared. The initiative was against Stern's wishes. He had been planning a mass breakout by his forty or so supporters held in Mazra'a and vetoed the idea of individual escapes for fear of prompting the authorities to tighten security at the camp. Nonetheless, the return of his most devoted disciple must have been very welcome at a time when there was little other good news.

With the capture of Becker and Reuven the need to deal with Morton and Wilkin became even more acute. Before an assassination plan was hatched, Stern felt a duty to do what he could to save the lives of the two robbers who, if convicted, faced death by hanging. Becker and Reuven pleaded not guilty and built their defence on a series of what the presiding judge described as 'astonishing' coincidences.

The case against them was not quite as straightforward as it seemed. The money had disappeared and was never recovered. A conviction required witnesses to stick by their testimonies and to repeat them in court. Given the dire warnings issued regularly by the Stern group as to what would happen to anyone who collaborated with the police against them, it could not be taken for granted that witnesses would speak out. The public knew very well that the threats were in deadly earnest. A few months before, acting on information provided by the unfortunate Arieh Mechachem, the police had arrested one Elihahu Moldovan, a nineteen-year-old who had arrived illegally from Czechoslovakia three years previously. He was found with a Nagant 7.62 seven-shot revolver – the Belgian-designed, Russian-manufactured handgun favoured by the Stern group, Russian revolutionaries and the Soviet secret police – and sentenced to six months in prison. A month later, on 16 November 1941, a young Jewish detective called Soffiof, who worked with Morton and was present at the arrest, was shot dead in Rehovot while returning from a trip to the cinema with his wife and child. Pamphlets distributed by the Stern group soon afterwards said the killing was 'a warning to all professional and amateur informers who hand over the fighters for Israel's liberty to the police'.[7]

Morton assumed from the outset that witnesses would be threatened. 'Because of the difficulties inherent in getting members of the public to give evidence against gangsters of this kind, the first thing we had to do was to collect up all our witnesses and keep them until the trial in a place where they could not be got at and intimidated,' he wrote.[8]

Stern was to discover that the task of dissuading the public from cooperating would not be easy. As Morton pointed out, 'the offence could not, by any stretch of the imagination, be described as either patriotic or political'. The shooting of the bystanders had resulted in a wave of indignation in Tel Aviv. Both the victims were Jews, one a blameless young man, the other a convert to Judaism who left four orphaned children and a pregnant widow. Even the robbers' counsel seemed anxious to disassociate himself from his clients. During the committal proceedings Max Seligman, the Jewish underground's attorney of choice, declared that he had 'been the object of criticism and even threats … for having agreed to defend the accused and asked the Court to endorse the fact that it was not possible for him to withdraw'.[9] As it turned out the witnesses stuck to their stories. Both men were eventually convicted and Becker sentenced to death by hanging. Much to Morton's annoyance, however, his sentence would subsequently be reviewed in the light of political sensitivities.

Seligman, who had been born in Cardiff and, according to Ted Horne, 'spoke Hebrew with a pronounced Welsh accent',[10] was not quite as blameless as his outburst suggested. He was well acquainted with Stern who, after the arrests of Becker and Reuven, sent him a message requesting a meeting. The rendezvous took place at midnight near the Tel Aviv zoo. While the two men talked, Avraham Amper and Zelig Zak, both armed with pistols, watched from a distance for any unwelcome arrivals. Seligman agreed to represent the robbers. When Stern asked whether it might be a good idea to kill Constable Stoodley, the Crown's main witness to the shooting of the passers-by, Seligman counselled against it. Stoodley had already given his account and if he were to be killed there would be no chance of unpicking his evidence in cross-examination.[11]

Stern's recklessness was growing by the day and he was now willing to countenance the riskiest actions. If he could not reach out to terrorize individual witnesses he could try to cow the Yishuv in general. At the same time he would remove the threat posed by the men whom he had come to regard as his greatest immediate enemies.

The decision to kill Morton and Wilkin was Stern's characteristic reaction to his now desperate situation. A less determined man might have concluded that the odds were so stacked against him that his only choice was to surrender. Yair was different. He still had a handful of followers and some deadly resources. The way out was to pull off a spectacular act of violence which, he believed, would transform the situation in his favour. It was clear that time was running out. He was, as an old friend and former mentor, Abba Achimeir, remembered, 'living like a hunted animal who spends his days in his lair and only ventures out at night'.[12] By now he was changing addresses constantly, moving between the few friends who were prepared to give him refuge. Roni was assumed to be under police surveillance, so visiting her was an invitation to arrest. One of those who sheltered Stern described how he would arrive at his flat in the early hours of the morning, and 'knock quietly on the door. We would open up and without a word he would collapse on the bed and fall asleep immediately.'[13] Then, before dawn, 'he would slip away, even without us noticing it and without eating anything'. He carried a small bag containing the Tanakh (the Hebrew bible) and phylacteries, the ritual items that Orthodox Jews use for morning prayer, including a box with sacred texts, strapped to the head. Sometimes when there was nowhere to go he would doss down in a bomb shelter.

It was the faithful Svorais who eventually rescued Stern from his vagabond existence. At the end of December, Zelig Zak heard of a small flat that might suit the couple, who had a small daughter, Herut. The apartment had originally been a laundry room and it sat on the roof of a newish but already quite dilapidated block at 8 Mizrachi Bet Street in the Florentin area of Tel Aviv. It was named after David Florentin, who bought the land in the 1920s to build homes for his fellow Greek Jews, many of whom were destitute as a result of a huge fire that had devastated Thessalonika. By the mid-1930s the ground floors of many buildings had been turned into workshops and stores. The narrow streets of Florentin attracted the poorer of Palestine's new immigrants drawn there by the prospect of work. The block-long terraces of apartment buildings also offered advantages to those outside the law. Uri Avnery, who had rejected Stern's leadership during the power struggle with Raziel, had a flat there, and appreciated the fact that in the event of a police raid you could run along the roof and escape 'down any stairs you wanted'.[14] Only half a mile away to the south lay Jaffa. And standing imposingly on the main road that ran between the Arab town and Tel Aviv was the newly built three-storey reinforced concrete headquarters of the CID where Morton and Wilkin had their offices.

As Moshe Svorai had just escaped from prison, it was left to Zak to arrange the rental with the landlord. He turned up with Tova, whom he introduced as his sister, married to a man named 'Bloch'. He explained that she was sick and would be spending most of her time indoors. Her husband was a long-distance lorry driver supplying British Army depots, which would account for his frequent absences. The landlord swallowed the story and on New Year's Day 1942 the family moved in. The flat was discreetly situated. It was reached by six flights of stairs, fifty-nine steps in all, the staircase running from a front door that opened directly onto the street. The family would be living in a space that measured a mere twenty-eight square yards. Within the flimsy walls were contained a small entrance hall, a cramped living room that doubled as a bedroom, a galley kitchen and a toilet-cum-shower room with plumbing so temperamental that the lavatory flooded every time the shower was turned on. There was one small window in the hall on the left as you entered and another in the kitchen. A larger double window was set into the back wall of the living room. It measured about three feet wide by four and a half feet high and looked out over the flat roof of the block at the residents' washing flapping in the Mediterranean breeze.

Three days after the Svorais moved in Stern turned up for a meeting at the flat. He arrived carrying a large suitcase. Asked by Moshe what it contained, Stern replied: 'this is my folding bed.' The man who had charmed Polish ministers and officials and wowed professors with his brilliance had been reduced to the status of a vagrant. Svorai insisted that, despite the obvious dangers, Stern should move in with them. He resisted briefly before submitting and that evening unfolded his camp bed for the first time in the Svorais' tiny dwelling. To nosy neighbours he would be introduced as 'Mr Azaria'.[15]

Despite all evidence to the contrary, Stern believed that if his fellow Jews only understood what he was trying to say they would rally to his cause. Even though the eyes of not only the British but also their enemies in the Haganah and the Irgun were upon them, the group still managed to distribute leaflets and even to transmit two broadcasts. They were beamed out hurriedly from the apartments of two staunch female supporters, Nelly Langsfelder and Julie Elazar.

The first broadcast was written by Stern and delivered by Moshe Svorai. It declared that the war raging all around was not a contest between democracy and totalitarianism but a struggle between two malevolent forces and had nothing to do with furthering Jewish national interests. It was 'a war between Gog and Magog'.[16] The second was read by Stern himself, the first and last time he spoke over the airwaves. It was a diatribe against his former Revisionist comrades whom he derided as being an 'absurd copy' of the left-wing Mapai and the Jewish Agency. He ended with a call to arms: 'Hebrew Youth! Do you want the nation to be redeemed? Do you wish for the conquest of the homeland? Are you ready to lay down your life for the resurrection of the Hebrew kingdom? Join the war of the underground army of battling Zion whose flag will one day fly over the walls of liberated Jerusalem!' The chasm between rhetoric and reality was vividly illustrated by the fact that, as soon as the broadcast was over, Stern and his helpers had to scuttle away, lugging the transmitter with them, when a police van was spotted next to the building.[17]

The time for words had passed. On 18 January, Stern called a meeting of his lieutenants. They gathered at a flat at 30 Dizengoff Street, the closest thing they had to a safe house. Dizengoff was one of Tel Aviv's busiest thoroughfares, swinging in from the east then bisecting the city from south to north, but the house was on a quiet, residential stretch at the eastern end. It had been rented by Zelig Zak, who in the meantime had been picked up but managed to escape while being transferred from the Jaffa lock-up to Mazra'a camp. Present at the meeting were Svorai, Levstein and Tselnik and the talk was all of killing. There was a new name on Stern's hit list: Binyamin Zeroni. The taint of suspicion had clung to him ever since his miraculous escape from Jerusalem police headquarters following the assassination of Cairns and Barker. Moshe Rothstein had also planted doubts about where Zeroni's real loyalties lay. Zeroni's personal attacks on Stern and the imputation of cowardice, contained in the charge that he never went on operations, had settled the question once and for all. The four men agreed that he should be executed for treason.

They also decided to begin planning the assassination of a British official, Oliver Lyttelton, who, as Minister of State in Cairo, was the senior political figure in the region. According to Yitzhak Shamir, Stern had entertained the idea for some time. It had been 'born one spring evening in 1941' at a meeting in Tel Aviv. 'It was part of his total concept of how we should fight, not just the British in Palestine but the British Empire as such: to try to put out of action the people who made policy and moved the pieces on the Palestine board.'[18] Even though Lyttelton was in Egypt, Stern claimed to be in contact with Jewish soldiers in the British Army there who would be prepared to help. The main business of the day, though, concerned Morton and Wilkin. Levstein brought the group up to date on how his plans were progressing: all, it seemed, was going very well. The date for the assassination was set for two days' time – Tuesday, 20 January.

Levstein would later describe the plan in gloating detail. His testimony is invariably coloured by the compulsion to present the police in the worst possible light, but there is no reason to doubt the technical specifics of the operation, which match those of police reports. He 'started with the assumption that Morton's desire to capture [our] members outweighed any considerations of personal safety on his part. Besides, I knew that he used to get personally involved in his operations.'

On this premise, Levstein laid his trap. One of his team would explode a small bomb in his room so the neighbours could hear it (in fact witnesses said two small detonations were subsequently heard). He would scatter a trail of chicken blood inside the apartment and on the stairs outside, giving the impression that a bomb-maker had injured himself while constructing a device. The explosion would automatically alert the police. 'I knew the news would immediately reach Morton at the CID headquarters in Tel Aviv, and he would come over to apprehend the wounded person and use him to find out about the rest of the organization.'

On arrival, Morton and his colleagues would see the blood trail and follow it up to its apparent point of origin. Then the real bomb would go off. The site chosen for the attempt was at 8 Yael Street, a three-storey building in a tree-shaded residential road lined with Bauhaus-style apartment houses, just behind Dizengoff Circle. Two of Stern's supporters rented a room there, a breeze-block and tile construction perched on the roof, similar to the Svorai residence in Mizrachi Bet Street.

Levstein spent several days preparing. 'I rested during the day, and at night I would go out to 8 Yael Street where I was going to lay the trap for the British brutes.' The bomb would be hidden inside the room on the roof. Inside it, next to the door, was 'a chest where I hid 55 pounds of blasting gelatin [gelignite], the best explosive we had at the time. I put it inside a well-sealed tin box. Inside the explosives I attached five detonators, connected in a row, each inside a primer made of exploding cotton or TNT to increase the explosion … Around the explosives I put 33 pounds of nails of all kinds.' As a finishing touch, the shrapnel was 'soaked in salicylic and sulphatic acid, to aggravate the wounds'.

The bomb would be detonated by remote control via a command cable, disguised as a radio aerial that ran from the rooftop across to 13 Zamenhoff Street, a house in the road behind. The roof there was rather higher than that of 8 Yael Street. From this vantage point, the man charged with triggering the bomb would have a clear view of anyone arriving to investigate the initial, 'come-on' explosion, and know exactly the best time to press the bell-push that would send a battery-powered electric current racing down the two thin wires to spark an almighty blast.

Levstein's plan did not end there. He decided to plant a second bomb to catch Morton and Wilkin. The reasons he gave for doing so are confused and contradictory, as will be seen later. This one was buried by Levstein the night before the attack in a flowerbed next to the path that led from the gateway of 8 Yael Street to the house. The command wire ran over the fence to 10 Yael Street next door and up a drainpipe to the roof where the second operator would be stationed.[19]

The two men he chose for the job were individuals he calls 'Baruch' and 'Yehoshua'. Baruch was 'an old and devoted member' who 'had all the qualifications for the job'. His true identity is unclear.[20] Yehoshua, who 'from the day he joined the underground as a child became a legend of self-sacrifice, devotion and courage', was Yehoshua Cohen, a nineteen-year-old Palestinian-born farmer's son. He would gain notoriety six years later as the man who fired the shots that killed the UN envoy to Palestine, Folke Bernadotte.

Baruch was posted on the roof of 13 Zamenhoff Street, and Cohen at 10 Yael Street. Levstein claimed that both were given very firm instructions. 'I told them in no uncertain terms that the trap was intended for Morton and Wilkin,' he wrote. 'If those two did not show up it was not to be used.' Baruch said he had once been questioned by the detectives and 'there was no way he could fail to identify them'.[21]

If all went according to Levstein's meticulous plan, the Stern group were poised for their greatest coup yet. First would come the minor explosions that would raise the alarm and bring Morton and Wilkin running to the scene. They would climb to the roof whereupon Baruch would judge the right moment to press the button and send them to their doom. What, then, was the purpose of the second bomb, buried in the flowerbed? Levstein would write many years afterwards that he planted it 'so that in case Morton and Wilkin survived the bomb on the roof they would be trapped by the one I

... put on the [pathway] from the street to the door of the building'.[22] But in the next sentence he gives another explanation. He had 'no doubt' that they would come to Yael Street as soon as they heard news of the initial small decoy explosion. But if by any chance they did not, they would 'surely come after the main bomb on the roof went off'. This makes no sense. He claimed he had given strict instructions to Baruch not to press the trigger unless he was certain he was blowing up Morton and Wilkin. If the pair failed to show up there would be no 'main bomb' explosion. It seems more likely that Levstein realized there was no guarantee that Morton and Wilkin would be first on the scene. The bomb he had planted on the roof might therefore claim some unintended victims. But the two policemen would surely come hotfoot once news of the big blast reached them. The bomb in the pathway would give him another chance to kill the right men.

On the technical side, Levstein's plan worked brilliantly. According to Morton's report, 'at approximately 9 a.m. on 20.1.42 an explosion occurred in a small room on the roof of No. 8 Yael Street, Tel Aviv. Some five minutes later a further small explosion occurred.' The inhabitants of the house thought an air raid had begun and ran down to the bomb shelter. As they emerged a crowd of people were gathered in the street looking up to where smoke was pouring from the windows of the rooftop flat. At this point a patrolling policeman turned up and went with the landlady up the stairs to the roof. He ordered her to lock the door and then descended to await reinforcements.

Meanwhile, a member of the public had reported the explosions to Tel Aviv police headquarters. The senior officer there was a deputy superintendent called Solomon Schiff, the highest-ranking Jewish member of the Palestine Police Force. Schiff was forty-five years old. He had been born in Kishinev, the scene of the great pogrom that inspired the poem the young Avraham Stern had recited to the students of the Jerusalem Gymnasium. After his family moved to Palestine he served in the Jewish Legion in the First World War and joined the PPF in 1923, shortly after its formation. He appeared to be a devoted servant of the Mandate. Three months before, he, his wife Rachel, his seventeen-year-old daughter Akiva and eleven-year-old son Yosef had all become naturalized British citizens.[23]

Schiff's first act upon hearing the news was to call Morton at CID headquarters to tell him about the explosions. Morton recalled later that he wanted to know 'could I go along there with him to see what it was all about?' Morton was, for the moment, otherwise engaged. 'As it happened, the weekly Area Security Meeting, attended by the District Commissioner, the Brigade Commander and his staff officer, was then in progress in my office,' he wrote. 'I felt that I could not very well walk out and leave them, and the matter did not seem urgent enough to warrant breaking up the meeting.' He therefore 'told Schiff that I would be along as soon as I could, suggesting that he should go ahead without me'.[24]

Schiff had already dispatched a party of men to the scene, led by a Jewish officer, Inspector Ze'ev Dichter. With him went a British inspector, George Turton, who had just been transferred to the area and had reported for his first day's work that morning. Schiff put the phone down and together with his deputy, Inspector Nahum Goldman, drove the half a mile or so to the scene. On arrival Schiff found the street full of children from a school in Zamenhoff Street. When the first blasts were heard their teachers had hurried them off to the air raid shelter. They had now re-emerged and were hanging around to watch the developing drama.

Schiff led the party into the house and up the stairs to the roof. They opened the door and walked across the reinforced concrete to the apartment. The door was locked. Schiff ordered it to be forced open. When this was done they all stood back. Schiff led from the front. He took the first step through the door, followed by Goldman, Turton and Dichter. As soon as Dichter crossed the threshold, Morton reported, 'there was a violent explosion and all four walls of the room, which were of concrete blocks, were blown completely away and the roof of reinforced concrete collapsed'.

Schiff was 'blown through the wall and landed in the garden below and died instantly'. A mattress in the room floated down to land next to him. The rest of the furniture was 'blown to pieces'. Turton and Goldman lay trapped beneath the rubble. Dichter was hurled across the roof, where only the parapet saved him from sharing Schiff's fate. Two Jewish constables, who had gone onto the roof but had not entered the room, escaped with minor injuries. Goldman was taken to the Hadassah Hospital where he died at 5.30 the following morning. Turton went to the Assuta private hospital where both his legs were amputated. He died at ten o'clock that night. Dichter eventually recovered.

The blast finally brought at least one of its intended victims to the scene. Morton and a party of CID detectives raced to Yael Street and began to poke around in the debris of twisted reinforcing rods and shattered concrete while a police photographer snapped the scene. The pictures show Morton in sports jacket, flannels and trilby, notebook in pocket, peering below a great chunk of concrete for clues. The hunt soon turned up the second bomb, buried just below the surface of the flowerbed at the entrance. Why had Yehoshua Cohen not detonated it when Morton arrived? Later he would let it be known that he had been inhibited by the presence of so many innocent bystanders. His story seems to stand up. Morton reported that occupants of 10 Yael Street who rushed up to the roof after the big explosion spoke of seeing a man there who 'warned the people to keep away as there might be a second explosion'. They 'observed that this man was holding something in his hand which he took pains to conceal from the occupants of the house'. Both he and Baruch were able to slip away in the confusion.

In his report Morton was sure that the 'infernal machine', as the police and press referred to such bombs, was not aimed specifically at him. Though there was 'no doubt whatever that this outrage was deliberately planned and executed with the intention of killing some senior police officers … it is difficult to believe that it was intended for any one particular person.' Rather, it would appear that 'the intent was to intimidate the police and terrorise the public in order that no future action should be taken against the gang who perpetrated it nor justice done to those of them who are already in custody'.[25]

Stern and his men had pulled off the most spectacular act of violence against the British that Palestine had yet seen. They had failed, though, to break free of the pursuing Furies. They tried to make the best of the bodged job. A leaflet, written in a grandiose style that indicated the hand of Yair, was rushed out to 'clarify' the event to the Yishuv. The justification started with a denunciation of Britain's refusal to allow 'refugees from the death camps' to enter Palestine, and urged readers to wake up to the fact that 'the Mandate government is the *enemy* of Zionism'.[26]

As the instrument of an oppressive ruler the police were thus fair game, be they British or Jewish. The British, at least, were 'doing their duty'. But 'a Jew who hands his fellow Jews who fight for the freedom of their people over to the enemy, is betraying his national duty. He is a traitor and an enemy of Israel.'

The leaflet went on to libel the dead men. Schiff was 'a man who served the foreign rulers with his club', beating anti-British demonstrators and assaulting prisoners. Turton was 'the executioner of Shlomo Ben-Yosef', a reference to the fact that he apparently had been present when the Irgun's first martyr was hanged in Acre prison in 1938. It did not mention that Turton had also won the King's Police Medal for Gallantry, for defending single-handed a train carrying Jews from a strongly armed Arab gang.

Schiff was buried on the afternoon that he died in a coffin draped with the Union Flag and the blue and white colours of Zionism. The ceremony took place at the Nahalat Yitzhak cemetery on the eastern edge of Tel Aviv. All the pomp that the Mandate could muster was on display to mourn its faithful Jewish servant. 'A long file of wreath bearers – followed by a party of constables carrying rifles headed the procession,' reported the *Palestine Post*. At its head was 'the officer's grey charger, with his riding boots thrown over the empty saddle'.[27]

The following day it was Goldman's turn. He was forty-two years old and left a wife and three daughters aged sixteen, thirteen and three. At a service in Tel Aviv's Great Synagogue a rabbi quoted David's lament for Saul and Jonathan from the Second Book of Samuel: 'They were pleasant in their lives and in their death they were not divided.'[28]

Schiff's British colleagues looked on, uncomprehending and angry. 'I couldn't understand why Schiff and Turton, who only a year before had been decorated for rescuing Jews under fire [should be killed],' said Alec Ternent, a CID officer in Jaffa. He heard mutterings of 'Jewish bastards'.[29]

But the official voices of the Yishuv were also united in bafflement and outrage at the killings. The head of the Jewish Agency's political department, Moshe Shertok, led the chorus, expressing the 'utter horror' felt at the crime. He went on: 'The Jewish Agency will wholeheartedly support whatever effective measures may be taken in order to track down the murderous gang and free Palestine and the Yishuv from the nightmare of hold-ups and assassinations.'[30]

It was not just the establishment that was appalled by the killings. The draping of twin flags on Schiff's coffin was no mere gesture. Some years later, Efrem Dekel, the head of the Haganah's intelligence department, revealed that Schiff had been a long-standing sympathizer who on at least one occasion had deliberately dragged his heels to give members the chance to move an arms cache in advance of a raid. Nahum Goldman had been helping them since his earliest days in the police, 'passing on bits of information of interest to the Haganah' and taking 'special pains to send warning of impending searches for arms in Jewish villages'. He 'regarded this as the duty of a Jewish policeman and carried out this duty to the day of his death'.[31]

If Morton was right and Stern had really hoped that the bomb blast at 8 Yael Street would 'intimidate the police and terrorise the public', his gamble had gone terribly wrong. From now on, every hand in Palestine would be against him.

NINE

'Al-Ta'Amod!'

One week after the killing of the three policemen a special meeting of the District Security Committee was held in Geoffrey Morton's office at CID headquarters in Jaffa. The seniority of those present indicated the importance of the subject under discussion. They included the chief of police, Alan Saunders, the head of the CID, Giles Bey, and a representative of the Chief Secretary, all of whom had come down from Jerusalem. Also in the room were the military commander of the area, the District Commissioner and Captain C. H. Wybrow, the Area Security Officer.

There was only one topic on the agenda – 'The Yael Street Bomb Outrage' – and conversation was brisk and to the point. The military commander started by asking 'what measures were being contemplated' in response to the crime. Saunders replied that the police proposed a 'general round up of the group' and assured him that 'every means would be taken to secure the perpetrators ...'[1] The District Commissioner intervened to insist on clarification that 'the general cleanup referred to the Stern Group and not the IZL [Irgun] generally'. Saunders confirmed that this was the case.

The 'S. of P.' (Morton) then entered the discussion. He produced some leaflets which had been distributed 'admitting various crimes including the recent assassinations' which he took to be the work of the Stern group and not the Irgun.

It was now that Wybrow – who ran a rival intelligence network to Morton's – dropped a bombshell. The reason for the District Commissioner's concern not to lump the Irgun in with the Stern group became clear. In this matter at least, it seemed that the Irgun were firmly with the British. Indeed, relations were so good that they appeared to be offering to bring their British friends the head of their number one enemy in Palestine. Wybrow told the meeting that 'information was forthcoming from IZL and Jewry generally that Stern could be liquidated and would be liquidated provided that [those] promising to do so could be given a safe conduct ...' He added that he 'hoped to be able to determine the whereabouts of Stern shortly'.

It was a remarkable offer but Saunders was having none of it. The record states: 'The IGP (Saunders) said that if information on Stern's whereabouts could be obtained, the police would liquidate him and there would be no occasion for Jewry to undertake this task.' The discussion was deemed sensitive enough for those present to agree that 'a formal record of this meeting should not be published'.

Why the sensitivity? What was meant by 'liquidate'? In the context of what Wybrow said, it seems clear that the Irgun were proposing to kill Stern. Otherwise why would they be seeking safe passage for their men? From Saunders' mouth the word is more ambiguous. It crops up in other security apparatus documents as a term for 'shutting down' or 'rounding up' and is not necessarily as dramatic as it sounds. However, Saunders was an articulate man whose reports are models of clarity and precision. In saying that it was the job of the police to 'liquidate' Stern, he does not make clear that he is employing the word in a different sense from the one in which it has just been used, one that did not imply an extra-judicial killing. In the light of what was to come, the word undoubtedly has a sinister ring.

The meeting had been convened to get results. That very afternoon the call for action was answered with a resounding success. At 3.30 p.m. Morton had a tip-off from 'a Jewish source' that on the day of the Yael Street bombing two men had sublet a room in a flat on the third floor of 30 Dizengoff Street and had not left it since. The main tenants of the three-room flat were a married couple. The informant added that the lodgers received visits from 'other suspicious characters'.[2] The information set Morton's bloodhound nose twitching. 'There was no positive information to connect them with the Stern Gang,' he wrote, 'but the circumstances were so unusual that I felt sure (for once) that this was what we were looking for.'[3]

There were few detectives around when the information came in but Morton decided that 'there was no alternative but to go and investigate in person and without delay'. A light presence was anyway an advantage, for 'any elaborate police activity might have resulted in the escape of the men and would certainly have brought half Tel Aviv to the scene to watch and to hinder'. In his memoir Morton admitted to some misgivings before setting off. How did he know that he was not being lured into another Yael Street trap? He claimed later that the informant's interest in possible reward money persuaded him this was not the case.[4] Nonetheless, he wrote, 'I must admit quite frankly that I did not relish my task one bit. Stern had proclaimed on many occasions that he and his followers would never be captured alive, but would blow themselves up, taking as many policemen as possible with them.'[5]

Morton would repeat this claim in connection with the death of Avraham Stern. Though Stern's literary output was full of bloody imagery and declarations of his willingness – indeed, yearning – to die for the cause, there is no record of him having ever once (let alone 'on many occasions') issued a *public* threat of the sort that Morton describes. Throughout his life he had shown an aversion to living out the fantasies that permeate his poems. His men, by contrast, were up for any risk and willing to draw a gun and shoot their way out of trouble when cornered – as Yehoshua Becker had demonstrated only a few weeks before. Where Morton got the idea that Stern and his group were determined, if the worst came to the worst, to go out in a blaze of suicidal glory remains a mystery.

Morton arrived outside 30 Dizengoff Street at 4 p.m. He instructed three men to form a loose cordon round the house and climbed the stairs to the top floor. With him were Sergeants Ken 'Busty'

Woodward and Daniel 'Happy' Day. According to his memoir – which chimes in most details with his official report delivered the day after the event – Morton rang the bell on the door of the flat on the right. 'After a moment's delay the door was opened by a woman who was apparently expecting to see an acquaintance, for there was a smile on her face and her mouth was opening to speak – until she saw who was there,' he wrote. Immediately 'the smile froze, her jaw dropped, her eyes nearly popped out of her head, and an instant later she turned and fled down the corridor behind her into a room at the far end'.

The details given by the informer were precise. The men were holed up behind the first door on the left off the corridor. Morton 'drew the gun from the pocket of my raincoat and, with my left hand, gently turned the handle of the door. To my great surprise, it gave under my grasp.' He pushed it open and stepped inside. He had taken the inhabitants completely by surprise. According to his contemporaneous report, 'one man was lying on the bed facing me, whom I immediately recognised to be Zelig Zak, a known member of the Stern gang who escaped from custody recently, and two on the bed to the left, all were fully dressed'.

'I said to them "Don't stand up!" (in Hebrew, al-ta'amod!) They ignored my order and started to rise. I again ordered them to stay where they were, but they immediately jumped up and I saw one of the two men on the far bed grab at an overcoat which was lying on the stool beside the bed. I shot him. As I did so the other two sprang towards me and knowing them to be dangerous men and believing that they were armed, I shot them also.

'I fired altogether seven shots into the room, but I am not able to remember how many I fired at each man. I fired only long enough to ensure that they were disabled and could not shoot me or members of my party.'[6]

In the space of a few seconds the room had been turned into a shambles, puddled with blood and reeking of burnt gunpowder. The noise of the explosions from Morton's pistol would have been literally deafening in the enclosed space. It faded away to be replaced by the groaning and cursing of the injured. Zelig Zak lay on one bed, severely wounded. Avraham Amper, Stern's old comrade from the Polish training camps, was sprawled on another. The third man, Moshe Svorai, was on the floor, shot through the shoulder, thigh and jaw.

Morton shoved another clip into his pistol and ordered a search of the room. According to his report, when Woodward delved into the pocket of the man who had reached for his overcoat (it was Svorai), 'I saw him find, in one of the outer pockets thereof, an automatic pistol.' Morton then 'observed Sgt. Day open a drawer in a small cupboard, beside the bed on which Zelig Zak was lying and saw that it contained two hand-grenades'. At that point he 'heard firing from the garden below, where I had posted members of my party to prevent any escape'.

The shooting was coming from the gun of Constable Alec Ternent. Ternent was twenty-four years old. He had been brought up in a tough part of Birkenhead where his father was a commercial traveller. He spent several years in the Liverpool Scottish battalion of the Territorial Army which gave him a taste for service life. He arrived in Palestine at the age of nineteen and for the last year or so had been based in Jaffa, latterly working in the CID alongside Morton. He was greatly impressed by him. 'Morton was completely fearless and one of the few men I have met in my life who I would follow anywhere,' he testified in middle age. 'He inspired a tremendous amount of confidence in all his subordinates.' He was clever as well as brave and could 'come straight from some shoot-up or other nasty incident, take off his tie and dictate the most succinct and really brilliant report'.[7]

Ternent had taken up his post on a pathway that ran along the side of 30 Dizengoff Street, pistol at the ready. Morton had instructed him and the other officers manning the cordon that 'under no circumstances should they allow anybody to escape from the house'.[8] It was a typical, white, cement-skimmed Bauhaus-style detached apartment building. The path was flanked by flowerbeds planted with shrubs and flowers. As he stood there he heard shots coming from the top floor. Then there was another noise – the sound of a latch being opened. He looked up to see a man clambering through a small window and reaching out to grab a vine that climbed conveniently up the wall. 'I was amazed,' he remembered later. 'Through my head [ran the thought] is he a killer escaping? Is he one who's managed to elude the net?' All he had heard was firing: 'How could I tell who'd shot who?' He had no doubt that the man was guilty of something for when the raid began 'anybody who was innocent, reading his Bible or the *HaBoker* [a newspaper], would have stayed put'.

The man began lowering himself using the creeper and the adjacent downpipe as handholds. He half turned and Ternent saw he was 'rather pasty' – a result perhaps of long weeks spent hiding indoors – and had 'darkish hair'. When he had descended a few feet Ternent shouted at him in Hebrew not to move. The man, though, 'maintained a grip with one hand and moved … the other'. Ternent assumed that he was reaching for a gun. 'I didn't give him a chance,' he said. He fired four times and the man 'half fell, half sort of crashed down the vines' to the ground. It was Yaacov Levstein, who had been in the lavatory when Morton and his men burst through the door.

Soon afterwards more police turned up, led by Tom Wilkin. At some point an ambulance arrived and the wounded were given first aid by medics from the Magen David Adom, the Jewish equivalent of the Red Cross. The least badly wounded was Levstein, who had received a flesh wound in the rump from one of Ternent's shots. When a request was made to remove the injured men Morton denied it. 'I refused to allow them to be transported other than to the Government Hospital in the Government Ambulance and under a strong Police escort, and this was eventually done,' he stated in his report.

Before they were driven away, Morton took Ternent to one side to hear his account of what had happened. Morton was 'acting like a father … [taking] me by the hand and saying "good show"'.[9] While they were talking an important visitor arrived – Alan Saunders, who had earlier been at the special meeting of the District Security Committee, called to plan the elimination of the Stern gang. Morton marched over to him and came to attention. Saunders can hardly have dared hope for such dramatic results so soon. At a stroke, Morton had neutralized Stern's explosives wizard (Levstein), his bodyguard and all-round enforcer (Zak), his most devoted disciple, intelligence chief and newly appointed Tel Aviv commander (Svorai) and his old and trusted comrade from Polish days (Amper).

What had they all been doing together under the same roof at such a dangerous time? In his memoir Levstein maintains that the flat in Dizengoff Street was 'chosen because it was considered one of the safest places in Tel Aviv … and the police could not possibly know who was using it'. He admits, though, that this was a rash assumption to make. 'Since the attack on Yael Street a witch hunt had been unleashed against [us],' he wrote. 'The British knew it was the right time to liquidate the fighting underground. Public leaders, the press, and even the man on the street, were caught up in the British propaganda …' Furthermore, Zak, whose picture had been widely distributed since his escape from the train to Mazra'a, had 'rented the apartment from a family unknown to us, a cardinal sin in the underground'.

Despite the obvious risks it was decided to use the room to hold a weapons and explosives training session on Tuesday, 27 January. The instructor was Levstein, who was currently operating out of Jerusalem. He arrived early in the morning and class began soon after. Amper, Zak and Svorai listened as Levstein explained the workings of a hand grenade and the rudiments of laying charges. The session lasted until mid-afternoon. As they did not dare go out in daylight, they relaxed, waiting for nightfall. Levstein wrote that Svorai lay on the bed in the corner of the room reading the memoirs of one of the Russian socialist revolutionaries whose *modus operandi* they were now imitating. Zelig Zak 'was stretched out on a cot to read a newspaper, and Amper sat on a chair next to the window and told me about his adventures when he escaped from Poland through Russia and Turkey ...' Levstein left the room to go to the lavatory so his highly coloured rendition of what happened after his departure comes second-hand.[10]

Moshe Svorai gave several accounts of the event, which are by and large consistent. He related that he had put down his book and was sitting on one of the two couches in the room talking to Amper when 'Morton broke in holding a pistol'. The policeman then shouted in Hebrew, 'Who murdered Schiff?'[11] Then, rather than telling them not to get up, as Morton claimed, he said the policeman ordered them to raise their hands. 'We indeed got up, we raised our hands and he started shooting at us,' he said, 'first at Zelig, then at Amper and then at me.' He saw someone picking up his coat, in order, he alleged, to plant a pistol in it. He also maintained that when the Jewish medics arrived the police 'did not allow them to approach us' and they lay there for two hours before they were treated. Svorai and Levstein would maintain stoutly for the rest of their lives that the three men in the room offered no resistance to Morton, Woodward and Day. They had nothing to resist them with, as they had no guns, and the weaponry that was found there had been planted by Wilkin. The charge that the wounded were denied first aid would also be repeated many times.

Morton never wavered from his account, which was backed up in court by Sergeant Woodward when Svorai and Levstein went on trial. Nor did he express the slightest doubt that he had acted well within the law. Under cross-examination at the trial of Svorai and Levstein, he gave cool, confident answers to the lawyer for the defence:

Counsel: What were your instructions to the police?
Morton: To use all means to prevent the escape of the suspects.
Counsel: What were they?
Morton: All means.
Counsel: Did you give permission to shoot?

Morton: No, I did not say it.

Counsel: In accordance with the Police Ordinance, is it allowed to shoot anybody to prevent his escape, or when he shows an attempt to escape?

Morton: According to the ordinance it is not permitted but this was a special case.

The President of the Court: In what way was it special?

Morton: The people were suspected.

Counsel: Is it allowed to shoot anybody who is suspected?

Morton: I wanted to prevent losses amongst the police party.

Counsel: Is it allowed for a policeman to kill anybody if he does not like him?

Morton: I am a police officer and I did my duty.[12]

Morton clearly believed that he had little to fear from accusations that he had exceeded that duty and the circumstances allowed him to take no chances whatsoever. In his report he states baldly that 'on searching the flat it was observed that the door of the lavatory was locked and that the key was on the inside. I called to whoever was inside to come out and receiving no reply fired four shots through the wooden door.' The fact that he felt no need to justify this action suggests that, indeed, 'this was a special case'.

When asked about it much later, Alec Ternent did not try to hide his intentions when he aimed his gun at Levstein. 'He was the first person I ever fired at in anger in my life and I meant to kill him,' he said. 'I meant to shoot to kill [and] it was a bad aim when it hit him in the arse.'[13] Morton was careful in his report to stress that Ternent had his backing. 'I desire to add,' he wrote, 'that I gave the Police personnel implicit [sic] instructions that under no circumstances should they allow anybody to escape from the house and B/C [British Constable] Ternent was carrying out these implicit instructions when he shot and wounded Yaacov Levstein.'

Morton appeared confident of the approval and backing of his superiors. That was by no means guaranteed, particularly when the action was as robust as it had been in the Dizengoff Street raid. A few months previously, in October 1941, MacMichael had ordered a thorough report on the activities of the Jewish underground and their relationship with the Jewish Agency and other major institutions of the Yishuv. The memorandum that resulted concentrated mainly on the Haganah and its new commando unit, the Palmach, and the Irgun. The Stern group is represented as a bunch of Chicago-style gangsters, devoid of any ideological impetus, who operated 'on the plane on which guys are merely bumped off, rubbed out or put on the spot'.[14] It was 'a menace to society but ... not politically important'.

The Haganah and the Palmach, and to a lesser extent the Irgun, were linked to legitimate political bodies with strong political connections, particularly in America. MacMichael already feared that the 'Zionist Juggernaut ... will be the cause of very serious trouble in the Near East'. He concluded that in dealing with the underground it was best to tread carefully because the danger they posed was 'infinitely less easy to meet by the methods of repression which have been employed against Arabs'.[15] The Stern group, however, had no powerful friends abroad and had been forced to seek alliances with Britain's enemies. It followed, therefore, that in the campaign to shut them down, the same considerations did not apply.

Morton had proved astonishingly efficient in pursuing the goal. Within hours of the special meeting he had gone a long way to achieving Saunders' declared objectives. In a single operation he had conducted a 'general round up' of members as well as capturing one of the perpetrators of the Yael Street outrage.

The police had already correctly surmised that Levstein had been behind it. In his report Morton refers to him as 'having conceived and executed' the attack. The evidence that he said was found at the flat confirmed it. As well as a loaded automatic and two hand grenades there was a length of fuse and 'batteries similar to that used in the Schiff case'. With Zak's capture another file had been closed. He was believed to have been the man who, two months before, had killed the Jewish constable Soffiof as he walked back from the cinema with his wife and child.

None of this would have been possible had Morton not received an accurate tip-off. Where had it come from, and why? In his book Morton refers only to a 'Jewish source' and suggests that the main motive was money. The Stern group believed the information had come from the couple from whom Zak had sublet the room.[16] Svorai claimed later the husband was a member of the Haganah.[17] Whoever gave the tip-off, their motive was not financial gain. Morton's reference to money may have been an attempt to put Stern's followers off the scent. His book was published in 1957 when memories were still fresh and the thirst for revenge lingered.

Writing to Giles Bey nine days after the shootings, Morton revealed that 'the information leading to the arrests of these four gangsters was passed to me by a member of the public through the intermediary of two Jewish members of my staff'. He pointed out that, although a decision had been made to offer two hundred pounds each for information leading to the arrest of Zak and Svorai, the notices advertising the rewards had not yet been published. 'The fact that this information was forthcoming even though no reward had been offered is in every way commendable,' he declared. He went on to ask for one hundred pounds to be disbursed to the informant and twenty each to the Jewish officers, for 'you will appreciate that all Jewish members of the CID at the present time run very grave risks, and I do feel that work such as this should be handsomely rewarded'. Giles responded with a cheque.[18]

There was, it seemed, no shortage of money available in the hunt for the Stern gang. A decision had already been taken the day before the special meeting to offer a thousand pounds for 'information leading directly to the apprehension of 'Avraham Ben Mordechai Stern alias "Yaer [sic]"'. Five other names were on the list, carrying rewards of between four hundred and one hundred pounds. They included those of Hanoch Strelitz and Binyamin Zeroni, whom the CID appeared not to know had split from Stern. The inducements came with a threat, intended to draw the net yet tighter. The public were warned that 'any person who knowingly harbours or conceals or assists in any way' any of the wanted men would be subject to the full force of the emergency regulations.[19] Morton had asked the Jaffa–Tel Aviv area Public Information Officer for some images for the wanted posters. He responded with 'eight snaps of Herr Stern as requested'. He went on: 'I understand that you are not only next on the list, but that you are very badly wanted by the gentleman referred to above and his honourable associates.' He concluded: 'I do heartily hope that you will get him and them before they get you.'[20]

TEN

'It Doesn't Matter If They Kill Me'

Avraham Stern's face was everywhere. It gazed down from hoardings and out of the pages of the newspapers. The photograph was rather unflattering. The subject stared sullenly at the camera with dark stubble shading his chin and cheeks, his mouth set in a resigned, unhappy line. The picture had been taken after his arrest in 1939 and it created the desired effect. Gone was the romantic, dandy revolutionary; in his place was a seedy-looking gangster.

The thought of his mother having to see her son's image plastered over the walls of Tel Aviv with a thousand-pound price on his head filled Stern with anguish. 'Dear and beloved mother,' he wrote in what would be his last letter to her. 'It pains me without limit that you are pained. But you know me and you know that the things they are saying about me are based on lies … may God grant that we see better days.' He signed it with his childhood nickname, 'Mema'.[1]

For months he had been able to keep up only intermittent contact with Roni, usually through letters delivered by courier. One day he decided to risk a night-time foray to see his long-suffering wife face-to-face. With Amper and Zak lying gravely wounded in hospital he had to rely on Yitzhak Tselnik – a graduate of the Polish training camps and now his chief lieutenant – to accompany him to the rendezvous. Roni arrived with her mother. Even though the couple's circumstances were more desperate than ever, they had forgotten or perhaps deliberately abandoned their previous agreement not to have a family and she was now two months pregnant. They walked the darkened streets together for an hour. Stern seemed in good spirits, joking and murmuring endearments to Roni in Russian. When they parted his last words were: 'You aren't angry with me, are you? Tell me you aren't angry. Tell me you love me.' There was one further communication. He sent a note asking for clothes and enclosing five pounds. In it he remarked how it was only in the last few days that he had come to understand 'how good it is that we will have a child'.[2] Roni sent back a parcel of garments for him, including some silk socks.

If Stern remained in Tel Aviv he was bound to be caught. If he ventured out he was certain to be recognized and few would have any qualms about turning him in. Stern's behaviour had dissolved the code of solidarity that made even law-abiding Jews reluctant to hand over one of their own to the British. The lavishness of the reward would also help to dispel scruples. A thousand pounds was a lot of money, enough to buy a substantial villa in Tel Aviv, and everyone was on the lookout. The *Palestine Post*, under the headline 'Policeman Who Looks Like Gangster', had related how 'a Jewish plainclothesman unfortunate enough to bear a likeness to the much sought Abraham Stern has twice found himself dragged before the police since the publication of the reward notices. An Australian soldier seized the man in the street yesterday and brought him up to a Police Constable demanding the [money] on the spot.'[3]

Stern would be no safer if he stayed put. The unusual ménage in the rooftop flat in Mizrachi Bet Street was sure to attract attention. The roof was a busy place, with the other tenants coming and going throughout the day to hang up and take down their washing. How long could it be before someone began to wonder about the furtive figure flitting around behind the shutters of the apartment of 'Mrs Bloch'?

There were just two of them there now. Moshe was only a mile or so away, recovering from his wounds at the Government Hospital in Jaffa. Tova did not dare visit him for fear of being followed. With Stern in residence, the flat was no place for a little girl and Herut was being looked after by her grandmother.

He passed the days writing and reading – Israel Zangwill's *Memoirs of a Social Revolutionary* and a novel by Vicki Baum. The main contact with the outside world was through a thin, bespectacled woman called Hassia Shapira, a telephone operator at the newspaper *HaBoker*. She would deliver food and domestic supplies, carry messages and letters from the dwindling band of people willing to have anything to do with Yair, and take away his replies. Her comings and goings provided more fodder for gossipy neighbours. Tova told anyone who asked that the visitor was a friend who was looking after her while she recovered from her illness. By now the pretence had become a reality. Tova had developed a liver condition, which caused her acute pain in her side.

Stern had to move, but where to? Roni's brother, Nehemia Brosh, would claim later that at this time the head of the Haganah, Eliyahu Golomb, came up with an unexpected offer. He proposed to hide Stern on a remote kibbutz and put the word around that he had fled abroad. Given the organization's alliance with the British and its hostility to Stern, this seems remarkable. Brosh's explanation was that Golomb had heard from the Haganah's contacts inside the police that a decision had been reached that Stern would not be taken alive, and he wanted to spare him from the vengeance of the CID. The Haganah certainly had many agents among Jewish members of the force. It is possible that one of them had formed this impression from conversations or documents relating to the manhunt. In any case, Brosh said, Stern turned the offer down. He could not run away and hide when his men were in prison or lying in hospital under police guard.[4] He could at least, though, try to move to somewhere less hazardous. Stern's presence in the Svorais' flat was a measure of his desperation. He had nowhere else to go. Ever since he had moved in, he, Moshe and Yitzhak Tselnik had tried to find safer alternatives. One idea was to move him to an ultra-religious neighbourhood where the inhabitants' complete absorption in their own lives made them oblivious or indifferent to the activities of outsiders and there was a reduced risk of betrayal.

Another was to smuggle him to Jerusalem in the back of a furniture lorry. This seemed to have the most chance of success and Tselnik was charged with organizing it. The operation was supposed to take place at the beginning of February.[5]

Every day brought new disasters. On 1 February, five days after they were shot by Morton, both Avraham Amper and Zelig Zak died of their wounds. According to Yaacov Levstein, he and the others had maintained a defiant front despite their injuries, threatening a hunger strike unless they were treated by Dr Marcus, a local physician who sympathized with their cause. They had 'fasted for one day when Amper and Zak seemed to be doing better. Zak woke up and said that he felt strengthened by his wounds. Jokingly, he added that he was now bullet-proof. Amper also seemed to be in good spirits and sent regards to his friends and relatives.'[6] The next day, though, they woke 'pale and listless. At noon Zak suddenly collapsed, and by the time the nurse came in he was dead. About an hour later Amper suddenly took a turn for the worse and expired.'

The photographs published in the newspapers on 3 February showed Stern and five other wanted men. Pictured with him were Yaacov Polani, Binyamin Zeroni, Hanoch Strelitz, one Aharon Zukerman and Nahman Shulman, a low-ranking member of the band who was reported to have been hanging about 8 Yael Street before the outrage. Shulman was arrested the same evening.[7]

Those still at large had four choices. They could wait to be picked up. They could act like the 'anonymous soldiers' of Yair's imagination, fight on, and, in all probability, meet the same fate as their comrades in Dizengoff Street. They could flee. Or they could give themselves up. Polani, who had a four-hundred-pound bounty on his head, took the third option and disappeared to a kibbutz at Maale Ha-Hamisha, in the hills west of Jerusalem.[8]

On 4 February, Strelitz and Zeroni, who, despite being far more important than Polani, merited bounties of only two hundred pounds each, gave themselves up. There are two versions of how this came about. According to police chief Alan Saunders, following the quarrel with Stern they had made up their minds that it was time to make their peace with the British. The police were ignorant of the split when 'the two men approached the CID through intermediaries with a view to surrender'. Negotiations were still in progress at the time of the Yael Street bombing. Saunders was well aware of the potentially sobering effect that the subsequent shootings in Dizengoff Street had on the rest of Stern's past and present associates. He wrote that, 'unnerved, perhaps, by the vigorous police action at Dizengoff Street and the sight of their photographs in the press side by side with those of Stern and other desperate men, Strelitz and Zeroni surrendered unconditionally at an address in Tel Aviv'.[9]

A slightly different account circulated later which showed the pair in a less timorous light. According to this, they insisted on certain preconditions before handing themselves over. They approached the British through an intermediary, Yitzhak Berman, a Ukrainian-born, London-trained lawyer who was also a senior figure in the Irgun's intelligence bureau. He was to offer their surrender, subject to three guarantees: they would not be handed over to Morton in Jaffa but to the CID at their headquarters in Jerusalem; they would not be tortured; they would not be put on trial but sent under the emergency regulations to a detention camp. Berman, who went on to become a government minister, claimed later that he took the offer to Dick Catling who pushed it up the line to Giles Bey. Giles agreed. Strelitz and Zeroni were whisked off to Jerusalem in Catling's car and the British kept their word, sending them off to Mazra'a to join their brothers-in-arms.[10]

The following day, Aharon Zukerman, described by an informer as the group's 'secretary' in Tel Aviv, followed their example. He had imagined that the police knew nothing about him. He was having breakfast in the Shederoth café in Allenby Road in Tel Aviv when he opened his newspaper to see his own face staring back at him above an offer of a hundred-pound reward. According to Giles he surrendered 'unconditionally' at CID headquarters, though again there is another account stating that via Berman's good offices he managed to strike the same deal as the others. On 10 February, Baruch Moisevitz, whom the police believed to have been leader of the group in Tel Aviv at the time of the Yael Street bombings, and was perhaps the man mentioned by Levstein in his account of the attack, was arrested 'on information supplied by secret sources'.[11]

Whether or not he was bypassed by these arrangements, Morton must have felt great satisfaction at the way things were going. One way or another, the Stern gang was being mopped up. Furthermore, the vigour the police had shown – exemplified by his own actions – had sent a strong message to other potential enemies that the game was not worth the candle. 'It is generally believed among the more politically-minded Tel Aviv Jews that the tempo and determination displayed by Government and Police to root out and destroy the Stern movement will have far reaching results,' he wrote to Giles Bey on 3 February.[12] 'If successful [this] will serve as an effective deterrent to other individuals and groups who, in the future, like Stern, may become possessed with the idea that without political and party backing, and with public sympathy they can overawe the nation and set up [a] "Chicago administration" against which the government would be powerless to act.'

This was a succinct but fairly accurate assessment of what Stern had been aiming to do. All his life he had tried to fit his talents and ambitions into the confines of institutions and organizations – the Hebrew University, the Revisionist movement, the underground. His nature ensured that each attempt ended in failure. The name he had been born with and the name he had chosen for himself revealed the problem. Stern, by coincidence, means 'star' in Yiddish, one of the languages spoken in Suwalki. From childhood he had been a performer, revelling in the limelight of theatrical productions and recitals. His desire for attention was evident in his dress. The man who proclaimed his willingness to endure misery, filth and death felt uneasy if he was separated from his silk socks. Behind this apparently harmless, even touching vanity lay something much more dangerous.

Stern was incapable of sharing centre stage with anyone. To act alongside him meant accepting a minor part, and those who questioned his right to the top billing, such as Raziel, Strelitz and Zeroni, were first confronted, then rejected.

He picked his own roles – poet, dreamer, lover, international wheeler-dealer. The greatest of these was that of 'Yair'. Yair was the man he wanted to be, a feared and fearless warrior, noble and self-sacrificing, whose dedication would lead him to a redeemer's death. Now the performance seemed hollow and ridiculous. His poetry was steeped in blood, but he had never felt the rush of horror and excitement that came with looking a man in the eyes as you shot him dead or pressing the button that exploded an infernal machine. But the drama was not over yet. There was still another act to come, still time to bring the theatre to its feet.

Later his followers would claim that he knew the end – a violent one – was coming but was fatalistically resigned to it. It would not mean extinction but redemption. Binyamin Zeroni testified that 'Yair dreamed of death. In conversations and discussions between us he always focused on death ... whereas I thought you must fight for an idea, he said you had to die for it. He would often say "it doesn't matter if they kill me".'[13] Yitzhak Tselnik would maintain later that before the Dizengoff Street shootings Stern had seen his capture and trial as an opportunity to denounce British policy in Palestine. After the bloodbath 'it was clear to him he wouldn't be taken prisoner but instead would be shot on the spot'.[14]

On 11 February, Dick Catling summed up for the benefit of Giles Bey the actions taken by the police since the Yael Street outrage. Two of the Stern group were dead. Eighty-five more were locked up; three were serving jail sentences, six were on remand and facing trial and the rest were being held under emergency regulations.[15] That amounted to a clear majority of the known membership of the group. The organization was in smithereens, morale had evaporated and, of the old command echelon, only the leader remained at large.

On 7 February, Hassia Shapira arrived early at the flat and announced that she thought she might have been followed. It was a feeling rather than a conviction. Stern told her she must from now on stay away from Mizrachi Bet Street. Their only trusted link with the outside world was, for the time being at least, severed. What were they to do for food? Tova decided to go down to the local grocer's shop and ask the woman who owned it if she would deliver provisions as her helper had herself fallen ill. '"Don't worry, Mrs Bloch," the nice lady answered,' wrote Tova some years afterwards.[16] '"I can bring you the goods at home but only in the evening."' The following night the shopkeeper duly turned up. When she knocked on the door, 'Yair went into the wardrobe and I closed the door on him. The weary shopkeeper sat for a minute that went on and on. She had many interesting stories about her customers ...' When the Good Samaritan finally left, Tova waited until her footsteps had faded from the stairwell and 'hurried to open the wardrobe door so he could finally breathe air'.

Tova admitted that she found such incidents very trying. Stern, by contrast, emerged from his confinement 'wearing a pleasant smile and in a good mood'. He tried to calm her down but her nerves were fraying. Yitzhak Tselnik was still trying to find a refuge for Stern in Jerusalem. On the evening of 9 February he came to report on that and other matters. The procedure was for Tselnik to wait some way off for Tova to descend, walk to an alleyway up the street and, by showing herself, signal that it was safe for him to go up. That day, she related afterwards, as she emerged from the front door she noticed a man 'wearing a hat and dressed in a black coat' who followed her. The street was lined with stalls, illuminated by electric light bulbs, and after passing her the man turned back to examine her face. Whether or not he recognized her, she claimed that she recognized him: he was one of the detectives who had burst into their flat in Tel Aviv when Moshe had been arrested along with Yaacov Polani and Yehoshua Zettler the previous May. She had encountered him a second time after Polani and Zettler had escaped from the police station, when detectives paid another visit to the apartment believing they might be hiding there. She climbed back up the stairs, flustered and distressed, and told Stern what she had – or might have – seen. Was she positive the man was a policeman, he wanted to know? She was not. Perhaps it was her nerves making her imagine things.[17]

Half a mile away from Stern and Tova's claustrophobic hideaway, Geoffrey Morton was struggling to close the circle around his prey. This was no longer a straightforward police operation. The hunt for the perpetrators was now intensely personal. Svorai claimed that when he burst into the room at 30 Dizengoff Street, Morton had shouted Schiff's name – demanding to know who had murdered him. There is no mention of this in Morton's testimony as, perhaps, is to be expected. In the light of Morton's record and writings, however, it does not seem altogether improbable.

Morton brought to his police work a belief in the sanctity of authority that was in its way as hard and fierce as Stern's nationalist zeal. It stretched back sixteen years, to the moment of revelation when a single burly constable had quelled a mob of rioters at the Elephant and Castle. Since then he had suffered many disappointments and some disillusionment. But he had kept faith, and been rewarded for his fidelity. To be a policeman was to be far more than a mere enforcer of the law. He saw himself and his colleagues as the custodians of a system that formed the foundation of civilized life. An attack on one policeman was an attack on all of them and, by extension, on society itself; or at least British society and therefore the best example of it.

By declaring war on the British police Stern had established himself as an enemy of everything Morton held sacred. Morton had never met Avraham Stern but he had formed a strong opinion of who he was and what he stood for. Morton was well informed about his opponent's background. He would have known about his academic record and his cultured tastes – enthusiasms that Morton, the music lover, shared. None of this mattered.

Nor did the fact that Yair had merely overseen operations miti-
gate his guilt. He had come to represent all the bad that was done
not just in his name but by the Jewish underground in general. It
was this perception that had led Morton, against all his policeman's
training and instincts, to blame Stern for the death of his friend
Wally Medler in Jaffa four years earlier, even though there was no
evidence to connect him to the case.[18]

Now Stern was alone, cornered and helpless. The *mano a mano*
was reaching its end. It was time for the reckoning. But where was
he? It seems that at this point neither the police, the Haganah nor,
despite their earlier claim, the Irgun had any idea where Stern might
be. His image was everywhere, offering the public the prospect of an
easy thousand pounds. The eyes of every policeman in the land
were peeled for Palestine's number one gangster, and every informant was on the alert to pull off a lucrative coup. Yet it would not be
a tip-off that led the police to the door of 8 Mizrachi Bet Street but
an extraordinary sequence of events that began in the ward of the
Government Hospital, just over a mile from the CID building near
the Jaffa seafront, where Yaacov Levstein and Moshe Svorai were still
being treated. What happened there, wrote Morton, would 'provide
us with the clue for which the whole police force was watching.'[19]

ELEVEN

'Avraham, Avraham'

The two survivors of the raid on 30 Dizengoff Street were making a good recovery. Since their arrival, security at the hospital had been stepped up and guards were placed on all the entrances.[1] The detention ward was on the ground floor and contained six beds. The prisoners were watched around the clock by two police sergeants, one of them an Irishman named Arthur Daly. Morton had known Daly since they were constables together at the Mount Scopus depot. Daly was the camp bugler and Morton recalled how 'many a time I had watched with amusement when, on one elbow, he had blown perfectly the morning Reveille in the direction of the open window without getting out of bed'.[2]

Daly had distinguished himself in other ways. In 1936 he was awarded the British Empire Medal for an act of exceptional selflessness. The citation read that while on duty at Tel Aviv railway station 'he saved the life of a woman who fell on the line beneath a moving train by throwing himself on top of her and holding her in position until safe to rise'. He was known for his good grasp of Hebrew, and had a streak of cunning that would prove invaluable in closing the ring around Avraham Stern.

According to Morton's official report, the day after the prisoners were brought in from the Dizengoff Street shootings, 'Sgt. Daly came to me and suggested that useful information might be forthcoming if he were to offer his services to the prisoners as a go-between, in order to take information to their friends and relatives outside.' Morton told him to go ahead but emphasized he should make it clear that he expected to be paid for his trouble

– this to allay suspicion that the sergeant was acting for any other motive than money.

The arrangement began working immediately. That same day, Yaacov Levstein accepted an offer from Daly to deliver a note to his mother, who lived not far from the hospital in Rambam Street, in south Tel Aviv.[3] He admitted that the genial Irishman soon charmed them. 'Dailey [sic] did his best to befriend us and put us at our ease,' he wrote.[4] 'He told us he was Irish and had Jewish friends.' Given their admiration for the IRA, being Irish was a great advantage in winning the confidence of the Jewish underground. Yitzhak Shamir chose 'Michael' as his *nom de guerre* in homage to Michael Collins, the IRA leader. Irishmen, even those in British uniform, if they appeared sympathetic, might be regarded as fellow victims of imperialist oppression.

Daly seems to have played the part to perfection. Levstein related how, when the Irishman asked if he wanted him to deliver a message to his parents, he 'jumped at the opportunity'. His mother had pleaded with him to give up the underground life and lived in a state of perpetual anxiety. He 'knew how worried' his parents were and 'how much better they would feel if they got a direct message from me'.

Morton said that 'subsequently several notes of an innocuous nature ... were passed backwards and forwards between Levstein and his mother through the intermediary of Sergeant Daly'.[5] He was a welcome visitor. Daly became 'quite friendly with my parents', wrote Levstein. 'He would stop to see them, chat with them, enjoy my mother's home-made cookies and even received a shaving kit in return for his good offices.'[6]

On Wednesday, 11 February, the hospital's medical officer examined Svorai and Levstein and found them in satisfactory health. He reported that they were now well enough to be discharged from hospital. This meant that very soon they would leave the comparative comfort of the ward for a cell, in the prison in the Russian Compound in Jerusalem, where they would await trial on what in

Levstein's case might be capital charges. Levstein says that the news was broken to him by Daly who suggested that he might like a visit from his mother before he left. He replied that he would be happy to see her.

In his memoir Morton elaborated on Daly's stratagem. The sergeant solicitously pointed out to both Svorai and Levstein that for the move 'they would need some clean clothes – those in which they had been captured were caked with blood, and they would not want to don the uniform normally worn by convicted prisoners'.

Until this point Svorai had not taken up Daly's offer of help. Morton says that he had mentioned in casual conversation that he had a wife and child in Tel Aviv. However, he could hardly ask Daly to communicate with his family without bringing trouble down on Tova. He was about to relent. According to Morton, 'after some hesitation, Yaacov Levstein wrote a note to his mother asking her to bring him some clean clothes down to the hospital the next morning'.[7] Svorai 'at first refused to take any similar steps, but eventually agreed to add a note for his wife to the bottom of the Levsteins' letter to his mother'. Svorai told Daly 'Mrs Levstein would know how to get in touch with his wife'.[8]

This was an encouraging development. Up until now the translated notes had revealed nothing. The discovery of Tova Svorai's address might provide more clues as to Stern's whereabouts. There was nothing then to suggest that Tova might be harbouring him – though, given the couple's closeness to Yair, it must have occurred to Morton that there was a chance that this was the case.

Then, slowly, that chance began to seem a real possibility. As soon as he received the notes Daly hurried to Morton's office. Svorai's caution had not entirely deserted him. Morton said that his note to Tova had been 'written in an obscure Russian dialect in Hebrew characters and it was very difficult to translate'.[9] There was a delay as he 'got an agent in Tel Aviv to do it for me'. He hesitated to ask one of his staff. The reason he gave for this was that he 'felt this was not a matter in which to implicate my Jewish colleagues'.[10]

The inference is that he feared the contents of the letter might be leaked to Stern sympathizers.

At 8.30 that evening he received back the translation from the unnamed 'agent'. It was clumsily expressed but there could be no mistaking the import of two key phrases in Svorai's letter. He started off 'Shalom my Tova', then proceeded to reassure her he was in good health. 'I can imagine your worries and fears, especially after the other two died,' he wrote. 'I feel well and you know I always wish to tell you the truth.' Far from being concerned about himself he was distressed at not having news of her, particularly as she had been ill. 'I am worrying about your wellbeing as I know nothing of what is with you and of our guest,' he declared. The word 'guest' gleamed from the typed page like neon. Just in case the police missed the clue, it was repeated again a few lines later: 'I am worried because I have not seen or heard from you,' he persisted. 'There is no need to worry anyhow, consult with our guest.'

The coy reluctance to name the 'guest' could not fail to arouse the interest of the CID. Perhaps it was Stern. Perhaps not. Whoever it was, it seemed highly likely they had something to hide. In order to find out, Morton had first to discover the whereabouts of Tova, and for that he needed the help of Mrs Levstein, who, Moshe Svorai had told Daly, would know how to reach her. It was now the middle of the evening. Sergeant Daly, changed out of his uniform and dressed less obtrusively in civvies, set off for the Levsteins' home in one of the ornate turn-of-the-century Ottoman houses lining Rambam Street. He handed Mrs Levstein her son's letter and mentioned that there was an attachment from Moshe Svorai who believed she would be able to pass it onto his wife. According to Morton's report, 'Mrs Levstein informed Sgt Daly that she was at a loss to know what to do with this note as she did not know the whereabouts of Mrs Svorai'.[11] Nonetheless, after Daly left, a watch was kept on the house. Midnight came and went. No one arrived and no one left. It seemed that Mrs Levstein was telling the truth.

There was heavy rain overnight. Up in the rooftop apartment at 8 Mizrachi Bet Street, it drummed on the windows and bounced off the flat, concrete roof. Inside the bed-sitting room Tova and Stern slept, she on the couch, he on a divan that slid out from underneath it. In the previous few days, Stern's famous sang-froid had begun to melt. They lived in continual fear of discovery. The previous day the cistern in the tiny bathroom had flooded. The landlord had promptly sent round a plumber. When he arrived Stern once again had to climb into the wardrobe. He was forced to squat there for half an hour, in among Tova's dresses, while the workman fixed the leak.[12]

The flat felt like a prison. Stern paced the cramped space, smoking, talking and writing. He scribbled poetry incessantly, pouring out a torrent of rage and despair. One ran: 'And all Tel Aviv became hell/and every house became [a] gallows/and everyone in it became a detective'. His words showed he was reaching the end of his endurance. 'Mad pouring rain and ardent, bitter cold./Where to rest my tired head? Where to hide my shivering flesh?' He cried out to 'My God, the God of revenge/The God of the Fighters of Freedom'.[13]

At other times he told Tova of the guilt he felt about the trouble he had caused his mother and Roni and the anguish they must experience as they pictured him jerking on the end of a British hangman's rope. 'When he said "neck" he would make a gesture with his hand to illustrate it,' Tova remembered.[14] He talked bitterly about those who had let him down over the years, among them David Raziel and Hanoch Strelitz, who had abandoned the struggle rather than stay and fight for their ideals. He found it hard to sleep. On Wednesday night when Tova went to bed he stayed at the table, writing and smoking, finally tiptoeing to his bed at four o'clock.

Tova would describe the night of 11/12 February 1942 as bitterly cold, 'freezing my bones in a way that hadn't happened for years'. At six o'clock, an hour before dawn, she heard a scratching at the door. 'I raised my head and opened my eyes and looked across at Yair's bed,' she wrote. 'I could see he had woken too.' Who could it be? Everyone from their immediate circle was either dead, locked up or had gone to ground. The scratching was familiar. It was the signal Hassia gave when she visited – but she had been told to keep away. The noise continued. Tova glanced nervously at Stern. He nodded and she rose and padded the few steps over the cold tiles to the entrance. Tova turned the lock and opened the door. A gust of cold air filled the hall. There, framed in the doorway, her glasses gleaming, was the thin, anxious figure of Hassia Shapira. Tova pulled her inside and shut the door.

Hassia explained why she had disobeyed instructions and risked the visit. She was carrying an important message – potentially a life-saving one. It came from Nehemia Torenberg, an Irgunist of long standing from the Rosh Pinna community who had followed Stern after the split. He was conveying an offer he had just received via an intermediary from the new Irgun leader, Yaacov Meridor. Apparently the Irgun's attitude towards Stern had softened. Having told Captain Wybrow that they were willing to 'liquidate' their former comrade, they now wanted to offer him sanctuary, just as the Haganah had earlier. Stern's mood seemed to lighten as he read the letter. He considerately told Hassia to climb into bed with Tova to warm herself up. Then he sat down at the small table in the hall to write his answer. Politely but firmly, he rejected the offer. 'My answer of course is no,' he replied. 'I am not one of those who voluntarily give themselves up to the police or do the bidding of the left or the right.' In a reference to the Haganah proposal he added, 'the left is also willing to look after me if I hand myself over to them'. He was, however, prepared to cooperate with the Irgun if they were planning action against the British. If the Dizengoff Street shootings and the ongoing treatment of refugees in the camp at Athlit had 'opened their eyes and revealed to them the true face of foreign rule' then he would be willing to listen to their plans.[15] The letter was the last Stern wrote. He could not have wished for a better last testament, proof for all who came after him of his tungsten-hard determination and unquenchable fighting spirit.

Dawn came just after seven o'clock. By 7.30 there were people about on the streets and it seemed safe for Hassia to slip away to carry the reply back to Torenberg. Stern was anxious once more. He paced up and down, a few steps forward, a few steps back, a prowling, troubled figure. 'Suddenly,' Tova remembered, 'I saw that Yair had stopped. He was holding onto the door that separates the hallway and the room. He pushed it backwards ... I went over to him and he whispered: "Tova, they are watching us through the slats in the shutter."'[16] It was only eight o'clock. Could the landlord or his wife have decided to hang out their washing early? She prayed that they had not. The landlord was a friendly man who was in the habit of stopping to chat and ask after Herut, the Svorai's little girl, now staying with her grandmother. She crept to the window. There was no one outside. The slats were half open to let in a little light. She pulled the lever to lower them. They both relaxed.

Tova moved around in her housecoat, laying the table for breakfast. It was the same one they always ate, a 'three-storey' sandwich made up of bread, cheese and jam, washed down with a cup of tea. She cleared away the plates and put a joint of meat in the oven in the galley kitchen to roast for the following day's Shabbat supper. Then she tidied away the bedding and lay down on the sofa to read. A few feet away, Stern sat at the table, blue carpet slippers on his feet.[17] The table was covered with strips of white paper. His pen moved steadily over them, covering them with his neat handwriting.

Tel Aviv was by now properly awake. Outside in Mizrachi Bet Street the vendors had set out their stalls and were chatting among themselves and bantering with the shoppers. The cafés were full of people drinking coffee and reading newspapers. All the news, it seemed, was bad. The Japanese were at the gates of Singapore. In Libya, Rommel was building up supplies for another push on Egypt. From German-occupied Europe leaked awful tales of Jewish persecution – massacres and round-ups, disease and famine. The columns combined to radiate a mood of impending crisis.

That morning Geoffrey and Alice Morton set off as usual from their mellow stone bungalow at Sarona for their places of work. The drive took about ten minutes, south along the Haifa–Jaffa highway. The cold, wet night had given way to a bright day. To the left as they drove stood orange groves and Arab villages, looking much as they had for centuries. To the right, the modernist apartment houses and office blocks of Tel Aviv gleamed clean and white in the morning sun. The car pulled up outside CID headquarters and Morton alighted and entered the building. The Jaffa High School for Girls, where Alice taught geography to Arab students, was only a short walk away.

Morton's day got off to a bad start. The surveillance of the Levsteins' home in Rambam Street had taken them no nearer to Tova Svorai and her mysterious guest. That line of inquiry seemed to have reached a dead end. Half a mile away at the Government Hospital, Moshe Svorai and Yaacov Levstein's stay was almost over.[18] Now they were about to exchange a hospital ward for a cell in the Jerusalem Central Prison, whose high, cavernous rooms and wide, flagged corridors had once been the Marianskya, a hostel for Russian women pilgrims to the Holy Land. Levstein was in surprisingly good spirits. 'It was a beautiful spring day, full of sun and the singing of birds,' he remembered.[19] 'I was happy to be recovering and looked forward to seeing my mother. I knew she would feel much better once she saw me. After all, she had once said that prison was a safe place for me, since she did not have to worry constantly something was going to happen to me.'

According to Morton's official report, Mrs Levstein arrived at the hospital at 9.30 a.m. with clothing for her son. She was met by Sergeant Daly who 'took her into the courtyard of the hospital and took the clothes from her, pointing out to her the window of the [ground floor] ward in which her son was accommodated'. He 'subsequently allowed Mrs Levstein to stand in such a position as she could carry on a clandestine conversation with Zvorai [sic]'. Daly then 'entered the detention ward and appeared to be busy with the other prisoner'.

Yaacov Levstein's account differs slightly. He says that he and his mother talked first. They were speaking in Russian and Daly ordered them to switch to Hebrew. Aware the policeman spoke this well, Levstein was careful not to say anything revealing. 'Once he realized that he did not stand to gain anything from my mother's visit, he motioned to her it was time to leave,' he wrote. It was then that Svorai made his fatal intervention. Levstein claimed that 'as my mother was about to leave Svorai turned to her and said in a clear voice: "Perhaps you can give my regards to my wife who lives at 8 Mizrahi B[et] Street."'

The effect on Daly was electric. He 'lunged across the room as if bitten by a snake', rushing to a telephone outside the door of the ward. Levstein recalls: 'I fell back on my bed, my heart pounding violently. I knew something terrible was going to happen.'

Svorai never denied the essentials of the story. In a conversation with Stern's biographer, Ada Amichal-Yevin, he said that when Mrs Levstein appeared at the window he let Yaacov speak first and 'then I asked her, did you see Tova? She told me no, she hadn't as she didn't know where she lives.'[20] When Moshe was arrested Stern had been installed chez Svorai for four weeks. Everyone knew the arrangement was a bad one and the last thing he had heard was that plans were in hand for him to move to Jerusalem at the beginning of February. 'I did not imagine that on 12 February he would still be in the apartment,' he claimed. 'So I said what I said – Mizrachi B 8.'

In Geoffrey Morton's official report, Daly heard Svorai give Mrs Levstein the address more precisely as '8 Mizrachi B Street – on the roof'. He also says that, rather than phoning, 'he obtained a relief from Ajani Police Station [the nearest to the hospital] and came and reported the matter immediately to me'.

When Daly reached CID headquarters with the information, Morton 'immediately dispatched Inspector Wilkin and a party of CID personnel to visit the roof … following myself a few minutes later'. Normally he was the first to rush to the scene of any drama, but as he explained later, he was expecting an important call from Jerusalem. Despite the colourful circumstances in which it was obtained, the information was after all fairly slight. The 'guest' might turn out to be an innocent party. Or he might be worthy of police attention, but have already flown the coop. After a dozen years of police work Morton was well used to false alarms and dud tip-offs.

So it was Wilkin who set off first, along with his assistant and friend Sergeant Bernard Stamp and other policemen. When Wilkin arrived at 8 Mizrachi Bet Street, Morton reported later, he immediately threw a cordon round the house to prevent anyone escaping. Then he and Stamp mounted the stairs to the little flat on the roof. Tova was reclining on the sofa where she would lie to ease the pain in her inflamed liver, when she heard a 'light, delicate knock on the door. Yair got up from the quiet of his chair. His blue slippers with the soft soles did not make any noise. He went straight to the wardrobe and got in. I closed the door after him. Only then did I approach the outer door and open it.'[21]

Standing there were 'the red-haired English officer Wilkin' and two other detectives. Tova appeared to have met Wilkin before – possibly during the raid on the flat in Keren Kayemet Street – for she was familiar with his 'sweet-talking' manner. According to her account he asked her: 'Tova, why didn't you come to see the injured Moshe?' She 'evaded an answer or gave a short reply'. Wilkin continued: 'I've come to take clothes for Moshe. He's moving today to the prison in Jerusalem.'

Tova went into the living-room-cum-bedroom and fetched vests, pants and handkerchiefs from a drawer and took down Moshe's suit hanging on the back of the door. She gave them to Wilkin who seemed in no hurry to leave. Instead, she said, he kept up his 'smooth-tongued' chat. '"Take my advice," he said politely. "Persuade Moshe to give up his fight against the British. What good is it doing him? After all, he's got a sick wife and a little girl. It's time he took care of them because he's never going to defeat the British."'

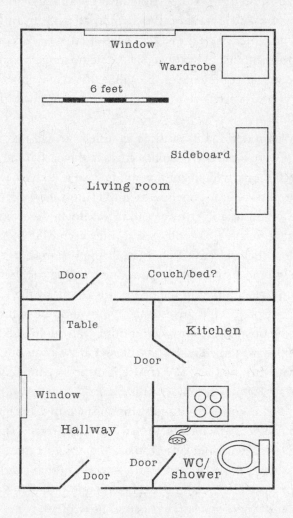

Tova was desperate not to prolong the encounter and said nothing. Her apparent serenity ruffled Wilkin for, she claimed, his 'face became red with anger' and he shouted 'you are murderers, you are thieves, all of Stern's people!' He ended the tirade by promising that, like Zak and Avraham, they would all end up in Nahalat Yitzhak, the cemetery on the eastern edge of Tel Aviv. This provoked Tova into an outburst of her own. She 'could no longer be silent and I said in a strong, confident voice: "Wilkin, listen to what I'm telling you. It will be my privilege to see all of you running away from our country."'

Now Wilkin decided it was time to search the flat. According to Tova there were more than two detectives in the party. One of them left to fetch more residents of the building, so as to have witnesses to back up the police if anyone tried to claim they were planting evidence or mistreating Tova. Wilkin sat down to examine the papers lying on the hall table. Meanwhile, according to Morton's report, the other detective – Bernard Stamp – started to work his way through the apartment, opening and shutting cupboard doors first in the kitchen, then in the bed-sitting room. By the end there was only one place left to investigate … the wardrobe in the corner.

'When he opened the door,' wrote Tova, 'Yair couldn't be seen at all. The closet was filled with suits, dresses and a coat. But then he reached in with his hand. Of course it came in contact with the body of Yair. He pulled him towards him.'

Later, Morton could not disguise his satisfaction at the ignominious circumstances in which Stern had been discovered. 'This tough gangleader, master-mind of terrorism, organiser of mass murder and assassinations by the dozen, arch-enemy of Britain and the war effort, this would be Quisling, had been found hiding in the wardrobe under the petticoats of his hostess,' he wrote.[22]

Tova claimed that as Stamp pulled Stern out he saw the policeman's hand move to his hip pocket and she assumed he was going for his gun. 'I sprang up … and stood between Yair and the detective,' she wrote. '"Don't shoot," I said. "Or if you do, shoot me."'[23]

She had no reason to fear. Wilkin was in the room now and standing in front of Stern. He was 'shaking his finger and saying "Avraham, Avraham" like a good father scolding his child.' Stern stood 'pale and quiet' saying nothing, his nostrils quivering slightly. The detectives sat him down on the sofa. Stamp stood over him, holding his two wrists in one big hand and covering him with his pistol with the other. Another detective stood in the door, his gun drawn. Wilkin ordered Tova to sit next to Yair on the couch. He showed the neighbours one of the Stern 'wanted' portraits and referred to him as a 'murderer'. This provoked further histrionics from Tova who urged them not to believe him. The frail figure sitting next to her was 'a great Jew who loves his people and land'. Stern at last spoke. 'Tova, it's not worth replying to him,' he said. Then he asked for his shoes, which were lying in a corner. She brought them over, 'black shiny shoes', and Stamp released his grip so that Stern could put them on. Tova noticed the clock on the sideboard next to the sofa. It read 9.40 a.m. Then there was a commotion and 'at once the place was filled with English detectives, tall with light faces and hair. Their mood was exuberant ...' Geoffrey Morton had arrived.[24]

The first thing Morton says he did on reaching the flat was to order 'the removal of Mrs Svorai to CID headquarters'. A later report written by Alan Saunders for the benefit of the Chief Secretary claimed she was 'hysterical and began tearing off her clothes'.[25] Tova maintained that a policewoman took her into the kitchen and searched her. Then she changed her housecoat for a dress and was escorted down the stairs by two policemen. A small car stood alongside the kerb. She was surprised to see Wilkin standing next to it. Parked across the street was a van which she assumed was there to take Yair to the police station. The escorts ordered her to get into the car. She saw Wilkin gazing up towards the rooftop apartment which was hidden by the parapet of the building. Nonetheless she, too, pressed her face against the window and stared upwards.

In that cramped flat Geoffrey Morton was looking for the first time on the face off the man he had been hunting for so long. The

178 · PATRICK BISHOP

atmosphere in the room can only be imagined. From the door to the window set in the far wall the distance was twelve feet eleven inches. From side to side it measured just over twelve feet. In it were crammed a divan, a wardrobe and a sideboard. The tiny space was crowded with big British bodies. Morton and Stamp were both six feet tall and there was at least one other policeman present, all towering over the small figure hunched on the couch.

The truth of what happened next would be endlessly disputed. For the next fifty-four years of his life, Geoffrey Morton would find himself again and again having to defend his version of events, fighting several legal actions to defend his honour when his account was contradicted. The basic story was told when he sat down the day after the event to compose his report for his superiors in Jerusalem. The document does not lie in any of the official archives but was discovered tucked away among the papers of Alec Stuart, which, after his death, Morton arranged to be placed in the Department of Documents at the Imperial War Museum, London.[26] It is written in flat police language, devoid of drama or emotion. After Tova Svorai's departure he wrote that he 'instructed Stern to exchange his slippers for walking shoes'. (According to Tova he had already done this, though the detail does not seem important.)

At the time 'Stern was sitting on the edge of a settee and just as he finished lacing his shoes he took a leap towards the window opposite which he was sitting. He dived under the arm of No. 67. B/Con. Hancock, S.N., who was covering him with a revolver and passed behind Sgt Stamp who was examining the contents of the buffet [sideboard].' Stern was 'halfway out of the window when both Hancock and myself fired practically simultaneously'. He was hit immediately, 'the first bullet catching him on the side of the head by the ear'. Then 'he swung round and received other bullets as he fell one of which passed through his heart'. It seemed to Morton that 'he died immediately'.[27] From the back of the police car Tova heard the shots. She screamed to the people in the street: 'Plainclothes police have murdered Yair Stern!'[28]

When Alan Saunders came to write a long report on the evolution of the Stern case for Chief Secretary Macpherson, he described the killing in the same way that it had been presented to him by Morton in his initial account. Stern was 'half-way out of the window when he was shot by two of the three policemen in the room, bullets entering the side of his head near the ear and the left side of his chest'. These two reports would form the basis of the official explanation of the shooting, to be repeated in press statements, internal documents and responses to parliamentary questions. It was summed up in a sentence that, by now, as Morton was the first to admit, was discredited: Stern had been shot while trying to escape.

The detectives gathered up the papers scattered on Stern's desk to take them away for translation. A journalist from the newspaper *HaBoker* who arrived on the scene reported seeing two plainclothes policemen, one of them a Jewish officer carrying the body down the stairs, covered in a grey sheet.[29] It was put in an ambulance and taken to the Government Hospital in Jaffa.

There was a procedure that had to be followed before Stern could be buried. Moshe Svorai and Yaacov Levstein were in bed in the detention ward waiting to be moved to prison when a Jewish detective called Yosef Brenner entered with another officer and told them they had a duty to perform. Brenner led Svorai to a room in the hospital where a body lay stretched out under a cover. Morton was waiting for them. The cover was pulled back to reveal the body of Avraham Stern. Svorai was asked if he recognized it. He replied that he did not. The process was repeated with Levstein. He, too, claimed he did not know the man.[30]

That afternoon, at four o'clock, Stern's wife, mother and brother gathered at an open graveside in the Nahalat Yitzhak cemetery. Roni had heard of her husband's shooting on the radio. She travelled from her home at Ramat Hashavim about ten miles north of Tel Aviv to the apartment in the city where Stern's brother, David, lived with their mother, Liza. David set off in search of more details, 'hoping that Yair was only wounded and arrested'. He returned to find policemen in the flat, come to tell them that Avraham was dead. The body arrived at the cemetery in a car of the Chevra Kadisha religious burial society and was taken into a room for ritual purification. Then it was taken to the grave and lowered in. As David recited the Kaddish prayer for the dead, British police watched from a distance.[31]

Before it left the hospital, a photograph was taken of the corpse. It shows the body stretched out on what looks like a concrete slab, on top of a blanket. The head rests on a metal plate. Three bullet-entry wounds are visible on Stern's thin, narrow torso – one below his left shoulder blade, one over his heart and one in his left side. There appears to be another through his left ear. His thick hair falls back in waves and his cheeks are clean-shaven. His eyes are half shut – but they seem almost alive. His mouth is relaxed; you sense the beginning of a smile. He looks strangely contented.

TWELVE

'The Blood of Your Brethren Is Calling to You from the Grave'

For a day or two after the shooting the official telegrams that whizzed incessantly between Jerusalem, Cairo and London purred with satisfaction at a job well done. When the news reached the Colonial Office in London, a senior official, Sir Stephen Luke, circulated a report in which he expressed the hope that the killings of Stern and his henchmen might serve 'not only to stamp out the Stern group itself but also seriously to discourage terrorism of the type to which the group resorted'.[1] One of the recipients scribbled a note in the margins of his report: 'Most satisfactory'. Another crowed 'the Stern gang has been liquidated'.

Major-General Douglas McConnel, the army chief in Palestine, was equally delighted with the outcome. He informed the War Office that 'within the short space of three weeks since the Schiff murder the untiring efforts of the police have resulted in practically the entire destruction of the brains of the gang ...'[2]

In a world dominated by soldiers, sailors and airmen, it was, for once, the turn of the police to warm themselves at the hearth of official approval. There were gongs in the offing. At the top of the list was Geoffrey Morton who was put forward for the King's Police Medal, awarded for 'distinguished service'. The citation recorded how he had 'performed dangerous and arduous duties in a manner beyond praise'. It went on: 'To his personal efforts have been very largely due the success attending the rounding up of dangerous criminals. He has repeatedly shown outstanding coolness and courage of the highest order.'[3] It was only what everyone was saying.

Captain Wybrow, the Area Security Officer with whom Morton had clashed in the past, sent a note praising the 'splendid way you have cleared up the Stern Group ... the part you have played in this reflects great credit on your courage and tenacity'.[4]

As Morton would be the first to admit, the recent triumphs had been a team effort and several of those involved in the routing of Stern and his followers would get a share of the credit. Police Medals for 'meritorious services' were dished out to Dick Catling, Sergeant Daniel Day and the man who set Morton on the fatal trail – the charming but dangerously deceptive Sergeant Daly.

Stern's shooting was presented to the outside world as a satisfactory outcome that required little justification. A bad man had got his comeuppance and the precise circumstances of how he met his end were not elaborated on. MacMichael wrote in a telegram home that Stern had been shot 'while trying to escape or resist',[5] a formula that would be repeated mechanically in official statements in the months to come. The question of why it was necessary to shoot dead an apparently unarmed man was never addressed and at first no one seemed inclined to raise it. The Reuters news agency report, printed in many British newspapers, described Stern as a 'gangster' who had been killed 'while attempting to resist the police'. The Jewish press seemed unconcerned about the exact details of Stern's demise. Bad news from the war front forced the story onto page three of the *Palestine Post*. It repeated the claim that 'the notorious gang leader' had been 'shot dead while making a bid for freedom'.[6] The Hebrew-language press also gave limited attention to Stern's death and the normally voluble Jewish Agency made no official comment. To help keep public opinion onside, some anonymous government propagandist produced a pamphlet designed to blacken Stern's name further. Those who picked it up would learn 'the amazing story of his attempts to ingratiate himself with the Axis'. It went on: 'We are able to reveal ... that while the gang were ready to add the role of fifth-columnists to their other infamies, Stern himself was prepared to drive a devil's bargain with the Italians.' However, 'even they could not swallow the pretensions of this cheap double-crossing gunman whose success in murder and robbery has evidently given him the idea that he might rise to be a Quisling'.[7]

The apparent equanimity with which the public took the news was welcome. But the wiser heads in the administration doubted that the relief that the elimination of Stern had brought would last for long. In Government House, Sir Harold MacMichael reviewed events with his cold, appraising eyes. Three days after the killing, he cabled the Colonial Secretary with his conclusions. The tone was sombre and cautious. He started off by listing the positive results to date. Police action had resulted in the death of Stern and 'two other terrorists' and the 'detention of the majority of the principal members of the gang'.[8] Other arrests had been made and the hunt was on for the remainder of the band.

That was the upside. There followed a dispiriting catalogue of caveats and warnings. The first concerned the fundamental legal difficulties inherent in dealing with tightly knit, ruthlessly dedicated underground organizations of which the Stern group was a classic example. 'It will not be possible, because of the lack of evidence identifying individual members with criminal acts, to bring the gang to trial before the Courts,' he wrote. In the case of the most spectacular charge against the group there was no evidence that would stick even in a wartime tribunal. 'While there are grounds for believing that at least the leaders tried to come to an arrangement with Italy,' MacMichael judged 'there is … no such evidence of this as would secure convictions.'

He went on to report a 'very disquieting development'. It had been brought to his notice that 'membership of the gang increased from about 100 to 300 during the period immediately preceding the murder of the police [officers], when the leaders appeared to have immunity and their terrorist activities appeared to be invariably successful'.

The tone of MacMichael's report was a posthumous tribute to the effectiveness of Stern's methods. Even in death he was capable of rattling his enemies. Sir Harold's anxiety was revealed in the dramatic measure he now proposed to counter the threat that he believed the Stern group still posed to Palestine's security.

The unlikelihood of obtaining convictions meant that the authorities would have to resort to the emergency regulations to keep Stern's followers locked up. MacMichael had come to the conclusion that this was not enough. It was 'most doubtful', he wrote, 'whether the detention of known members will of itself be sufficient to break up the gang finally and completely, or to provide adequate discouragement to the undertaking of similar activities by other hidden organisations'. As long as there were Sternists in captivity 'there is always the possibility, despite any precautions taken here [that an] attempt at rescue or break out will be made'.

Drastic remedies were in order, which MacMichael now unveiled. 'The most effective measure,' he wrote, 'would be the deportation of those members of the gang who are in detention, provided that accommodation suitable for the detention of terrorists with their criminal and seditious record could be arranged in the country of reception.' MacMichael had already obtained the army's support for the idea. 'I consider, and the military authorities emphatically agreed, that deportation and detention in, for example, the West Indies, would be the only measure sufficiently rigorous to eradicate this terrorist organisation.'

The High Commissioner was effectively admitting defeat. The inference was that the security services of Palestine were neither capable of completely eradicating the menace posed by a small band of extremists, nor hanging on to those they had managed to lock up. Rather than dealing with the problem he would prefer it was shunted off to someone else.

It was a surprising attitude from a man who had never shirked the challenge posed by the Arabs, whose rebellion he had helped to crush with notable ruthlessness. Behind it lurked a deep pessimism about how events in Palestine would develop. The war was far from decided but already Sir Harold was peering into the future, where he could discern the almighty struggle for possession of the Holy Land that would erupt as soon as circumstances allowed. A short time before his report on Stern's killing he had sent to Luke in London what the recipient described as 'a most formidable account of the Jewish secret quasi-military organisations'.[9] MacMichael attached a commentary in which he 'expressed very grave apprehension about the possibilities of a Jewish resort to arms if they fail to gain the post war political concessions which they are now demanding'.

Luke was impressed. 'It seems to me,' he noted, 'that it is vitally important that the most drastic measures should be taken to maintain public order in Palestine, not only because of the war, but because the end of the war will produce immediately a most delicate, dangerous and electric situation in the Middle East.' Hitherto the threats to public safety had come mainly from the Arabs. Today, though, 'there can be little doubt that they come from the Jewish side'.

Luke was all for backing the deportation proposal. Given the condemnation that the Yael Street bombing had provoked within the Yishuv, he was inclined to think that 'the adoption of drastic action against the ... group would not produce the violent revulsion of feeling that would normally be the result of Govt. action along these lines'. However, he warned, 'we cannot safely assume that we should have the Jewish authorities and community with us'.

For the moment most of Palestine's Jews seemed to accept the British line that, by shooting Stern, the police had rid Palestine of a dangerous outlaw. Saunders had noted in his report to Chief Secretary Macpherson, written eight days after the event, that 'the news of Stern's death has been received by the man in the street with relief'.[10] It was true that the precise details given about how he met his end were vague. Within the administration there seems to have been no appetite to establish them, for no internal inquiry was ordered into the circumstances of Stern's death. For public consumption the killing had been given legal cover by the Jaffa coroner, an

Arab, whose inquest into the death of Stern returned a verdict of 'justifiable homicide'. The same conclusion was reached in the cases of Amper and Zak, both of whom died of the wounds they received at 30 Dizengoff Street. The fact that the verdicts were given by an Arab was later cited as evidence of an official cover-up. As all the deaths occurred within the jurisdiction of the Jaffa coroner's court, however, it followed that the inquest would be held there; and Jaffa was an overwhelmingly Arab area.

The present state of calm could not be relied on. Jewish public opinion was like Lake Tiberias. For much of the time it might look placid, but it needed only a breeze to whip the surface into menacing combers and, as Saunders went on to warn, the wind was already freshening.

'There have been a number of reports ... that politically minded persons and certain organizations view the shooting at No. 30 Dizengoff Street and 8 Mizrahi B Street with disfavour on the grounds that it [sic] was unnecessary and brutal,' he wrote. He cited the evidence of a pamphlet which had begun to appear in the streets of Tel Aviv on 17 February, dealing with the two incidents. The headline was 'MURDER' and it purported to 'correct the facts which have been distorted with criminal intent by the murderous gang of the Palestine Gestapo'.

There followed a denunciation of the police actions of the last six weeks and of Morton in particular. The rather clumsy police translation from the Hebrew read: 'The four men caught at 30 Dizengoff Street *did not fire at the Police*. The stories about an "exchange of shots" is a criminal lie. The British Gestapo entered the house and opened fire immediately, although the men lifted their hands and surrendered. Jacob Levstein, when he saw that surrender was ineffective, threw himself on the ground so that the police should think him dead. The Gestapo officer MORTON kicked him and when he discovered that he was still alive, shot him.'* It went on to claim that

* Levstein, of course, was not present in the room.

the wounded men had been tortured while in the Government Hospital in Jaffa which had resulted in the death of Zak and Amper.

Then it dealt with the events of 12 February. 'And last of all the story of the filthy murder of Abraham Stern which the "poor" police invented that he was shot "resisting arrest". The gang of police murderers entered the room fully armed, ordered his girl-friend out of the room, so that she should not witness the crime and UNLAWFULLY MURDERED HIM COLD-BLOODEDLY WHILE UNARMED WITHOUT TRIAL OR JUDGEMENT.' It concluded: 'LISTEN ISRAEL. THE BLOOD OF YOUR BRETHREN IS CALLING TO YOU FROM THE GRAVE.'[11]

If the denunciation had been the work of the embittered remnants of Stern's band it would have had little significance. But Saunders believed the pamphlet had been issued not by Stern's friends but his erstwhile enemies – the Irgun Zvai Leumi. This was a far more worrying prospect. Since the start of the war the Irgun had by and large respected an agreement to do nothing to harm the British, and actively cooperated on many occasions. If Captain Wybrow was to be believed, they had gone so far as to offer to take out Avraham Stern. Did this mean that the truce was at an end?

Saunders also recorded another troubling development, emanating from the opposite end of the political spectrum. He had received other reports 'stating that certain well-known figures, including Dr Magnes of the Hebrew University, have been asked to approach government with a request for an inquiry'.[12]

Judah Leon Magnes was one of the most respected figures in the Yishuv, a monument of rectitude and reasonableness. If he was disturbed by the circumstances of the death of his talented but troublesome former charge, how long would it be before disquiet – which adept propaganda might fan into anger and violence – spread to the rest of the Jewish community?

Stern was dead but it seemed that his memory would continue to trouble Palestine. Nor had his departure removed the threat of further action by those of his followers who were still at large.

Saunders believed that it was 'unlikely that the organisation has been completely exterminated'. It was highly probable that the diehards would be bent on revenging their lost leader, and Geoffrey Morton was surely near the top of their list of targets.

Morton wrote that within an hour of the shooting an armed guard was put on his house in Sarona. From then on he and Alice were under constant protection by a team composed of Sergeant Stuart, who had been with him at Mizrachi Bet Street, Constable Ternent, who had shot Yaacov Levstein as he shinned down the pipe at 30 Dizengoff Street, and Sergeant Shand, serving in the anti-narcotics branch, who had volunteered for the duty. They all bore the first name 'Alexander' and henceforth the three Alecs, as Morton dubbed them, 'were always there, unobtrusive but ready to go anywhere at any time of the day or night and to tackle any job'. The trio 'virtually became members of the family, and on the odd occasions when we went to a cinema, or out for a walk on the Tel Aviv sea front, two of them invariably went with us'.[13] Wilkin, meanwhile, moved out of the Tel Aviv flat where he spent his spare time with Shoshana and into Jaffa police headquarters.

For the moment, at least the threat seemed limited. Those Stern followers who were not in custody were keeping their heads down, concentrating on staying out of the clutches of the British until the hue and cry had died down and they could start to plot their revenge.

In Jerusalem, MacMichael's attention was now diverted elsewhere. As the month of February wore on, he found himself drawn deeper and deeper into a grim drama that would come to be seen as a symbol of the heartlessness of British rule in Palestine. Illegal Jewish immigration had been a continuous problem for the British authorities since 1934. When war broke out, efforts to block it continued as strenuously as before. The reality of what Nazi occupation would mean for the Jews was soon clear and became shockingly more apparent with every passing day. None of this had dented the determination of the Colonial and Foreign Offices to keep out refugees, regardless of the fact that many were fleeing in leaky, often unsanitary boats from death and enslavement. Towards the end of 1940, two ships carrying 3404 Jewish men, women and children arrived off Haifa after sailing from the Black Sea. They were stopped by the Royal Navy and those on board interned ashore. Later they were put on board a requisitioned French liner, the *Patria*, with the intention of deporting them to camps in Mauritius. Before it departed, however, a team from the Haganah boarded the ship and planted a bomb with the intention of preventing her from sailing. When it exploded the *Patria* sank and 260 were drowned.

The British relented and allowed the survivors entry to Palestine but the Yishuv blamed them rather than the Haganah for the tragedy. The incident did nothing to change official thinking. And no one was more intent on upholding the policy than Sir Harold MacMichael.

On 11 December the *Struma*, which had been built in 1867 as a luxurious steam yacht for the Marquess of Anglesey but had suffered a drastic change of fortunes over the years, sailed from the Romanian Black Sea port of Constanta. It was crammed with 769 Jews fleeing from the pro-Nazi and murderously anti-Semitic Iron Guard. The ship, which had latterly been used for transporting cattle, was dirty, freezing cold and the diesel engines broke down constantly. On 16 December she reached Istanbul where she was interned by the authorities. The Turks asked the British ambassador, Sir Hughe Knatchbull-Hugessen, whether the refugees would be accepted in Palestine. If not, they would be sent back to Romania. Knatchbull-Hugessen replied: 'from the humanitarian point of view I did not like [the] proposal to send the ship back into the Black Sea' and suggested that if the refugees reached Palestine 'they might despite their illegality receive humane treatment'. The ambassador had spoken out of turn. The last thing the current Colonial Secretary Lord Moyne and Foreign Secretary Anthony Eden and their officials wished was to establish a precedent.[14] 'If we were to accept these people, there would of course be more and more shiploads of unwanted Jews later!' exclaimed one Foreign Office official, Charles Baxter.[15] The ambassador was ordered to make it clear that the refugees could not enter Palestine, but to say no more than that; certainly not to suggest an alternative course of action. For ten weeks the problem went back and forth while the refugees shivered aboard their stinking ship. A proposal to at least allow the children in collapsed when, after finding no one else who was willing to offer sanctuary, the Turks lost patience and ordered the ship to be towed back into the Black Sea. On 24 February, shortly after parting company with the tug, there was an explosion – apparently caused by a torpedo fired from a Soviet submarine – and the *Struma* sank, with the loss of all but two of the refugees on board.

When the first unverified reports reached the Palestinian authorities they were kept out of the press by the censors. On 26 February, the facts were confirmed and the Yishuv went into mourning. Almost every Jewish worker in Palestine observed a one-day strike and leaflets appeared in the streets denouncing British barbarity. MacMichael's firm support for the official line was well known. One flier carried his picture. His eyes stared out, seemingly indifferent, below beetling eyebrows and a vast, domed forehead. Underneath his picture were the words: 'Wanted for Murder'. Nor would Lord Moyne's leading role in the affair be forgotten.

Why had the British authorities behaved so cruelly? The official justifications were practical and political. If the Jews were allowed unfettered access to Palestine, they would place an impossible burden on an infrastructure already creaking under the strain of war. Another wave of immigration was also likely to inflame Arab feelings – and the British were anxious to avoid encouraging already well-established pro-Axis sentiments. A final excuse that appears in the correspondence was the fear that German agents might be hidden among the refugees. This concern was simulated. No spy was ever uncovered among the 'illegals' – for, as Dick Catling pointed out, 'an enemy agent would have been too conspicuous. He'd have been unmasked by the Jews themselves.'*[16]

The brutal pragmatism of the British seems partly a reflection of the resentment felt by the Palestine administration and those in London who directed it. '[To them] it seemed so unfair,' wrote one historian of the episode. 'Britain was engaged in mortal combat against Nazi Germany ... why should she be lumbered with other responsibilities, why should she divert valuable manpower and shipping from the war effort?'[17]

The position, though, was untenable. The story of the *Struma* caused deep unease in Britain and outrage among American Jews, whose perceived ability to influence Washington's attitude was respected and even feared by the government. Once again, Britain's Palestine policy performed an ungainly *volte-face*. On 5 March the Cabinet ruled that any Jews who reached Palestine 'should be treated with humanity' – although this still meant that they would be penned up in camps until somewhere else could be found for them. A few days later Harold Macmillan, then a minister at the Colonial Office, told the House of Commons that Britain would strive to ensure that there was no repeat of the *Struma* catastrophe.

Repentance came too late. The affair burned into the consciousness of the Yishuv. Those who had previously believed in the ultimate benevolence of British rule were forced to think again; those who doubted it had their suspicions confirmed; and those who denied it had their convictions strengthened. In this atmosphere, Avraham Stern's message did not seem quite so crazy. Events would soon show that there were still men around who were determined to act upon it.

* However, the Germans *did* try to infiltrate Jewish agents by other means. See reference in note 15.

THIRTEEN

'Hatred Was Aflame in Their Hearts and the Need for Vengeance Burned'

Just after eight o'clock on the morning of Wednesday, 22 April 1942, the Deputy Inspector General of the Palestine Police, Michael 'Mac' McConnell, stepped out of the front door of his house in the Jerusalem suburbs and walked round to the garage. Spring was well advanced, birds were singing in the trees and the dawn freshness was already wilting under the brassy Palestinian sun. As the veteran policeman, who had served in the force since its earliest days, backed his car out of the garage his servant stood in the drive to see him off. When McConnell drove away an object fell from underneath the vehicle. The servant walked over and picked it up. It exploded instantly, blowing off both his hands. He died soon afterwards.

Three hours later a little boy was playing by the side of the road near the home of McConnell's boss, Alan Saunders. An unusual object caught his eye. A policeman happened to be passing and the child pointed it out to him. What the policeman saw was a zinc box, attached to a long wire. The wire stretched for a hundred yards across a neighbouring field and terminated in an electric switch. Later examination revealed that the box contained seventy-three 'fingers' of gelignite, wired to detonators and packed around with six pounds of iron rivets.

Someone, it seemed, was trying to decapitate the high command of the Palestine Police and it was not difficult to guess who. The Public Information Officer informed the local newspapers that 'the bomb was similar to those used by the murderers of Inspectors Schiff, Turton and Goldman in Tel Aviv'.[1] Stern's master bomber

Yaacov Levstein was safely behind bars. It seemed he had left behind a team of adepts to carry on his work.

Nine days later, at 8.15 a.m. on Friday, 1 May, Geoffrey Morton opened the door of his American saloon car parked outside the bungalow in Sarona and slid his large frame behind the wheel. His wife, Alice, got in beside him. They were joined in the back by Sergeants Alec Stuart and Alex Shand, each carrying a Thompson sub-machine gun. The precaution was clearly justified. Not only had remnants of the band tried to kill the chief of police and his deputy, they had already made what appeared to be one abortive attempt on Morton's life. Morton's journey to his headquarters took him past an orange grove surrounded by a stone wall on the outskirts of Tel Aviv. A few weeks previously, he wrote, 'a sharp-eyed police patrol noticed that the cement surrounding one of the big stones which formed the wall had been carefully chipped out and that the stone could now be quickly removed from inside the wall. The implications were pretty sinister ...'[2] Since then the route had been kept under surveillance – but not very efficiently, as Morton and his passengers were soon to find out.

In the back seat Alex Shand was scanning his side of the road for anything suspicious. 'Suddenly there was an explosion ... the car was rocked from one side of the road to the other.' He jumped out and saw 'a great hole in the road. It was obvious it had been set off by remote control some hundred yards away.' His first reaction was 'great anger ... I think I was the only one who spoke. I said "you bastards!"'[3]

The car was destroyed. By a miracle, nobody had been hurt. The Mortons appeared extraordinarily composed. As is sometimes the case with narrow escapes from death, the grim scene quickly morphed into bizarre comedy. Shand remembered an Arab taxi driving up and Alec Stuart ordering it to stop. He jumped into the front seat and in doing so put his foot through a mandolin. 'He got his foot stuck in this thing and he was kicking it off in the road. I thought it was a very funny sight.'

A police car picked them up and took the party to Jaffa, where Alice insisted on carrying on with her duties at the High School for Girls. 'After I had cleaned her up a bit, my wife taught all the morning with a splitting headache,' Morton recorded proudly.[4] Everyone had heard the explosion and initially thought it was an enemy air raid. Alice, displaying the coolness that would sustain her throughout her adventurous life with Geoffrey, did not enlighten them and they only learned the true story when they read it in the next day's newspapers.

The investigation soon established that the bomb had been dug into a camel track that ran along the side of the road – planting it in the tarmac would have been too conspicuous. The command wire ran into an orange grove over a hundred yards away. The bomb was funnel-shaped to direct the blast. It was made of about sixty sticks of gelignite, packed with iron rivets and tamped inside a length of drainpipe. Human error had saved the Mortons and their bodyguards. Shand believed that if the operator had 'pressed the plunger when [the bomb] was in line with the front wheel, the full force of the explosion would have hit the centre of the car. As it happened they hit the rear. It happened to be a slope-backed car ... and it didn't get the full force of the explosion. That was our luck.'[5]

This bore all the hallmarks of a job by Stern's men. But which ones exactly and what was their strategy? In Jerusalem, the hunt for the perpetrators of the McConnell bomb outrage produced quick results. The day after the attempt a 'trusted source' gave the names of six Stern followers in the city. Two of those named were picked up in a raid, along with another who had not been on the list, a Turkish-born waiter named Nissim Bachmaris, who worked at the Palatin café. Under Dick Catling's patient interrogation, Bachmaris's denials of any involvement with the group broke down and he started to gush information. He led them to a house in Givat Shaul, a new quarter still under construction in the north-west of the city, where Moshe Bar Giora, who had been involved in the attack, and another man were living. A search produced bomb-making materials. An ambush was laid and late on the evening of Thursday, 30 April, two men were seen approaching the house. When challenged they ran off. One was shot and wounded in the thigh, the other was captured. The wounded man was identified as Ezra Sharoni. The other was Bar Giora. The combined operations had been very effective. 'There is little doubt that these arrests broke the back of the organisation in Jerusalem,' Alan Saunders concluded.[6]

In Tel Aviv, events moved equally swiftly. In the early hours of the morning after the attempt on Morton, the police picked up a man named Yosef Nikolaievski wandering shoeless in the north of the city. When questioned he at first claimed he had been taking a nocturnal dip in the nearby Yarkon river. After questioning by Alec Stuart, Alex Shand and Tom Wilkin, he eventually provided a very different explanation. He was, he confessed, a long-standing follower of Avraham Stern. Four days before, in his room in Tel Hai Street, he and five others had built a pipe bomb packed with rivets and seventy pieces of gelignite. He identified one of the men as Yehoshua Cohen, who had been on the neighbouring roof of 8 Yael Street when Schiff and the others were killed. The job took all day. That evening Nikolaievski delivered the bomb to the flat of one of his confederates, Eliahu Levy, then went to see a film at the Mograbi cinema. As he told Tom Wilkin, he got home just after midnight and was 'about to retire when I heard the bell ring twice. I opened the door and I saw six or seven men.'[7] He tried to slam the door shut but was overpowered, dragged outside, blindfolded and handcuffed, bundled into a car and driven off. After a while the car stopped on some rough ground and Nikolaievski's mystery captors started to question him.

'They asked me where the landmine was which was in my house the previous day. I told them that I didn't know what they wanted from me.' His memory clearly needed jogging. Now they 'handcuffed me behind the back, placed a rope through the handcuffs and hoisted me in the air so that my feet were off the ground. They again demanded that I should tell them where the landmine was.

As I was in great pain I told them to let me down and I would tell them everything.'

Nikolaievski gave them half the story, admitting his part in the bomb-making but giving phony names for his confederates. He was set free but the following night he received another visit from the same men. The torture was repeated and this time he gave up the name of Eliahu Levy. They returned for a third time in the early hours of the morning and, after handcuffing and driving him around for half an hour, cut him loose for the police to find.

Who were Nikolaievski's night callers? According to Shand they were members of the Haganah. The wave of arrests that followed suggests the CID were being given valuable help from very well-informed Jewish sources. By 12 May, nine men and a woman had been arrested. They included Shimon Lokshin, who had planted the bomb intended for Morton, and Nehemia Torenberg, who had passed on to Stern the Irgun's offer of salvation. Some had given themselves up, including Yitzhak Tselnik, the man closest to Yair in his last days and his effective deputy. A few other significant figures were still at large, however, notably Yehoshua Cohen, who it was thought had triggered the bomb aimed at Morton.

Most of those in detention kept their mouths shut but some spoke quite freely. One, Yitzhak Reznitsky, who had been part of the plot to kill Morton, gave an interesting account of the dynamic that had driven the group's survivors to attack the British establishment head on. Alan Saunders' report on the round-up operations says that Reznitsky told his interrogators that the killing of Schiff and his colleagues at Yael Street 'produced a state of turmoil within the Stern Group. Members were shocked and displeased by the action and the movement was in danger of liquidation.' However, the police actions that followed brought them back into line. 'The severe methods employed by the police ... including the shooting of Zak, Amper, Sevorai [sic], Levshtein [sic] and Stern himself ... convinced the members of the Group of Government's intention to crush their organisation at any cost, and it was decided to fight back.'[8]

Saunders judged that the Jerusalem bombs and the attempted killing of Morton were 'intended to advertise this fact and ... to indicate the Group's determination to eradicate its particular enemies in the CID'. Stern's death certainly sparked a thirst for revenge among the boldest of his followers. 'Heavy darkness descended on their hearts and minds,' wrote Yaacov Banai, an early chronicler of the group. 'Hatred was aflame in their hearts and the need for vengeance burned.'⁹ Ezra Sharoni was sitting with Nehemia Torenberg in a café in King George V Street, Tel Aviv, when they heard the news. They struggled 'to avoid crying', he remembered, years later. 'We sat in shock and shortly afterwards parted, determined to prepare a plan of attack.'¹⁰

According to Nathan Yellin-Mor, who would be one of the triumvirate who revived the group's fortunes, hatred was focused on one man in particular. 'The first goal for a revenge attack was perfectly clear – Geoffrey Morton, the murderer of Yair.'¹¹ The problem was how to get at him as 'he took strict precautionary measures ... there was no chance of harming him in a direct attack'. He confirmed that a first attempt to plant a mine in the wall of an orange grove had been foiled when the device was discovered.

The vendetta against Morton was personal. By killing Stern he had put not only himself but those around him in mortal danger. Having scoped out his route to work, the would-be assassins knew very well that Alice was always at his side. The Jerusalem bomb had been more in the nature of business. After the initial discovery, more mines were discovered in the area around Saunders' house. The planned operation, it turned out, had not been aimed specifically at him: the police chief's house happened to be on the way to the Mount Zion cemetery, where McConnell would have been buried had the car bomb hit its intended target. The mines, wrote Yellin-Mor, 'were intended for the heads of government and senior ranks of the police and C.I.D.' who would have come to McConnell's funeral. Thus, a child's discovery averted a spectacular outrage that might have wiped out a sizeable number of the British elite in

Palestine, from Sir Harold MacMichael downwards. By going after Morton and the Mandate's top brass, the plotters believed they would have at least the tacit approval of the Yishuv. 'In the minds of those seeking vengeance,' wrote Yellin-Mor, 'the *Struma* disaster had created the right climate of opinion among the public.' It was a judgement that was shared at least in part by those responsible for Palestine's security.

As it was, these operations used up the last reserves of strength of an exhausted and enfeebled organization. Almost all the key figures and most of the veterans were now locked up – 150 of them by the police count. For those who remained on the outside, further attacks on the British were too hazardous. The main aim now was to free their comrades, detained in Mazra'a and the other main compound holding emergency regulations prisoners at Latroun, halfway between Jerusalem and Tel Aviv. For the time being, escape plans would absorb most of their time and resources.

Geoffrey Morton had been gratified by the avalanche of letters and telegrams he received from Palestine's notables, Jewish and Arab, congratulating him on his lucky escape. One, from a fellow officer, Assistant Superintendent Henry Bennett Shaw, who would go on to become third in command of the PPF, mentions some act of kindness Morton had shown him. It gives an idea of his standing with his peers, not merely as a policeman but as a human being. 'My Dear Geoff,' he wrote. 'First of all I should like to congratulate you on your recent miraculous escape but also to thank you for your very nice and sincere letter as real friends are few and far between, but believe me old boy, it is at times like these that one appreciates them to the full. I do hope that for our sake and your dear wife that they shift you from Jaffa soon …'[12] Other correspondence came from people he had never met. One letter arrived from someone he knew only too well – Max Seligman, counsel to some of Palestine's leading Jewish desperados and a formidable courtroom foe. 'My sincere congratulations on your happy escape,' he wrote. 'Although this sort of thing may mean business for me professionally, you know that I deplore and abhor it.' He went on to pay Morton a considerable compliment. 'There is no need to tell you that with all our clashings, I do really appreciate your attitude and courtesy in regard to the various matters in regard to which I have had to approach you, and I am glad of your escape and hope that you will be spared to win the laurels which you deserve.'[13] This was all very gratifying and carried the ring of sincerity. But the tone was that of a respectful and even affectionate adversary. No one assumed that the battle between the Stern group and the British powers was over, least of all Morton's chief, Alan Saunders.

Saunders was worried that two major regional dramas, coming within a few weeks of each other, had had a toxic effect on mainstream Jewish public opinion. He quoted the opinion of a 'leading member of the Revisionist Party' who 'stated recently that whereas the original Group enjoyed little, if any, public support, the circumstances of the shooting of Stern, coupled with the feeling aroused by the "Struma" tragedy had caused some people to wonder if Stern's "idealism" was not, after all, worthy of serious thought'. He concluded that 'mere arrests and administrative detention is not likely to deter the fanatics from the present Stern group' and that 'further acts of terrorism are to be expected'.[14]

It was clear by now that MacMichael's solution of deporting the problem en masse to some remote corner of the empire was not going to work. London was sympathetic. The problem was that there were simply not enough ships to spare, even if some colonial governor could be persuaded to take in a boatload of hardened and violent hotheads. 'Much as I should like to help the High Commissioner it seems the practical difficulties are too great at the moment,' sighed Sir Cosmo Parkinson, Permanent Under-Secretary at the Colonial Office. He did not rule out the measure for ever for 'the situation might so develop that we should have to move these ruffians, whatever the inconveniences involved'.[15]

So what was to be done? MacMichael's room for manoeuvre was circumscribed by the fact that the *Struma* affair had grabbed the attention of public figures in London who were now keen to know more about what was happening in Palestine. They were led by the tireless Josiah Wedgwood, whose support in 1939 for armed insurrection against colonialist oppression had so gratified the Irgun. Wedgwood had reacted to the news of the shooting in Mizrachi Bet Street by dropping a note to Viscount Cranborne – 'Bobbety' to his intimates – who had taken over from Moyne as Colonial Secretary at the end of February. 'Dear Bobbety,' he wrote. 'Who on earth (and off it) is Stern and what have your Palestinian rulers done now?'[16] Now a peer, he tabled a question in the House of Lords on 2 June publicly asking Cranborne 'when and under what circumstances a Palestinian Jew named Stern was killed while attempting to escape?' The minister replied by listing the group's crimes and repeating the formula that Stern and 'two other terrorists' had been killed 'while attempting to escape'.

Faced with scrutiny from London, the perceived change of mood among the Yishuv and the realization that Stern's followers were not going to be defeated by force alone, MacMichael and the security apparatus of Palestine settled for a policy of appeasement.

The shift in approach was never openly acknowledged but it was apparent in many ways great and small, and Geoffrey Morton was alert to, and resentful of, all of them. He noticed a telling change in terminology in official correspondence. In the months leading up to the death of Stern his organization had been routinely referred to as the 'Stern Gang'. Within a few weeks of the event this contemptuous phrase had disappeared and it became again, as it had been before, the more respectable-sounding 'Stern Group'.

Ten days before the attempt on his life, Morton had been angered by a memorandum he received from Superintendent Laurence Harrington, addressed to the officers in charge of the five divisions in the Lydda area under his command. It passed on an instruction from Jerusalem that henceforth 'in all cases where it is intended to prosecute Jews who may be found contravening the Firearms Ordinance, the approval of the Inspector General [Alan Saunders] in writing must be obtained before referring the case to the Military Court under the Emergency Regulations'. Morton would later describe this as 'the most disgraceful official document it was ever my misfortune to receive'.[17] He pointed out that 'at that time illegal possession of firearms could be punishable on conviction with the death penalty and during previous years many Arabs had been so charged, had been convicted and duly executed'.

The new instruction meant that there would be one rule for Arabs and another for Jews: 'Whereas Arabs could continue to be prosecuted at the discretion of local police without reference to anybody', Jews could not be charged 'without first submitting the case through the Assistant Inspector General CID in Jerusalem for onward transmission to the Inspector General himself, who had no doubt been instructed to refer such cases to the High Commissioner'.

Morton was convinced that the edict originated in London. Whatever its origin, however, it was clear that the Mandate powers were now anxious to avoid anything that might inflame Jewish public opinion. On 6 March, Yehoshua Becker and Nissim Reuven, perpetrators of the wages snatch in Tel Aviv in January in which two Jewish passers-by had been shot dead, were convicted and sentenced at the Court of Criminal Assize in Jerusalem. Becker was condemned to death. Reuven got fourteen years' imprisonment. Three weeks later the convictions were upheld and the sentences confirmed in the Court of Criminal Appeal. Morton and his colleagues 'felt certain that Becker would pay the full penalty of the law for a clear case of murder, as many Arabs had done in the preceding years'.[18] The Jews Morton spoke to, though, were 'completely confident that he would not be executed'. Morton was sufficiently alarmed to raise the subject with Jerusalem, only to be told he was 'talking nonsense'. The matter preyed on his mind. Writing an intelligence summary for his superiors he took the opportunity to point out that if Becker were reprieved, 'any gangster cornered in possession of a firearm would have every incentive to try to shoot his way out'.[19] This intervention made him 'thoroughly unpopular' in high places. In any case, 'it made no difference – in due course Becker was reprieved without any official explanation as to why this was done, and those terrorists who were not already in the bag took on a new lease of life'.

Such appeasing gestures from the authorities themselves were unlikely to have much effect. What was needed was a démarche that might result in a cessation of hostilities, such as the one that had been worked out between the security services and the Irgun. Stern, after all, was dead. Perhaps after a decent interval, his followers' fury might start to abate to the point where an accommodation was possible. In May, MacMichael was informed that an offer to mediate between the Sternists and the authorities had been received from an unlikely quarter. Josiah Wedgwood informed 'Bobbety' Cranborne that he had been approached by Eri Jabotinsky, son of the late Ze'ev, with a proposal that he travel to Palestine to try to talk sense into the large number of Sternists behind the wire. Jabotinsky had come to know Stern well when they had both done time in Mazra'a.

Since his release he had been living in New York where he watched events in Palestine with dismay. Stern, he wrote to Wedgwood, had been a 'personal friend'. He stressed the purity of his motives and defended him from the charge of collusion with the enemy. As Jabotinsky saw it, 'Stern was slain in battle with the Police at Tel Aviv and thus became a hero and martyr for large sections of Jewish youth, even for those who in former times had been violently opposed to him'. He went on: 'The slaying of Stern is a personal affront to many hundreds or even thousands of Jews, and I am convinced that the actions of the Palestine Administration can only result in the fanning of a vendetta which may last for years and spread far outside the limits of Palestine.' Jabotinsky was offering to 'fly to Palestine in order to try and use my influence to negotiate [a] truce', and sought only 'airplane priority' and a guarantee that he wouldn't be arrested.

The overture was rejected by Cranborne. There 'could be no question of a truce with people who adopt such methods'.[20] Yet within a few weeks of Jabotinsky being told to mind his own business, two senior policemen set off on a mission that looked remarkably like an attempt to organize some sort of ceasefire. On the morning of 15 June Giles Bey arrived at Mazra'a camp accompanied by another officer called Ballantine. There, about a hundred Stern group members had been assembled in a hut to listen to a proposal being put forward by the visitors. It was delivered by Ballantine, a shadowy figure whose precise identity is unclear: there is no mention of him in the Palestine Police Force records, though he may have been a senior figure in the Nigerian colonial police on a temporary secondment.[21]

Ballantine left an account in a document marked 'secret' which described how he 'informed the persons present that I was new to this country and believed in making personal contacts with as many sections of the community as possible with the idea of (1) getting acquainted and (2) conveying to them the objects and purpose of a police force'. The gist of his message was that the Palestine Police had a job to do and were determined to do it, with the use of force if necessary. He flattered his audience by saying that he 'did not doubt members of the Group would be prepared to sacrifice their lives' to achieve their aims but the same applied to the police. This resulted in an inevitable 'exchange of lives' which was 'very foolish, childish and unnecessary'. He suggested that 'any lawful objects the group might have in mind would be at least equally worth pursuing by lawful and manly methods'.[22] The inference seemed to be that if they renounced violence they would be released.

Ballantine believed his address had gone down well. He was told by representatives from the audience that they wanted ten minutes to discuss the overture. Some then met him in the camp office and asked whether he would agree to allow an envoy safe passage to report his words to other members of the group. Ballantine replied that he didn't have the authority to grant the request and that he or Giles would pass it up the line.

Among those listening was Yitzhak Shamir. He later claimed that he had proposed that six Stern group members should be brought from detention in Acre to meet the Mazra'a detainees. This was done and they sat down to 'thrash out the pros and cons of the British proposal'.[23] Shamir's view was that 'we must do nothing, give nothing, exchange nothing – unless the British were prepared now, to pledge the post war creation of a Jewish state'. Instead they produced a set of counter-proposals, including the demand that the British hand over immigration control to the Jews, that were designed to be unacceptable. '[Ballantine's] spokesmen thanked us coldly and broke off further negotiations.' The encounter had taught them something that cheered them greatly: 'The Mandatory Government, at last, was becoming worried about' the Stern group.

This was a fair assessment. Ballantine's olive branch was indeed an indication of Britain's deepening concern about its situation in the Middle East. In the high summer of 1942, alarm was mounting among Palestine's rulers who were now extremely anxious to win whatever support and cooperation they could from their charges. On 26 May, after a lull of several months, Rommel's advance across the Western Desert resumed. A few weeks later the Germans were in Tobruk and on 23 June they crossed the Egyptian border, stopping, a week later, at El Alamein. In the Caucasus in late July, Hitler launched Operation Edelweiss. The objective was to seize the oilfields of the region, but beyond them a bigger prize beckoned. Success could force Turkey into the war on Germany's side, creating a vast new menace to Britain's Middle Eastern possessions.

In Palestine, the British rulers and the Yishuv establishment needed each other as never before. Jewish paramilitary organizations now represented a significant military resource, and none more so than the Haganah. The Mandate's security staffs spent much time calculating their strengths. In early July an intelligence report assessed the Haganah as being capable of mustering 41,600 men and women, excluding their members in the British Army and police. An earlier report had calculated that just over 24,407 rifles, handguns and machine guns were in Jewish hands. Thus, despite their numbers, the Haganah were still badly under-equipped. The need for the Jews to be able to defend themselves could not be more acute. They faced a war of extermination on two fronts – from the Arabs, who might choose to exploit Britain's difficulties to rise up against them, and from the Germans should they break the British in Egypt. It was inevitable that they should seek to acquire weapons by whatever means available, including stealing them from the army.

The authorities' attitude towards illegal arms had havered with the prevailing political situation, and the mailed fist alternated with the blind eye. In August 1942, the British knew that if the worst came to the worst, Jewish support would be most welcome and assumed that it would be forthcoming. This, surely, was a time for official myopia.

Geoffrey Morton's nature had always rebelled against the notion of selective justice. He was an intelligent man who recognized the complexities of the Palestinian situation. For him, though, the law was far more than a mere set of rules, to be bent or ignored as circumstances directed. It was the essence of everything he believed in, the bedrock of the society he risked his life to defend. His opposition to those who sought to undermine it – Arab or Jew, left or right – was unequivocal. By seeking to arm themselves the Jews were not only breaking the law, they were harming the British war effort. He freely admitted that he 'enjoyed pitting my wits against these illegal organisations, which, for their own selfish ends, were prepared to go to any lengths to undermine the war potential of the Allies at a most critical stage in the fighting'.[24]

Early in August, Morton received a tip-off which held the prospect of just the sort of police work he relished. The Special Investigation Branch of the RAF told him that a locally recruited Jew, Leading Aircraftman Zaks, had approached an RAF driver at a local ammunition dump with a proposal. He was offering big money for any rifles, machine guns and aerial bombs he could lay his hands on. Up to a thousand pounds was available for the right

Tom Wilkin relaxing on the beach at Tel Aviv. 'Wilkie' was one of the sharpest detectives in Palestine, feared and respected by the men he hunted.

Shoshana Borochov, Tom Wilkin's unlikely lover.

Fay Schreiber and Bernard Stamp. Their love-match created great difficulties for both, and his testimony given at the end of his life would challenge head-on Morton's account of how Stern died.

Loyal Zionist and servant of Britain, Solomon Schiff, whose death at the hands of the Stern group sparked outrage in Palestine.

One of the bodyguards who protected Morton, Alex Shand was fiercely loyal to his boss and found him 'strictly honest in everything that he did'.

Walter Medler (right) sunbathing at Athlit, south of Haifa, with fellow policeman Arthur Brument. 'Wally' was one of Morton's closest friends and his death at the hands of Stern's comrades hit the detective hard.

74

רצח!

סיר הארולד מק מייכל,

הידוע כנציב העליון לפלשתינה (א"י),

מבוקש עבור רצח

800 פליטים יהודים במימי הים השחור באניה "סטרומ"

MURDER!

SIR HAROLD MAC MICHAEL

Known as High Commissioner for Palestine

WANTED for MURDER

OF 800 REFUGEES DROWNED IN THE
BLACK SEA ON THE BOAT „STRUMA"

Cool, dutiful and impervious to sentiment, Sir Harold MacMichael became a hate figure to the
Jewish underground.

David Raziel. His intimacy with Stern turned first to rivalry and then to bitter enmity.

Binyamin Zeroni. He also quarrelled with Yair, telling him, 'The British will get you.'

Police mugshot of Zelig Zak, Stern's henchman who died after a showdown with Morton.

THE PALESTINE POLICE FORCE

REWARDS

REWARDS, as set out below, will be paid by the Government of Palestine for information leading to the apprehension of any of the persons named hereunder who are members of the organisation responsible for the explosion which occured at No. 8 Yael Street, Tel Aviv, on Tuesday, January 20th, 1942.

Abraham Ben Mordechai STERN, *alias* Yair.

Yacov POLANI *alias* Poliyacol

Nahman SHULMAN

Reward: £P.1,000   Reward: £P.400   Reward: £P.200

Zeroni BENYAMIN *alias* Ben Zvi, *alias* Yavniel, *alias* Aval, *alias* Kerner

Hanoch STRELITZ

Aharon ZUKERMAN *alias* Asck, *alias* Haivri

Reward: £P.200   Reward: £P.200   Reward: £P.100

and Abraham MAERI — Reward: £P.100

The most wanted men in Palestine. Notices like this appeared all over the country at the end of January 1942.

Relentless sleuth. Morton conducting inquiries (possibly with Alec Stuart behind).

Morton stoops to sift debris for clues following the bomb on the roof of 8 Yael Street, Tel Aviv, that killed Schiff, Goldman and Turton.

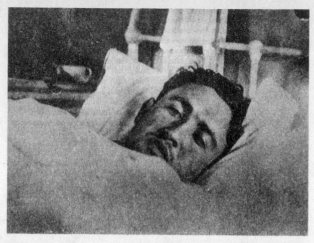

The Stern group's master bomb-maker Yaacov Levstein recovering in
the Government Hospital Jaffa after being shot by Alec Ternent.

The phoney ID card that Stern was trying to destroy when arrested.

stuff. Leading Aircraftman Watts reported the approach straight-away. Morton and his men now set about organizing a sting operation.

On 11 August, Watts told Zaks that he was detailed to drive a truck-load of ammunition from a dump near Ramleh to an RAF landing field near Gaza the following day. He was prepared to let him have ten boxes from his load in return for payment. Zaks was delighted and disappeared to Tel Aviv to 'make the necessary arrangements'.[25]

The following morning Watts set off in his lorry with fifty cases of ammunition on board. A short way down the road he saw a parked 'touring car' and opposite a man, who signalled him to stop. He then jumped in and they drove on, followed by the car. A few minutes later he was ordered to stop, just short of a track on the right that led to a kibbutz called Givat Brenner, a stronghold of the Haganah. The 'touring car' checked the road ahead. Several men from the kibbutz, who appeared at the junction, carried out a foot patrol at the same time. 'Both the occupants of the touring car and the scouts paid particular attention to an Arab taxi which had stopped a few yards from the Givat Brenner junction,' wrote Morton in his report. 'But after a thorough inspection of its occupants, which consisted of two veiled Moslem women, accompanied by baskets, suitcases and other paraphernalia, an Arab driver and fellah consuming bread and olives, they were apparently satisfied that there were no police in the vicinity.' They waved the lorry through some big iron gates into an orange grove alongside the track which belonged to the kibbutz.

The operation was watched closely by the two 'Moslem women' in the taxi. Sweating under their heavily embroidered dresses and veils were two of Morton's men, Sergeants Kenneth Hutchens and Ken 'Busty' Woodward. The driver drove slowly away. Down the road Morton, Tom Wilkin and several more officers were waiting. They drove back to the turning, meeting Watts and his lorry on the way. When the party arrived at the orange grove the gates were chained and padlocked. Woodward and Hutchens cut through the wire fence and raced through the trees in time to catch two men trying to hide the boxes in previously dug holes. Seven men were arrested and the car, which belonged to the kibbutz, impounded.

All but one of the prisoners were Givat Brenner residents. The other lived at a kibbutz nearby. When Morton sent a few policemen to search the kibbutz they were refused entry. An angry crowd gathered, a shot was fired, then the search party retreated, one of them nursing a badly bitten hand. A stronger force returned later and completed the task.

Before Morton could organize a search of the Givat Brenner prisoners' homes, however, he received 'urgent instructions from Jerusalem' to desist. This was despite the fact that one of those held was found in possession of notes listing a cache of 119 rifles along with a mass of other military equipment. Morton was not one to let the matter pass. 'In view of the notes found ... it is probable that the results of these searches would have been helpful in the investigation of the case,' he recorded plaintively in his official report.

It had been a classic Morton operation involving cunning, slick planning and psychological manipulation. The use of policemen in drag provided a touch of humour guaranteed to raise a laugh in messes the length and breadth of Palestine for years to come. The Givat Brenner caper, though, was to be Morton's last hurrah. The prisoners were sent for trial and most were convicted, and Zaks court-martialled and put away. All were members of the Haganah.

Alan Saunders had appeared to appreciate Morton's ruse. 'Your arrangements for the trap into which the accused fell were based on the best detective novel background,' he enthused.[26] Yet within a few days of this success, Morton received a very different missive from Saunders. 'The blow fell,' he wrote. He was 'informed that it had been decided that I had been working too hard and that for the sake of my health my wife and I were to be sent home on leave by air immediately.'[27] Morton was sickened by the news. 'The war was at its height; we had our backs to the wall in the Western Desert ...

things had never looked blacker and we were to pack up and go home to England for an indefinite period with no indication as to what my future was to be.' He 'argued to the point of insubordination'. His resistance produced a meagre result. 'The only concession I could obtain was that I would certainly be allowed to return to Palestine when I had had a good rest.'

Why had Saunders decided he could do without the services of one of his most effective officers at a time when Palestine was in such danger? There is nothing in the files that provides an answer. The strong suspicion must be that, with the Givat Brenner raid, Morton had overstepped the mark. Throughout his career he had bridled at the notion that political expediency should be allowed to restrain the pursuit of the guilty. He recognized the trait in himself and made no apology for it. 'As a policeman I doubtless took an oversimplified view of matters,' he wrote fifteen years after these events. 'To me a thing (in theory anyway) was either right or wrong, legal or illegal; if it was illegal, my job was to do all in my power to bring to justice the person responsible for it: it was equally my job to see that a man would be able to do without hindrance that which he was legally entitled to do.'[28]

This attitude had been more than apparent in a furious protest he directed to his bosses shortly before the Givat Brenner episode. A memo had crossed his desk revealing a plan by Saunders to release five low-level Stern group detainees. According to the Inspector General, they were now 'definitely hostile to the group's policy and have made known their change of front to their fellow internees'. He judged that their release 'would react considerably on the die-hards of the group without public security suffering in any way'. Morton and other senior officers had been asked if they had any arguments against the proposal. 'The most reasonable argument I can offer is the number of dead policemen for which these gangsters have been responsible,' fumed Morton in his reply. 'I would point out that it was exactly this policy applied to Messrs Stern, Levstein and Co which secured their release from internment following the double assassination of Inspectors Barker and Cairns in Jerusalem and which proved to be the death warrant of Messrs Schiff, Turton, Goldman, Soffiof ...' The 'blow' to the organization Saunders envisaged would 'prove to be a boomerang', he predicted.[29] He had already heard that Eliyahu Moldovan, whose arrest had resulted in the assassination of Soffiof, was also due for release. The news led him to send an anguished letter to his immediate boss, Superintendent Harrington. Despite his proven toughness and considerable pride, Morton did not hide his fears for his personal safety. 'As you know full well it is war to the end between the Stern gang and the Police in general, not to mention me in particular, and I am most apprehensive of retaliatory action which may be taken if Moldovan and other members of the gang are released,' he wrote.[30]

At a time when the British were anxious to keep Palestine's Jews on side, Morton was becoming a problem. The Givat Brenner sting – which seems not to have been referred up the chain of command for approval – was unlikely to improve relations between the authorities and the Haganah, who might be needed at any moment to shore up Palestine's defences. Morton's part in the raid on 30 Dizengoff Street and his shooting of Avraham Stern meant he was already a controversial figure in the eyes of the Yishuv. Judged from the viewpoint of political expediency, the perspective that Morton so despised, he was becoming more trouble than he was worth. It was time for him to go.

In early October the Mortons received two days' notice that there were seats on an aeroplane to take them out. They had just enough time to pile all their furniture and effects into a spare room in a police station before they departed. Morton's men at Lydda CID, Briton, Jew and Arab, gave them 'a most wonderful send-off – a farewell party which will always stand out for us as one of the greatest things in our not uneventful lives'.[31] Alice wrote in her diary that they left from Lydda at lunchtime on 16 September 'with about 30 police as escorts'.[32] Catling and John Scott came down from Jerusalem to wave them off, with Giles Bey, who was on their flight.

When they arrived in Cairo that afternoon the city seemed very relaxed and Alice noted there was 'hardly any effort to black out'. The Mortons put up at the Carlton, ate ice creams at Groppis and lunched at the Gezira Sporting Club with Mr and Mrs Giles. During a visit to the zoo they heard 'loud bursts of gunfire which made all the animals roar and scream'. It was a harbinger of things to come. Five weeks later the second Battle of El Alamein began. With victory, British fortunes in the war altered for the better. In Palestine, though, things would soon be changing for the worse.

FOURTEEN

'Terrorism Is an Infectious Disease'

The long journey back was an adventure involving flying boats and a stopover in Lisbon, where life was luxurious and Nazi officers gave Heil Hitler salutes in the hotel lift. After a month they arrived in a wintry, bomb-scarred London to begin a joyless and frustrating existence. The couple lodged at Calton Avenue with Geoffrey's mother, Sarah, a widow now since her husband's death in 1940. Geoffrey had been told he was on three months' leave. Time passed and there was no news of when they would return to Palestine. The waiting got on his nerves. In February 1943 he sent a long letter to Oliver Stanley, the latest in a series of short-lived Colonial Secretaries. Morton wrote that he found himself 'in peculiar circumstances. After prolonged consideration I feel that I am justified in presuming to bring my position to your notice.'[1]

There followed six double-spaced typed pages, starting with a precis of his awards and achievements, a record, he suggested, that was 'second to none'. It included the moment when he 'shot and killed outright Abraham Stern, the notorious Jewish gang leader, terrorist and fifth columnist … when he made a desperate break for freedom immediately following his arrest'.

He then turned to the circumstances of his departure from Palestine. 'In August last, the Inspector General, with the approval of His Excellency the High Commissioner, informed me that he considered that I had earned a rest and a period of relaxation from the strain of constant watchfulness, and that as a token of appreciation of the good work I had done, the Government was prepared to send my wife and me back to England by air.' He had 'received the assurance that everything possible would be done to ensure our return together' and 'there was no question of my not returning to Palestine at the conclusion of my leave'.

This, Morton, hinted, was not the full story and there were other forces at work. It was 'common talk in usually well-informed Jewish circles that I was to be removed shortly through Jewish pressure ... because I had dared to use fully my powers as a Police Officer and had thus created a most undesirable precedent from a Jewish point of view – one which they feared other Police Officers might later emulate.'

Finally, he appeared to get to the point. 'This, then, is the position in which I now find myself. When my wife and I arrive in Palestine in due course we must, from the minute of our arrival, take the same precautions for our safety as were necessary throughout 1942.' Despite all this he was still determined to return, for 'fortunately I do not suffer from nerves and I am quite prepared to carry on temporarily under these conditions if there is any prospect of a future solution'.

What did Morton mean exactly? Did he want to go back to Palestine or not? The confusing formula was repeated further down the page: 'Personally I can see no entirely satisfactory solution to my problem unless of course Palestine undergoes a radical change ...'

Stanley's reply is not recorded. The Mortons lived on in limbo. For a while he worked in the Crown Agent's office at No. 4 Millbank, the place where his career had begun, interviewing prospective candidates for the Palestine Police. At last, the Colonial Office made up its mind. They were to return to Palestine. In July 1943, he and Alice boarded a troopship for Durban and spent the next six weeks on the high seas as the vessel took lengthy detours to minimize the risk from U-boats. The last leg of the journey was by air then rail, travelling overnight in crowded, spartan cabins and compartments. It was by no means as much fun as the journey back to Britain, but Alice maintained her sense of humour. 'I shall be writing a book some day on "men I have slept with",' she joked in her diary.[2]

Geoffrey's new posting was in Jerusalem. They found digs in the German Hospice, run by German nuns, where the service was good but the food awful. They made friends with another youngish couple, Bernard Bourdillon, an administrative officer in the Government Secretariat, and his wife Joy, who lived up to her name. 'When Joy's laugh rang through the dining room – as it often did, for we were a cheerful party – it brought forth frowns of dis- approbation from some of the more elderly residents,' Morton remembered.[3]

Such companionship was a compensation for the boredom of his job. While visiting a tomb at the Pyramids during their Cairo layover on the way home, the Mortons' guide had told their fortunes. Geoffrey was promised there was 'a better position coming'. This turned out to be very wide of the mark. He had been promoted to deputy superintendent, but his new duties took him far away from the risky and stimulating work that he enjoyed. He was now in charge of the Criminal Records Office, which included responsibil- ity for the fingerprint department, the narcotics bureau and the headquarters of the Flying Squad. It was not as important as it sounded for 'most of these sections functioned automatically and needed little or no supervision from me'. He spent several mornings a week watching films in local cinemas in his role as police repre- sentative to the Censorship Board. His superiors appeared to have no intention of allowing him near any politically sensitive duties. Nonetheless, the threat from the Sternists meant he still needed around-the-clock armed protection, with Alec Shand and Ahmed Tamimi, a former Arab rebel whom Morton had won over and who now served as a police detective, serving as occasional bodyguards.

Palestine was relatively quiet. The defeat of Rommel at El Alamein and the failure of Operation Edelweiss in the Caucasus at the end of 1942 meant the German threat had abated, probably for good. The great Soviet victory at Stalingrad early the following year suggested the tide of war was turning. The minds of the Yishuv were now focused on what would happen when it finally ended. Already, though, those who were not prepared to wait that long were stirring.

The Stern group spent the months after Yair's death nursing their wounds and considering their next moves. The failure of Ballantine's peace mission had demonstrated the detainees' continued commitment to the cause. Their immediate priority was to maintain morale and cohesion. By the summer more than 150 members were held in the Mazra'a and Latroun camps and Jerusalem Central Prison. Conditions were mild. There was plenty of time for theoretical discussions and hashing out future plans. To put them into practice, though, required organization and resources on the outside. In the summer of 1942 there was little or none of either. If the group was not to atrophy, it was the prisoners who would have to resuscitate it.

On 16 August, Yitzhak Shamir and Eliahu Giladi broke out of Mazra'a camp. Their escape plan was as subtle as a grandmaster's gambit in one of the endless games of chess the inmates played, involving a complicated manipulation of the daily roll calls. Giladi, who had taken part in the Anglo-Palestine Bank raid, was notoriously violent and unstable. Expediency soon demanded that he be bumped off. Shamir was dour and utterly lacking in charisma, but he was – as the escape had demonstrated – a brilliant organizer. His treatment of Giladi proved that he was also just as ruthless and determined as his idol, Yair. For the next year he set about creating an infrastructure that would sustain the fighters when the campaign resumed. The new organization would be disciplined, secretive and bold. It would operate under a new name, Lohamei Herut Israel (Freedom Fighters of Israel), or 'Lehi' from its Hebrew acronym, which had been thought up by Yair before his death. First, though, it was necessary to organize another jailbreak. Freeing one's comrades was a sacred duty. Elaborate plans for a breakout from Mazra'a were among the papers discovered at 8 Mizrachi Bet Street when Wilkin and Stamp first searched the place. The prospect of escape sustained those who were banged up. Escape was more than

a mere morale booster. It was a necessity. Without a core of hardened operators, Lehi had no chance of resurrection.

On 1 November 1943, in a wadi near Latroun on the road
between Tel Aviv and Jerusalem, the dry earth of a slope stirred
mysteriously. A hole appeared, which grew wider and wider. Then,
one by one, men began to emerge from it, covered in dirt and struggling to suppress their hilarity. After seven months digging through
seventy-one yards of soil and stones, the twenty inmates of Hut 4 of
the Latroun detention camp were free. They were whisked away to
an underground bunker near Bat Yam. In the New Year of 1944, the
spirit of Avraham Stern was once again abroad in the land.

Among the escapees was Nathan Yellin-Mor. He, Shamir and
Israel Eldad formed the triumvirate leading an organization that
would become the spearhead of violent opposition to British rule
in the years ahead. Between them they combined the attributes of
the man they followed – Shamir provided leadership and efficiency,
Yellin-Mor, the journalist, the eloquence to analyse, articulate and
publicize the organization's goals, while Eldad – described by
Shamir as 'a believer in the Messianic aspects of the liberation of the
Land'[4] – invoked the quasi-mystical spirit which Yair had fostered
with his poetry and prose and which played an essential part in the
group's identity.

In death Stern's spell was as strong as ever. The second anniversary of his shooting was marked with leaflets and posters issued in
the name of Lehi, handed out wherever Jews gathered and pasted
up on city walls. The style followed the tone set by their leader and
was wordy and grandiose. Stern was a visionary and a martyr. The
other Zionist leaders had 'sold the Jewish nation for nothing' and
become 'slaves of the British ruler'.[5] Only he had seen 'the necessity
for fighting the foreign ruler, a thing which at that time was regarded
by the Yishuv as a crime'. Now, though, people were waking up and
'his doctrine is accepted by quite a number'. Frequently the tone
swells to a religious pitch. One pamphlet declared: 'OUR WAR IS A
HOLY WAR'. In this religion there was only one prophet – the

sacrificial figure of Yair. 'With his death his doctrine did not die but will be continued by his faithful servants and soldiers. His body has been taken from us but no one can take from us that doctrine which he taught us and for which he died.'

These were precisely the sentiments that might have been heard on the lips of an early follower of Jesus Christ. But there was nothing Christian about the rest of the Lehi message. One leaflet promised Yair's soldiers would 'honour his memory' with 'a tombstone of blood and fire'. Another, which mentioned MacMichael, Morton and Wilkin by name, promised retribution to any official who operated against them. 'Every foreigner and traitor in this country shall know that the days of January 1942 will not return … there is no way back. There is no compromise.'

By now Stern's disciples were already back at work and the High Commissioner was top of their hit list. MacMichael was the face of the British in Palestine, and in his haughty features they saw everything they hated about government policy. He had been held responsible for the manhunt that killed Amper, Zak and Stern and for the cruel pragmatism that sent hundreds of desperate refugees to the bottom of the Black Sea. Now he was accused of complicity in a much greater crime. By 1943 the scale of Hitler's extermination policy in Europe was widely known. In the light of this horrible knowledge, Britain's refusal to offer sanctuary in Palestine to his victims was unforgivable. As a consequence, one Lehi pamphlet raged, 'millions of Jews have fallen into Hitler's hands and have been destroyed … millions of Jews are now facing Hell, but the rulers of this country are continuing their criminal policy of closing the gates of Palestine …'

At three o'clock on the morning of 3 February 1944, a Christian Arab was driving his taxi past the entrance to St George's Cathedral, the very English-looking Anglican church on the northern edge of Jerusalem's Old City where the Mandate's rulers worshipped. He noticed two men perched on a ladder above the stone archway, stopped his car and walked back to see what they were up to. One of the men drew a gun and ordered him to clear off. He went straight to the nearest police station and told what he had seen, then returned with the police party. The men had disappeared. The taxi driver accompanied the police as they drove around the deserted streets. Eventually they spotted two men whom the Arab identified as the suspicious characters he had stumbled upon. When challenged they opened fire, killing the unfortunate taxi driver. Examination of the archway revealed electrical wiring had been installed, prior to placing an infernal machine which, it was assumed, was to be exploded when Sir Harold and his party attended that Sunday's service. It looked like a Stern gang job.[6]

The attempt confirmed that a new wave of violence was rolling through Palestine and in the next months outrages would become a weekly occurrence. Lehi leaflets had boasted that 'from now on the fighters for freedom will always be armed and use their arms whenever they are in danger.' On 14 February two Lehi men were pasting up wall posters in Haifa. Round the corner came Inspector R. D. Green and Constable H. E. Ewer. When they tried to arrest the billposters, they drew guns and shot the policemen down, mortally wounding both of them. In the next two months three policemen were killed and nine wounded in shootouts and bombings involving Lehi.

The police countered vigorously, shooting dead the Haifa commander Yerachmiel Aaronson while he was visiting Tel Aviv and arresting others, including Israel Eldad. Hassia Shapira was one of those caught in the dragnet, captured by Alec Stuart and Alec Ternent in a flat in Rothschild Boulevard, Tel Aviv. Inside her handbag they discovered a Colt automatic pistol and 'what appeared to be a home-made incendiary bomb'.[7] Before being sentenced to four years' imprisonment, she told the court that she was 'sorry the police entered my room deceitfully, thus robbing me of the opportunity to defend myself with my gun'.[8]

It was soon clear that Lehi were no longer a renegade band, operating in isolation. On 1 February came an announcement that the

Irgun had abandoned its policy of restraint towards the British until the war with Hitler was over. Its justification was that Britain was effectively Hitler's accomplice in the extermination of the Jews. 'There is no longer any armistice between the Jewish people and the British Administration in Eretz Israel,' it declared.[9]

The campaign had already started. Three days before, Irgun operatives had destroyed a number of British lorries in a depot in Jaffa. On 23 March they went much further: Irgun teams blew up the CID headquarters in Haifa, Jaffa and Jerusalem. In the mayhem four policemen were killed. The operations were launched at the same time as a Lehi shooting spree in Tel Aviv in revenge for the death of Aaronson, a few days before. These resulted in two more police fatalities.

The return of the Irgun to the fray reflected a change in its leadership. It was now commanded by Menachem Begin, a thirty-year-old Revisionist veteran who had been head of Betar in Poland before the war. He had arrived in Palestine in May 1942, having survived arrest and torture by the Soviet NKVD, eventual release and service in the Polish army of General Anders. After being given indefinite leave of absence from the military, he joined the Irgun in December 1942 and a year later had risen to the top. Begin had known Avraham Stern in Warsaw and admired him. There were nonetheless significant ideological differences between them. He dissented from Yair's view that Britain was a greater enemy to the Jews than Germany. However, it was the British who stood in the way of a Jewish state in Palestine, and once there, it was against the British that his energies were turned.

Begin was anxious to heal the old rift between the Irgun and Stern's followers. Doctrinal issues remained problematical and Shamir defended fiercely Lehi's right to organizational independence and freedom of action. However, from now on, the Irgun and Lehi would effectively work in partnership, doubling the threat that the Jewish underground posed to British rule. As MacMichael was to point out in a telegram to London, 'Terrorism is an infectious disease'.[10]

Geoffrey Morton watched the fresh spate of outrages from behind a desk. Occasionally he would be wheeled out to assist in an operation or allowed to supervise a non-sensitive case such as the seizure of a large quantity of narcotics. Once, after a rare outing on an arms search, he sustained the only wound he would receive in the course of his career, shot through the shoulder and hand when a colleague's gun went off by accident.

His frustration was apparent in a lengthy memo he wrote to his superiors on 15 March 1944. Morton's duties involved giving lectures to the Jerusalem Flying Squad. As he admitted in his report, he used these occasions to offer trenchant criticism of what he saw as an overly cautious policy regarding the use of firearms when confronted with potential danger. In one recent talk he had drawn a comparison between the shooting of Inspector Green and Constable Ewer and an event on the same day when a Sergeant Albutt had shot and fatally wounded an innocent Jew, Zvi Amramoff, who failed to stop when ordered to do so. The deaths of Green and Ewer were 'a tragic example of [a] failure to take necessary safety precautions'.[11]

Lehi had made it abundantly clear that they were prepared to shoot their way out of trouble rather than surrender meekly. Thus, when Sergeant Albutt encountered a man carrying suspicious-looking parcels who ran off when challenged, he was entirely right to open fire. 'If he had taken the other course and the man had escaped,' wrote Morton, 'I, and I believe most other police officers who are acquainted with the history of these terrorist groups, would have said that Sergeant Albutt was wrong in not shooting and in fact that he had failed in his duty in not doing so.' Morton hints that Albutt might be facing disciplinary proceedings as a result of the shooting. If so, Morton warned, 'it is hardly necessary for me to point out the irreparable damage which will be done to the morale of the British police of all ranks if this matter should be allowed to be taken further.'

There is no record of how events unfolded. Morton's tone, though, is that of a man who is reaching the limits of his endurance.

Beneath the events he is addressing he seems to be mounting a passionate defence of his own conduct in the case of Avraham Stern. In his memoirs he writes of 'a growing sense of frustration', looking on 'while my friends and comrades were killed one by one by terrorist organisations which seemed to be virtually immune from punishment'.[12] Both he and Alex Shand suffered 'from chronic nervous indigestion and were consuming vast quantities of stomach powder together'. After seven months back in Palestine he had had enough. He had told the Colonial Secretary that his continued stay in Palestine was conditional on the 'prospect of a future solution' and the situation undergoing 'a radical change'. But no one was expecting a happy ending and, while radical change was in the air, it was all for the worse. Sometime early in 1944, around the period he was delivering his despairing lectures to the Flying Squad, he asked for a transfer to another colony. According to Morton's memoir, the decision was in part due to Tom Wilkin. 'Wilkie was a frequent visitor at the Hospice,' he wrote. 'But it wasn't really to see me that he came. He used to try and get my wife by herself and say to her, "for God's sake, get him out of here before it's too late. He can't stay here. They're bound to get him if he does. You must get him away!"'

They left at the end of March, not a moment too soon. Lehi's hatred of MacMichael, Morton and Wilkin was unabated. The High Commissioner's time in Palestine was coming to an end. In July he sent his final dispatch to London reviewing past, present and future. It radiated pessimism. Nothing that had happened had persuaded him to change his opinion that 'the continuance of Jewish immigration on any considerable scale … would be disastrous to our imperial interests, to the security of the Middle East, to the Arabs, whose fear of a Jewish deluge is not without justification, and to the Jews themselves, for whom a process of gradual percolation … offers a far brighter future than does the attempt to obtain by force what is not theirs to take nor ours to give.'[13] The picture he painted was full of apocalyptic swirls. 'As the end of the war draws nearer, both Jews and Arabs are intensifying their efforts to prepare for the day of reckoning which they see looming close ahead,' he wrote. 'Determination is becoming daily stiffer; the bidding is getting higher; leaders are becoming more deeply committed by slogans and pledges; arms are being collected ...' He had little to offer in the way of a solution, except a return to the old partition plan.

Lehi had continued its attempts to hasten Sir Harold's own day of reckoning. On the afternoon of 8 August, MacMichael and his wife were driving on the Jerusalem to Jaffa road on their way to a farewell function when, three miles out of town, they were ambushed by a Lehi team. His aide-de-camp was shot through the lung and his driver through the neck. MacMichael himself was only slightly wounded and his wife escaped unharmed. The attackers were tracked to the nearby Jewish neighbourhood of Givat Shaul. When questioned, no one there had seen or heard anything. Their silence was the starkest demonstration of the sullen mood of the Yishuv and a taste of things to come. The authorities decided not to press the matter. The villagers were given a collective fine of five hundred pounds. It was not only the Arabs who pointed out the remarkable inconsistency of the official reaction. 'During the Arab revolt you only had to suspect someone had harboured or helped a rebel and his house was blown up,' recalled Ted Horne, who was serving with the Palestine Police at the time.[14]

Back in London, as they prepared for a new posting to Trinidad, the Mortons received some dreadful news. Tom Wilkin was dead. He had been transferred from Jaffa to Jerusalem in January and was living in a church hostel in St George's Road on the northern edge of the city. Each day he walked the mile or so from his digs up the hill through the Orthodox quarter of Mea Shearim to CID head-quarters in the Russian Compound. A Lehi team had been tracking his movements for weeks. On Friday, 29 September, after receiving the go-ahead from Yitzhak Shamir in Tel Aviv, they struck. The assassins were David Shomron and Yaacov Banai and the getaway car was driven by Yehoshua Cohen. Shomron was twenty years old and had never met Stern. 'The fact that Yair was murdered turned him into a symbol for us,' he said in May 2013, as he sipped coffee in a Jerusalem café.[15]

On the day, the pair 'dressed up to look like two Englishmen' in a 'nice jacket and a hat'. At 7.45 a.m. they took up their positions on what is now Helena Hamalka Street, a narrow thoroughfare lined with handsome old stone villas that climbs steeply up to the Russian Compound. As Wilkin stepped out of the hostel, a lookout signalled to them by tossing his beret in the air. The pair paced nervously up and down the pavement until they saw Wilkin coming towards them. They walked to meet him. 'Wilkin looked straight into my eyes,' Shomron recalled. 'He had one hand in his pocket – holding a pistol. In the other he was holding a briefcase.' The killers and their victim passed each other. Then Banai and Shomron turned round. Banai, as the senior man, had claimed the honour of shooting first. But Shomron 'started firing before him … at his back. He turned towards us and tried to pull out his pistol but didn't manage it …' The pair stood over him pouring eleven bullets into his body.

Wilkin was buried later that day at the Mount Zion cemetery, where fresh graves were being prepared daily. There was a huge turnout of fellow officers, the great and the good and their representatives. The bitterest tears were shed by a blonde, elegant woman who walked behind the coffin. Amid the pines, cypresses and oleander bushes, in the heat of the early autumn sun, Shoshana Borochov said farewell to her unlikely lover.[16]

FIFTEEN

'Striking a Blow against the Falsification of History'

In the autumn of 1944, the names of Avraham Stern and Lehi echoed round the world. On 6 November 1944 two young Jews shot dead Lord Moyne, now the British Minister of State in the Middle East, and his driver, as he arrived for lunch at his residence in Cairo. The handgun was the same Nagant revolver that had been used to kill Tom Wilkin as well as four other policemen. Moyne had been sentenced to death for his role in the *Struma* affair and his perceived hostility to Zionism. The wider purpose was to force the demand for a Jewish state onto the international political agenda and let the world know that there would be no peace until it was satisfied. Moyne's two killers, Eliyahu Bet-Zuri and Eliyahu Hakim, had never known Stern, yet when they spoke at their trial it was as if Yair himself were talking and they went to the gallows defiant martyrs.

The Yishuv was becoming inured to the underground's violence, but by killing Moyne Lehi had gone too far and for a while the Zionist establishment and the Haganah turned on them and their Irgun allies, cooperating enthusiastically with the British as they hunted the extremists down. The collaboration came to an end in the summer of 1945 when the Labour Party won a landslide victory in the first general election in Britain for a decade. Traditionally, Labour had been friendly to Zionist aspirations and had promised an end to restrictions on Jewish immigration to Palestine. The new Foreign Secretary Ernest Bevin soon made it clear that times had changed. He had been persuaded by his officials that a pro-Zionist

policy would make enemies of all the Arabs and seriously undermine Britain's position in a vital strategic area. The volte face was a
severe shock to moderate Zionists who believed Labour could be
relied upon to do the right thing. Avraham Stern's assertion that the
British were the enemies of the Jews rang truer than ever and, in
November 1945, Lehi, the Irgun, the Haganah and their shock
troops, the Palmach, joined together in a United Resistance
Movement to fight them.

By then the Mortons were in Trinidad where Geoffrey was
Superintendent of Police in Port of Spain. His life was far removed
from the daily struggle being waged by his old comrades against
assassination, intimidation and sabotage. Crime in Trinidad was
old fashioned and there was not much of it. In between his duties
he attended the races, went fishing and played bridge and tennis.
The Mortons had decided against having children while they were
in Palestine. Life was too dangerous. Trinidad was a good place to
start a family and in 1946 Alice gave birth to a daughter, Penelope.

In the summer of 1947 the Mortons were eligible for a long leave.
Few passenger ships stopped off in Trinidad but they were able to
find berths on a Norwegian tanker, which was calling at Port of
Spain en route to Venezuela, where they could pick up a liner to
France. Shortly before their departure, Morton heard some disturbing news. 'We had every reason to believe that we should be returning to Trinidad, but a fortnight or so before we were due to leave we
were informed – through high official sources – that two members
of the Stern Gang were on their way from France to Trinidad in
order to avenge the death of their leader,' he wrote in his memoir.[1]
The story was repeated some years later, when, around the twenty-
fifth anniversary of Stern's death, an Israeli newspaper carried an
interview with a Lehi veteran who described how, after Morton's
departure from Palestine in 1944, orders were issued to track him
down wherever he might be.[2] The trail stayed cold until someone
told a Lehi sympathizer in New York that he had met a policeman
in Trinidad who revealed to him that he was the man who had shot

Avraham Stern. An agent took a flight to South America that stopped over at Trinidad. There, he consulted the telephone directory and found Morton listed. A two-man Lehi team travelled by cargo boat to the island, reconnoitred the Mortons' house and drew up an assassination plan. Two further agents were sent by ship to carry it out, but by the time they got there Morton had gone, the State of Israel had been proclaimed and Lehi disbanded.

The story contains many holes. The *modus operandi* seems hopelessly amateurish for an organization as efficient and ruthless as Lehi had become. They had killed Moyne without too much trouble and in April 1947 would show themselves capable of planting an enormous bomb in the Colonial Office in London, which failed to explode only because of a faulty timing device. Morton would have presented a far easier target. However, recently released files reveal there was substance to the tale. A letter from Sir Stephen Luke at the Colonial Office to a colleague dated 18 April 1946 reports a warning passed on by the Special Branch from a 'Revisionist' source passing through London that the Stern group had drawn up an assassination list. On it were Sir Harold MacMichael, now serving in the Far East, and a 'Captain Morton, now believed to be in Jamaica or some other part of the West Indies'.[3] The authorities took it seriously, for before the Mortons' UK leave was up they were told they would not be returning to Trinidad, a decision that was taken, Morton wrote, 'because of information about the proposed activities of the Stern Gang in the island'.[4]

He was offered a new job in Nyasaland, a long, landlocked slice of south-east Africa, which was by his own assessment 'the backwater of the Colonial Service'.[5] He accepted it philosophically as he had 'no preconceived notions as to where I wanted to go next'. His time there was uneventful and rather enjoyable and he soon had two of the three Alecs – Stuart and Shand – who followed him into the service, for company. Unlike some of his colleagues, he liked Africans. He prided himself on his command of the local language, Chinyanja, and backed rapid promotion for outstanding local officers. He witnessed apartheid in South Africa, and detested it. It was, he wrote, 'based on the premise that the worst white man is a superior being to the best black man'.[6] By 1953 he had been promoted to Deputy Commissioner and he and Alice took stock of their situation. By now Penny had a brother, Geoffrey, born in October 1948, and it was time to think about their education. The local schools were inadequate and sending them to boarding school in England would cost money and mean they only saw them inter-mittently. Morton himself faced the dilemma that confronted every colonial policeman. He was forty-five years old: if he stayed on for another ten years, until the maximum retirement age, his pension would be better. However, he would probably have trouble finding another job and he 'had no intention of putting my feet up on the mantelpiece at that age and waiting to die'.[7] On the other hand, he wrote, 'I loved my job and the responsibilities and problems that went with it; I had worked hard and gained for myself a good status and an adequate salary, and it seemed not unreasonable to expect that I might in the not-too-distant future be offered a force of my own to command.'

In the end, he decided to quit while he still had the prospect of another lease of working life. In July they left for home, sent on their way with a round of farewell parties and ceremonies, sere-naded by the Police Band with a specially composed song called 'Chisoni' – 'Great Sorrow'. So ended a career that had taken him from the backstreets of the Elephant and Castle to the Zomba Plateau, plunging him in and out of innumerable adventures and excitements along the way.

Of all the dramas he had lived through, none was as powerful as his struggle with Avraham Stern. For the remaining forty-six years of his life he would never be able to shake off the consequences of the reckoning in the flat in Mizrachi Bet Street. Back in England he settled the family in Leckhampton, close to Cheltenham, and found a job working as personnel manager with Heenan and Froude, a sizeable engineering company.

By now the dream of a Jewish state had become a reality. In 1947 the power that Morton had fought so hard to uphold admitted defeat. Britain was exhausted after the Second World War. The Palestine conflict was tiny in comparison, yet the prospect of an open-ended struggle against an indefatigable and remorseless opponent was too daunting to contemplate. The continued policy of turning away the traumatized remnants of European Jewry from the gates of Palestine had depleted the moral credit Britain had amassed in the war and created friction with its crucial ally, America. At home, the mood was all for cutting and running. In 1947 Britain handed over the problem to the newly formed United Nations and in December announced that its twenty-eight-year Mandate would end on midnight, 14 May, the following year. Not even the most ardent imperialist mourned its passing. As officials, soldiers and policemen hauled down the flag a mood of sorrow, bitterness and regret hung in the air. The whole thing, it seemed, had been, almost from the beginning, a gigantic and stupid mistake. In the process of departure some of the records documenting the work of Morton and his colleagues in countering the endless trouble the steward-ship of Palestine had brought them went up in smoke. What was left behind was seized by the Haganah and, together with the papers that had been secretly copied by the organization's numerous Jewish agents inside the CID, placed in its archives. The information they yield provides much of the material for this book.

The Mandate was replaced by a UN proposal to partition Palestine into Jewish and Arab states. The Jewish Agency accepted the plan. The Arab Higher Committee did not. As the countdown to depar-ture continued the Haganah, Palmach, Irgun and Lehi battled with the Arabs. The day before the Mandate expired, David Ben-Gurion proclaimed the birth of the State of Israel. The announcement sparked an invasion by Egyptian, Syrian, Transjordanian and Iraqi forces. The subsequent year-long war ended in victory for Israel and its admission as a member of the United Nations. It did not, of course, bring peace.

When the dust settled, the victors sat down to write their accounts of the epic journey to statehood. Among them was Menachem Begin, by now the founder and leader of a right-wing political party called Herut. As commander of the Irgun, Begin had become the man the British feared and hated most, with a price of ten thousand pounds on his head. It was Begin who had been behind the deadliest action of the war against the Mandate forces. On 22 July 1946 his men planted bombs packed into milk churns in the King David Hotel in Jerusalem where the Mandate secretariat and military and CID offices were housed. The explosion brought down half of the southern wing of the hotel and killed ninety-one people, including forty-one Arabs, twenty-eight British and seventeen Jews.

In the eyes of his enemies Begin was a murderer, yet in his account of the struggle it was the British who had blood on their hands. The book was called *The Revolt* and in it he made plain his admiration for Avraham Stern, and his conviction that the British had shot him out of hand. He wrote that British detectives had 'foully murdered the unarmed ... Stern'. The book was published in Britain in 1951, while Morton was still in Nyasaland. News of its claims filtered through to him early the following year. Although he was not mentioned by name Morton's reaction was swift and dramatic. He sought the opinion of one of Britain's most effective advocates, Helenus Milmo, a former MI5 man and a member of the prosecution team at the Nuremberg Trials in post-war Germany. In Milmo's view, Begin's words constituted 'an infamous charge against a British official, acting in the course of his duty'.[8] He recommended an 'action for damages for libel ... should be brought against the publishers, printers and author in respect of it'. Of course Morton would have to clear it with the Colonial Office first, but the lawyer did not 'for one moment believe that [they] would be in any way obstructive or other than helpful'.

So it turned out. No objections were raised and the case was heard later that year in the High Court. It seems Milmo decided there was no chance of dragging Begin over from Israel so the defendants in the case were the publisher WH Allen, and their printers. Both parties collapsed immediately and issued profuse apologies. Morton was paid 'a substantial sum by way of damages' as well as his legal costs. In addition, a statement was read out by counsel in open court, reiterating the publisher's 'profound regret that they should … unknowingly have been responsible for the publication of a libel upon Mr Morton which … is as unwarranted as it was cruel'.[9]

The outcome seemed to serve as a rebuttal of a story that, in Israel, had come to be accepted as the truth. Almost every Jew, of whatever political stripe, believed Begin's version of events – that after capture an unarmed Stern had been shot in cold blood. In his statements to the court Milmo had repeated the original story that had been reiterated by the British authorities on numerous occasions and maintained ever since. In the initial 'statement of claim' Stern is said to have 'attempted to escape and whilst so doing was shot and killed by the plaintiff [Morton] acting in the course of his duty'. The version given out in court reads: 'after capture Stern made a dash for liberty, in the course of which he was shot dead by the plaintiff in the course of his duty.'

The successful libel action seemed to validate the official story. But within a few years of the action, a different version of events appeared. Surprisingly, it was provided by Geoffrey Morton himself.

In his first report, written within twenty-four hours of the incident, Morton had described Stern sitting on a settee in the living room of the flat and exchanging his slippers for walking shoes, as instructed. Then, 'just as he finished lacing his shoes, he leapt towards the window opposite', whereupon he was shot 'practically simultaneously' by Morton himself and Constable Hancock.

The revised account appeared in Morton's autobiography, *Just the Job*, published in 1957, four years after the High Court action. It is a well-written, wry and entertaining account of an adventurous career. By choosing to write it, he was positively embracing publicity. The decision was an affirmation of his pride in his record in the colonial police and evidence that he had nothing whatsoever to hide. Much of the action takes place in Palestine, but the incident for which he was best known takes up relatively little space. The few paragraphs he devotes to it, though, offer a significantly different interpretation of events from the one enshrined in the public record.

Fifteen years on, Morton was answering an obvious question arising from the original accounts. Why was it necessary to shoot a man who had no chance of escape? Here at last was an explanation. Morton repeated that after bending down to tie his shoelaces Stern 'suddenly dived under the gun of the policeman who was covering him and made a mad rush towards the open window leading on to the flat roof'.[10] He went on to explain the thought processes that raced through his mind at that moment.

'Although, as far as we knew, Stern had in the past directed the activities of his gang only from a safe distance, leaving his subordinates to do the actual dirty work on his behalf, I had no reason to disbelieve his oft-repeated threat to blow up himself and his captors at the same time if he were ever cornered to be an idle boast. The elaborate arrangements made at 8 Yael Street were an example of what they were capable of doing in this direction.

'Stern could not possibly have got away, for the house was surrounded and he knew it. What, then, was his object? I could only conclude that he had some infernal machine rigged up and that he was making a desperate attempt to reach it.

'None of the police in the room could get to the window before him, so, in order to prevent another shambles, I shot him dead. We did not find a hidden bomb, but that doesn't mean to say there wasn't one. In fact we did not look too closely, for without knowing its secret we might well have achieved the very effect we were trying to avoid.'

This explanation attracted no comment during or after publication. In the coming years, it would serve as the basis for Morton's case in three more libel actions he brought against authors who repeated the claim that he had shot Stern in cold blood. In 1964 he sued an American writer, Gerold Frank, his British publisher

Jonathan Cape, and their printers over passages in *The Deed*, a history of the Moyne assassination and the exploits of the Jewish underground. In the error-strewn text 'Captain' Morton was accused of torturing several of Stern's men, of killing him while his hands were manacled behind his back and allowing his body, wrapped in a bloody blanket, to be kicked down the stairs to the street. Frank also claimed that Morton, sensing an ambush, had sent Solly Schiff to his death rather than lead the raid on Yael Street himself. Once again, when confronted with the writ, the publishers folded. Once again 'a substantial sum in damages' was paid as well as Morton's costs and a comprehensive apology issued.

The two actions brought Geoffrey Morton £2944 for the injury to his reputation. In 1968, *The Terrorists*, by French author Roland Gaucher, was published in Britain by Martin Secker & Warburg. It repeated almost verbatim the claims made in the Frank book. The action came before the High Court early in 1972. On this occasion the publisher contested Morton's claim, arguing not that the allegations were true but that the offending passages did not bear the mean ing that the plaintiff attributed to them. Morton was called to give evidence and he made the most of the occasion. He gave a full account of his service career and detailed his commendations and awards. The accusation of torture clearly rankled. 'I never tortured prisoners and never allowed any of my officers to torture prisoners,' he declared. 'I regarded torture as a singularly pointless and fruitless exercise.'[11]

He went on to describe how he arrived at Mizrachi Bet Street to find Tova Svorai in hysterics and Stern sitting on a settee, 'with an inspector covering him'. He reminded the jury that 'Stern had always boasted he would never be taken alive and that, if cornered, he would blow himself up and the police with him'. He described once more how Stern had made a sudden dash for the window and repeated his fear that he 'might have some secret device which, by pressing a button or piece of wall or window would blow us all up'. He 'therefore shot him. I fired three shots. It was only on the third shot that he dropped.'

He said he had searched his conscience 'many times over this incident', but he concluded: 'I know of no other way in which I could have stopped him without, I thought, putting the lives of myself … and my men in jeopardy.'

Morton's testimony bowled the jury over. Secker & Warburg's counsel made no move to contest it. This time he was awarded £4000 in damages, nearly twice the average annual salary at the time. Mr Justice Lawson's summing up must have been pleasing to his ears. By bringing his action, the judge said, Morton was 'striking a blow against the falsification of history'.

Despite this victory, the story would not go away. Nine years later Morton felt compelled to bring a fourth action, this time against Weidenfeld & Nicolson for a passage in a biography of David Ben-Gurion that claimed Stern was 'murdered by the British'. 'He never wanted it to be accepted – [this] version of events,' remembered his solicitor in the case Richard Hargreaves.[12] 'He wanted to quash it. I explained to him that the longer he went on the smaller the damages would be … it didn't deter him. He would have gone on and on. He was that sort of man … very principled.' In a statement he prepared for the court he gave the fullest account to date of the story. Once again he made much of the suicidal threats he said had been issued by Stern. 'In his broadcasts and in his literature [he] frequently warned that neither he nor his men would ever allow themselves to be taken alive, and if they were ever cornered they would blow themselves up and take with them as many policemen as they possibly could. Knowing his great skill in the setting of booby-traps and in the use of explosives generally, this was not a threat we could take lightly.'[13]

Turning to the events of 12 February 1942, he described how, after getting the tip-off from Sergeant Daly about Moshe Svorai's reference to the 'guest' at 8 Mizrachi Bet Street, 'I quickly organised a party of police under Inspector Tom Wilkin to go and investigate, following on myself as soon as I had received an important phone call from my chief in Jerusalem, for which I had been told to stand by.'

At the flat Wilkin had found Tova Svorai and 'also, hidden in a wardrobe behind the lady's clothes, Abraham Stern himself'. Tova Svorai 'and another woman who had arrived from somewhere … [were] screaming their heads off and struggling with policemen who were trying to control them. Stern was sitting on a settee by the door and facing an open window leading onto a flat roof. A police officer was covering him with his revolver.

'As the women were being taken resisting and screaming to the top of the stairs I directed Stern to do up his shoe laces. He bent down and did so, and as he finished he made a sudden dive under the arm holding the gun, knocking it up, and sprang for the window.

'We all fully expected that, as he had so often threatened, if he were cornered Stern would have the means already prepared to kill himself and us with him. This could be motivated in many ways – by pressing a button, perhaps, or even a certain spot on any part of the room, or even by stamping on a certain spot on the floor. Of course the device and the means of setting it off could have been outside the window towards which he sprang.

'I knew he could not escape – and of course he knew it also. I therefore had to make a snap decision, with the awareness of his great skill in the use of explosives and of the need to protect my personnel and myself. I therefore opened fire and shot him dead, just as he reached the window.'

Morton had come to the conclusion that 'Stern was the architect of his own destruction … I have always had the feeling that he always intended it to happen in some such way. But for his threats and his great skill I should never have opened fire in such circumstances. But we were all living with this threat, and past demonstrations of his efficiency, in our minds.' He finished by declaring: 'I have never fired a gun of any kind since that incident.' The action dragged on for two and a half years but ended in an apology from the publishers and an award of £3000 in damages plus costs.[14]

The passages in the books were essentially repetitions of the hearsay that had done the rounds of the Jews of Palestine in the weeks after the shooting and had taken on the status of established fact. It seems to have emanated, initially at least, from the word of Tova Svorai and the crowd of bystanders who had gathered in Mizrachi Bet Street to watch the drama unfold. They, of course, did not witness the finale. None of the authors seems to have troubled to seek out the evidence of those who did.

When Morton launched his action against Gerold Frank and Jonathan Cape in 1964, the publishers took some steps to see if the claims in the book could be substantiated. Max Seligman, the genial fox of the Israeli bar, was put on the case. Seligman was on remarkably good terms with his old adversaries – indeed, he had been a guest that year at the annual reunion dinner of the Palestine Police Old Comrades Association in London. He used his contacts to seek testimony from Morton's former colleagues that would discredit Morton's story and enable his clients to claim justification as their defence. Among those he contacted was John Fforde, who had worked with Morton in Jaffa and had gone on to a long and successful career in the colonial police service. 'All the ex-officers of the Force to whom I have spoken in London and in Israel tell me that, despite the official statement which was issued at the time, it was common knowledge that Morton had deliberately murdered Stern who was handcuffed and in police custody at the time,' Seligman wrote.[15] 'It is understandable that Morton might not wish to admit to the murder, but you will doubtless agree that it is manifestly unfair that he should profit financially from it.'

Seligman now wanted to know whether Fforde could provide 'any information from your personal knowledge and if so, would you be prepared to give it, if required, on Affidavit?' The lawyer received a polite but unhelpful response. 'I am quite unable to confirm the allegation that [Stern] was handcuffed and in police custody at the time, and that he was deliberately murdered,' Fforde replied. He added that 'it was news to me that this is supposed to have been common knowledge ...' He sent a copy of his reply to Morton, with whom he kept up an affectionate correspondence, swapping family news and commiserating about the trials of advancing age.

Several more of Morton's intimates were approached from another quarter. In the late 1970s Binyamin Gepner, an Israeli author and publisher, began an exhaustive research project chronicling the deeds of the Jewish underground. Gepner had inside knowledge. He was a former Lehi man himself. He also had some credibility with the British. During the war he had thrown in his lot with them and joined a daredevil outfit called 'A' Force, operating behind enemy lines in the Balkans, where he won a Military Medal, before rejoining the underground.[16] Gepner was commendably anxious to hear the other side of the story and appealed through the pages of the Palestine Police Old Comrades Association newsletter for information. The events he was interested in were now a generation distant. Time had softened old enmities. Curiosity, and a courtesy that seems to have come naturally to many of the old campaigners, impelled a surprising number to cooperate. Among them were Alec Stuart, Alec Ternent and Alex Shand, all of whom knew Geoffrey Morton very well. Like Seligman, Gepner was keen to extract from them an admission that their old boss was guilty of shooting Stern out of hand. None of them would oblige. Instead, Gepner was treated to a recital from Shand of Morton's virtues. 'He was a very efficient man, [with] a tremendous lot of energy,' he said. 'Above all else he was strictly honest in everything that he did.'[17] Alec Ternent thought him 'completely fearless and one of the few men I have met in my life who I would follow anywhere'. As for any misconduct on Morton's part, 'I never saw him do it, I never heard of him doing it.' That applied to the circumstances of Stern's killing. 'I have every faith in the officer who pulled the trigger,' said Ternent. 'If he [said] he felt something awful was going to happen, then something awful was going to happen.'

At one point on the tape an exasperated Gepner snaps: 'You have blindly followed Morton's version as if you had learned the book by heart!' After three visits to Britain he failed to persuade anyone to confirm the charge he laid against Geoffrey Morton. His list of interviewees did not include another veteran of the old days in Jaffa, Sergeant Bernard Stamp, who had been in the room when Stern was shot. Stamp, though, had something on his mind. As the end of his life approached, he decided the time had come to share it.

SIXTEEN

'It's Nothing Like the Truth'

One sunny spring weekend in the late 1970s a journalist called Ilana Tsur gave a bar mitzvah party for her nephew in the garden of her villa near Tel Aviv. The celebration brought together far-flung members of her family, many of whom had not seen each other for decades. Among them was her uncle, a tall, erect man with a military bearing who was married to her mother's sister Fay. The couple had travelled from Hull in the north of England to be there. As Ilana ferried drinks and plates to tables set out under the trees she heard the Englishman mention a name she recognized. 'I heard the word "Morton,"' she remembered. 'It kept coming up – "Morton, Morton, Morton."'[1] Ilana was intrigued. She knew her country's history and the events of 1942. When she had a moment she asked her mother, Henia, why Uncle Bernard was talking about the policeman who shot Avraham Stern. 'My mother took me to one side and explained that he had been with him at the time. I was amazed. I later learned that it had been a family secret – a skeleton in the cupboard.'

Her journalist's pulse quickened. Ilana was a reporter for Israeli state radio and she had just stumbled on a historical scoop. People were still fascinated by the controversy over the shooting of Avraham Stern. Here, sitting in her garden, was Bernard Stamp, late of the Palestine Police, who was in a position to give an independent account of what had really happened in the rooftop room in Mizrachi Bet Street on the day Stern died. When the hubbub of the party subsided she approached him with an idea. Stern had a son, Yair, born five months after his father's death, who was also a journalist at the radio station. If Yair agreed, would Bernard be willing to be interviewed alongside him at the scene of the shooting?

'He was shocked at the idea,' Ilana recalled. 'Even after all these years he was scared that Lehi were after him.'

The lives of Bernard and Fay had been defined by the *coup de foudre* that struck when they first set eyes on each other on Tel Aviv's Gordon Beach in the days before the war. After her strictly observant father, David, had failed to prevent the match he cut off all contact with his daughter and ordered his wife to do the same. Though they were reconciled before his death he never saw Fay again. By falling for a Jewish girl, Bernard had created difficulties for himself with his superiors. The – not unreasonable – supposition was that pressure would be put on him by anti-British elements. 'He was … told that if he married my mother it would ruin his career and there would be no more promotion,' said his son Dan.[2]

In 1947 Palestine was no place for a British policeman to be, even one with a Jewish wife. He quit in November, still a sergeant, and the couple moved to his native Hull, where Bernard worked for the Post Office. They lived a frugal, decent life, bringing up a daughter, Iris, and a son, Robert Daniel, known as Dan. Neither parent spoke much about his time in the Palestine Police. 'You could always sense with my mother that there was something about those days they didn't want to talk about,' said Dan. 'I realised over time that they were frightened of retaliation.' Then, 'little bits were revealed to me and in later years it became more of a story'.

In June 1982, under his son's persistent prompting, he wrote down his recollections of the day Stern was killed, as a private record for the family. Three years later he had a stroke. After his recovery he remembered his conversation with his niece at the bar mitzvah party. According to Ilana, 'Fay wanted him to talk. She wrote to my mother to say that he was ill and I should come before it was too late.'

Ilana took her tape recorder and flew to London, then took a train to Hull. The interview she recorded lasted more than an hour.

Although Bernard Stamp was recovering from a stroke and close to the end of his life, his voice sounds strong and confident as at last, in his niece's words, 'he unloaded his heart'. This is what he remembered.

In February 1942, every detective at Jaffa police HQ was preoccupied with the hunt for Yair. 'The work we were on at the time was solely connected with looking for Stern,' he recalled. 'It was an obsession with the CID.'[3] On the morning of the 12th he was working in his office when Tom Wilkin came in and asked if he would join him on a search. The plainclothes detectives picked up a car and a driver and set off on the short journey to Mizrachi Bet Street, less than a mile away. It was a nice morning. A bright sun was drying the puddles from the overnight rain. They climbed the stairs to the rooftop flat and knocked on the door. A woman answered. It was Tova Svorai, though Stamp does not mention her by name. She seemed familiar. Tova, too, appeared to know him from a previous encounter. She asked them their business and they replied simply that they 'wanted to have a look round'. She 'saw there was no point in objecting' and let them in. It struck Stamp that 'she seemed a bit alarmed ... edgy'. He asked her whether she lived alone and she replied that she did. The pair then had a 'quick, basic look around'. Neither had much expectation of finding anything. They rarely did when they set off on raids that had been prompted by tip-offs.

Wilkin turned up some papers which seemed to interest him, but apart from that there was nothing suspicious. Then, just as they were coming to the conclusion that they had been sent on yet another wild goose chase, their eyes fell on something that 'was not exactly right'.

'We came across this shaving brush,' Stamp said, laughing as he recalled the moment. 'It was damp. I said: "She's been having a shave!"' The woman had just told them that she lived alone. The detectives' casual mood evaporated. 'That triggered the whole thing,' he said. 'If it hadn't been for that it would have just been "Oh damn, there's no one here, let's be off."'

242 • PATRICK BISHOP

They now set about searching the place thoroughly. In the living room was 'a sort of home-made wardrobe … a makeshift device for holding clothes'. It was covered by a curtain.

The two detectives paused. They pulled back the curtain and reached in among the hanging clothes. They 'pulled these aside – they parted quite easily'. Then they saw him, 'a man, crouching on the ground. A man helpless, unarmed, barefoot. He was in his underwear. I saw he had a pair of pants on and he had a vest on. That was all. He had nothing else on him.'

More than forty years on, Stamp's voice still rang with the drama of the event. 'There we were and there he was. And what could he do? There was this poor fella crouching there, terrified out of his wits. Two policemen standing over him. They were armed … he's crouching down. He can't do anything. He's not in a position to do anything even if he wanted to. To us he was harmless.'

Tsur asked Stamp if he recognized the crouching man. He replied that he did, and 'for a very good reason … I was one of only about two or three men in the police who had ever seen him before.' He had come across him one or two years before in Jaffa in the course of a round-up of Jewish extremists under the emergency regulations. They were questioned, details noted, and their homes searched before they were eventually released. Stamp himself had 'supplied his description' – presumably the one used on the subsequent wanted posters.

Stern did not know for sure that he had been recognized. They now saw that in his hands he 'had an identity card … he was in the process of tearing it up and putting some of it in his mouth'. Stamp took it from him and handed it to Wilkin.

They had their man. Wilkin took the next step. '[He] said, "We'd better get Morton." So he went to the door and shouted out [to the] the driver there. He said, "Will you go to tell Geoff that we've got him, or we think it's him."'

Tova Svorai was in the room with them. She did not seem to want to leave the man she had been harbouring. Stamp reassured her: 'I said, "Nothing's going to happen to him."' At this point a female neighbour was fetched, in keeping with the practice of having a witness present when a woman was first taken into custody to prevent subsequent allegations of improper behaviour.

Stamp dealt with Stern. 'I ran my hands over him ... "Put your hands up." Searched him. Nothing. "Open your legs." Nothing there. He'd no weapon on him. I said, "Well you can sit down now."' Tsur asked him, 'Did you tie his hands?' Stamp laughed. 'What for?' he replied. 'There were two of us there ... he was afraid, I could see that. He'd been caught you see, and he was afraid.' Even if they had wanted to restrain him they couldn't as they had not brought any handcuffs with them.

Stamp does not say how long it took between Wilkin sending the message back to CID headquarters and the arrival of Morton. But when he entered the flat 'the atmosphere changed straight away'.

'He came in and he said, "Just a minute Stamp." He called me over. We were down at the exit to the flat ... and he said, "You missed a chance, didn't you?" So I just said, "Well, what do you mean?" He just laughed, that's all. Ha! That's it you see. He didn't refer to it again.'

Tsur asked: 'What did he mean?' Stamp replied, 'Well, to my mind, he meant that I'd missed a chance of not [sic] disposing of this fellow everyone was looking for, because he was a wanted man. He was believed to be associated with the death of several policemen and that in Morton's opinion I should have shot him.'

'On the spot?' pressed Tsur. 'Well, very soon thereafter,' Stamp replied. 'I'd have to identify him first. But ... I'd missed the chance of not shooting him, not getting a medal, not getting promotion, not getting anything you see ... that was the interpretation I put on his remark.'

Stamp declared that he 'knew from that moment that there was going to be a bad end to the business, a violent end'. It was not long in coming. Morton had arrived with 'five or six other policemen'. He 'had his men around him and they sort of withdrew to the corner of the room … and talked in general … [then] they all came back in and regrouped'. Stamp 'thought at first that they were going to just drag him away'.

But then Morton dismissed Wilkin, leaving 'four or five' others with him. As well as Stamp they included Alec Stuart and Alec Ternent. They all 'just stood there, in a bunch … then Morton said something – "that's it" or something, I can't recall the words … he went over to Stern who was sitting [down], as far as I remember. [He] pulled him to his feet, dragged him towards the exit of the room … where there was a door leading to a window … and sort of pushed him and spun, he spun him round. And Morton shot him. Morton, revolver in his hand, shot him. Once. He went down. After the first shot, Stern went to the ground. From the force of the explosion he was knocked to the ground. Stuart, revolver in hand, fired a shot. I don't know whether it hit the victim or not. I can't remember. But Morton said, "Don't be a bloody fool Stuart, that's enough." He didn't fire any more rounds.'

'Had Stern made any attempt to escape?' asked Tsur. Stamp replied: 'No. I don't see how he could have escaped … there were at least three, four or more policemen there. We were all armed and I don't see what point he had in trying to escape. He was just pulled to his feet, spun round, and Morton shot him.'

He went on: 'The supposition was that he was going to be shot. Out of hand, there and then. In my opinion the fellow was doomed from the time the police came in there and saw that they had the right man in their possession, so that he was never going to get out [of] that room alive. I thought so and I think everyone in the room thought so.'

Tsur then went, line by line, through the passage in Morton's book dealing with the shooting. She started with his description of how, while bending down to do up his shoelaces, Stern 'made a mad rush towards the open window, leading on to the flat roof'. This brought an emphatic response. 'Ridiculous! Ridiculous! Honestly, it's nothing like the truth.'

Morton's assertion, offered in justification of his actions so many times down the years, that Stern had delivered an 'oft repeated threat to blow up himself and his captors at the same time if he were ever cornered' was 'hogwash ... I bet he can't produce one word of evidence that that was ever said except from his own mouth ...'

When it came to Morton's claim that he believed Stern 'had some infernal machine rigged up and he was making a desperate attempt to reach it', Stamp sighed. 'I've never heard of such rubbish in my life,' he said. 'If that was the case you've got the man in there, Stern, you've got Wilkin there, you've got me there before the main body of the police arrived. Wasn't that the time to spring a trap? Why wait until a lot more police came?'

Tsur went on to quote Morton's justification that 'the elaborate arrangements made at 8 Yael Street were an example of what they were capable of doing in this direction'. Stamp seemed bewildered. '*Where* street?' Tsur explained that it was the place Schiff and three other policemen were killed by a remote-controlled bomb. 'I never heard this story before about ... a sophisticated booby trap,' he said. 'I really know nothing about it ... I wasn't on that job. [This is] the first I've heard of anything like this.'

At one point it appears that there is an understanding between Stamp and his niece that the testimony would not be made public until after his death. Ilana Tsur can no longer remember if this was the case. In any event, her documentary was eventually broadcast on Israeli state radio in November 1986, more than a year before Bernard Stamp passed away. The contents of it were repeated in a long news feature in *Yedioth Ahronoth*, Israel's biggest-selling newspaper, under thick black type declaring, 'Yair did not try and escape – he was murdered in cold blood'. This was not a headline writer's hyperbole. At one point Tsur had asked Stamp bluntly, 'Did Morton murder in cold blood?' Stamp replied: 'I just can't think of any [other] way of describing it.'

Stamp's decision to come out with these charges after nearly half a century of silence must have been devastating to Morton. Until now the claim that he had killed Stern in cold blood had been made by participants in the struggle against the British, men such as Menachem Begin, or writers who either sympathized with the Jewish underground cause or who had repeated information from secondary sources as fact. Yet now the accusation came from the mouth of one of his own – a man who claimed to have been standing next to him when he pulled the trigger.

Morton seems only to have heard about it eight months after the event, when he was contacted by a London-based Israeli writer called Saul Zadka who sent him a translation of the *Yedioth* article and asked for his comments. There is no record of his response. He could take some comfort from the fact that Stamp's testimony was thus far confined to Israel. If it spread any further, he knew what to do. A few days after the communication he wrote to Alec Ternent, apart from Alice perhaps his closest confidant, telling him the news. The tone of his letter sounds cheerful and confident. He had no intention of replying in writing, he said, 'but if Mr Zadka or anyone else proposes to publish this article in this country they should be sure that they have a long pocket'.[4]

But time went by and nothing appeared in the English-language press. The spectral figure of Bernard Stamp flickered and faded and disappeared again into the mists of the past. Then, in August 1991, Morton received a letter from a journalist named Ian Black. Black was the *Guardian* newspaper's Jerusalem correspondent, a historian and an authority on the politics of the region. He quoted Stamp's interview with Tsur and pointed out the glaring discrepancies between his version of events and that presented in Morton's book and statements in court. It seemed, he wrote, 'only fair to seek your response to it'.[5]

He soon got it. As far as Morton was concerned, the incident was closed. 'A full investigation was carried out,' he wrote. 'An inquest was held by the Coroner for the district and a verdict of justifiable homicide was returned.' The account Black had outlined was 'inaccurate in practically every detail' but he 'had no intention of enumerating those inaccuracies for your benefit'. He closed by asking him to 'kindly refrain from communicating with me again, either by telephone or in writing'.

It was another six months before Black's article appeared, the cover story in the weekend section of 15–16 February 1992, almost fifty years to the day since the killing. It was titled 'The Stern Solution' and it gave a detailed and well-documented account of the circumstances around the event. Stamp's testimony provided an important source. But, on the advice of the paper's legal team, the accusation that Morton had killed Stern in cold blood was not repeated. There was nothing for Morton's lawyers to get their teeth into and no further libel action.

Bernard Stamp had nonetheless caused Geoffrey Morton a great deal of unhappiness. Why, after all that time, had he spoken out against his old boss? Ilana Tsur had probed her uncle's motivations. She mentioned the fact that Morton had made 'quite a lot of money' out of litigation.[6] 'I wouldn't go along with that,' he replied. 'Morton … in his way was a good police officer. He had commendations and medals and except in this incident where in my opinion he overstepped the mark, he was a good police officer. He wasn't an out-and-out villain who went around shooting people …'

When Morton considered the question his tone was sorrowful rather than angry. He laid out his response in yet another justification of his actions, written, it seems, for posterity. 'I had a high regard for Bernard Stamp,' he wrote.[7] 'He was a good Hebrew speaker and had a sound knowledge of Jewish affairs.' He mused that 'it was, I suppose, inevitable' that his marriage to a Jewish woman would have affected his career and 'no doubt he was bitter because of this'.

Nonetheless, he went, on 'it is inconceivable to me that he should come out with this story after nearly fifty years – in fact only after he had suffered a severe stroke. I fear that his mental as well as his physical faculties were sadly impaired.' He reflected that 'memories, for many of us, have become clouded with the passage of years'.

In fact Stamp had given the fundamentals of his story in the memoir he wrote at his son's prompting in 1982, three years before his stroke. There are several discrepancies in this account and in the Tsur interview, which in court a lawyer might fix upon to cast doubt on his reliability as a witness. For example, in the memoir he says he was one of the few policemen to have met Stern, a claim he repeated in the interview. He came across Stern after he was arrested in 'about September' of 1938 and not released until the outbreak of the war. This is at odds with the facts – Stern was in Poland in September 1938 and was not arrested until a year later. In the interview he says at one point that when Wilkin and he went to Stern's hideout they were armed, and at another that they were not. The dramatic story of the shaving brush which he mentions in the interview is not included in the 1982 account. He maintained that Alec Ternent was present in the room at the fatal moment. Yet Ternent left a written statement before he died emphasizing for the record that he had never set foot in the place.[8] In the same account he remembered Stern 'sitting on the side of the bed, behind him the bedroom window', whereas Morton places the bed *opposite* the window. His ignorance of the details of the Yael Street bombing seems curious – unless Morton was right and his recollection was impaired by the stroke.

When Morton confronted the testimony, though, he raised none of these points. Instead he made a far more devastating assertion, one that, if true, would fatally undermine Stamp's story. He wrote that 'in spite of what … Ian Black and Bernard Stamp himself have said – and I cannot stress this too strongly – Stamp was not, repeat not, in the room at the time of the shooting'.[9] He went on to explain that 'he had been there, but he was actually at that moment on the staircase between the ground and the first floor with Inspector Wilkin, trying to deal with the struggling and hysterical Mrs Svorai …'

This was quite a claim. If true, it would mean that Stamp had decided in his old age to invent, in startling detail, a malicious account of an event he had not witnessed. Unfortunately for Morton, there was counter-evidence that stated that Stamp *had* been in the room. What is more, it was Morton himself who had supplied it. The freshest account, the one written closest to the events they described, was the official report delivered by Morton within twenty-four hours of the shooting. It stated that while making his dash for the window Stern 'passed behind Sergeant Stamp who was examining the contents of the buffet'. It seemed that it was not only Bernard Stamp's memory that had 'become clouded with the passage of time'.

SEVENTEEN

'The Holy City'

Bernard Stamp's evidence is undoubtedly powerful. It is not, however, conclusive. Two other men were said to be in the room with Stern and Morton that day. To corroborate – or dismiss – Stamp's charge, their testimony is needed. One of those present was Sergeant Alec Stuart. He was among the PPF veterans the ex-Lehi man Binyamin Gepner talked to in the late 1970s. Gepner sat down with him in the Central Hotel in Cardiff and probed his memories of the day Stern was shot. On the recording you hear him asking eagerly: 'Now what happened in Mizrachi number eight?' Stuart's response is a dry chuckle. 'If you want to tell me something off the record,' coaxes Gepner, 'I'll switch the thing off.'[1] Stuart agrees: 'I think you'd better switch it off, actually.' His words are followed by an electronic click.

The next thing on the tape is a voice memo in Hebrew in which Gepner reports what Stuart allegedly said. The details add yet another layer of complexity to the episode and contradict elements of Stamp's story. In this version, Stuart was with Wilkin and Stamp when they went to the flat along with a dozen or so other policemen who formed a cordon around the building. He helped with the search and when it produced nothing went downstairs. When he returned after a few minutes he learned that Stern had been found. Wilkin told him to go to the office and bring back some handcuffs. He was *not* to inform Morton that they had arrested Stern. When he reached CID headquarters, though, he passed on the news immediately. He and Morton rode back together and entered the flat. When asked what happened next, Stuart allegedly replied: 'You know exactly what happened. He fired on him immediately from in front. He didn't shoot him from behind. He shot him with four bullets I believe. He was the only one who fired.'[2]

Why did he shoot, Gepner wanted to know? Stuart is reported to have replied: 'You know why. There is an official statement of his [Morton's]. That he [Stern] wanted to escape.' When Gepner pressed him on how this would have been possible when he was surrounded by policemen, Stuart would not be drawn. 'Over and over we discussed the killing of Yair,' he said, 'and he kept telling me: "You know exactly what happened."' Gepner was also curious as to why Wilkin told Stuart not to tell Morton that Stern had been arrested. Stuart is said to have replied that if he hadn't told him, then 'maybe they would have arrested Stern and not killed him'.

This second-hand testimony clashes at several points with Stamp's story. In Stamp's account there were only three in the original police party – himself, Wilkin and a driver. There is no mention of a dozen extra men, enough to throw a cordon around the building. He also says that, far from wanting to keep the fact of Stern's arrest away from Morton, Wilkin ordered the driver to go and tell him the news. Stamp also has Stuart opening fire on Stern as he lay on the ground, causing Morton to snap, 'don't be a bloody fool … that's enough'.

According to Gepner, Stuart said that only he and Stamp were with Morton when the shots were fired. What, then, of the sergeant mentioned in Morton's initial, nearly contemporaneous, report, 'B/Con. Hancock, S.N.'? Neither Stamp nor Stuart mentions him at all. Yet according to Morton he was not only there but fired 'practically simultaneously' with him.[3]

This is the only appearance of Hancock in the story. In all subsequent accounts Morton took sole responsibility for killing Stern. There is no mention of Hancock or Stuart firing his gun. An investigator might think this a curious omission. The fact that another policeman opened fire could be taken as confirmation that it was not only Morton who saw Stern making a sudden and apparently threatening movement, and reacted accordingly. This, surely, would reinforce the conclusion that the shooting was justified. Why in that case remove Hancock from the story? One explanation is that Morton did not welcome the airing of another narrative that might contradict his version. Another is that he wished to shield a colleague from the wrath of Stern's followers.

As Morton knew himself, the Sternists had long memories and he may have decided that, even many years after the event, it was unwise to expose a comrade unnecessarily. It was obvious that anyone who was present at the showdown was now in danger from the organization, and according to one story Wilkin had taken immediate steps to put himself in the clear. Yitzhak Berman, an Irgun intelligence chief and an intimate of Wilkin's, claimed the detective rushed straight from Mizrachi Street to see him, in order to have a witness who could vouch that he was not there at the time of the shooting.[4]

Stanley Neville Hancock remains a shadowy figure. There is no other mention of him in Morton's writings. The records show he joined the Palestine Police aged twenty in May 1939 and left six months after the date of the shooting to join the RAF. He was still in the air force in 1946, by which time he had been promoted to flight lieutenant. At some point between 1941 and 1945 he married in Jaffa, a woman called Else Schweikher, known as 'Peta'. She died in 1974. Hancock was last known to be living at an address in Edgbaston, Birmingham, but is no longer there and no further records are available.[5]

Rarely can a single act have produced so many differing versions of events. The confusion is not just restricted to the facts. In many ways, Morton's actions during the period ran counter to form. He appeared to revere the rule of law, as he demonstrated with his clashes with his superiors when he thought that, due to political considerations, it was being selectively applied. He was proud of his preference for guile and cunning over brute force.

He loved to tell a story of how, once, during the Arab revolt, he had persuaded a village in the 'triangle of terror' to hand over its weapons by the use of an elaborate trick. He first assembled the population and appealed to them to surrender their arms. When that had no effect, his men dragged one of the young rebels behind a house. Shots were heard and the party re-emerged carting away an apparently lifeless body. The men of the village promptly fetched their rifles, whereupon the young man appeared from the back of the police truck. 'There was an incredulous gasp from the villagers at this apparent resurrection from the dead, which turned first into a titter and then into a wave of hearty laughter at the realisation that they had been completely hoaxed,' Morton wrote.[6]

Morton was not, as even Bernard Stamp confirmed, someone who habitually 'went around shooting people'. Yet in Dizengoff Street and Mizrachi Street he had done just that.

These were tense days and anger was in the air. There is evidence suggesting that, following the killings of Schiff, Goldman and Turton, the police were operating in an atmosphere of greater licence. It is implicit in the special meeting of the District Security Committee in Jaffa on 27 January, at which Morton was present, when Alan Saunders talked of 'liquidating' Stern. Some policemen would later claim that it was assumed that, once caught, Stern was a dead man. Bernard Stamp told Ilana Tsur 'it was generally held that if that fella was caught he would probably get shot. It was sort of an opinion. There was nothing laid down in writing.'[7] This was echoed by Daniel Day, a sergeant who had been on the Dizengoff Street raid, when, during a visit to Israel in 1963, he told the newspaper *Maariv*: 'There was no other way of getting rid of him and solving the terror problem ... Stern would have been innocent for lack of evidence in a criminal trial or would have been held in a detention camp and soon run away.'[8] If it was true that there was an implicit understanding abroad that Stern was not to be taken alive, it would explain the failure of the authorities to carry out an internal inquiry into the circumstances of what was a very high-profile police killing.

An unwritten decision by the police to shoot Stern out of hand would not only have been criminal; it would also have been very

THE RECKONING · 255

stupid. It was true that, unless one of his men turned against him, there was little solid evidence to convict him. But locking him up in a detention camp would surely have meant he was effectively neutralized. By the time he was cornered Stern had become an embarrassment and a nuisance to both his former comrades and the Yishuv in general. He had repeatedly demonstrated an inability to compromise, towering vanity and a quarrelsome nature that would surely have led to his marginalization and possibly his death in some internal underground feud.

If events did unfold in the way that Stamp claimed, then Morton would have been well advised to keep quiet when passing references were made to a story that, anyway, was being constantly overlaid by bigger events. Instead, defending his reputation became close to an obsession as he issued repeated legal challenges, which, if the verdicts had gone against him, would have resulted in his financial ruin. As it was, he won quite handsomely. By some accounts some former colleagues were irked by his success and felt there was something improper in the fact that he had made money out of libel actions. The notion that Morton was financially motivated does not sit easily with a man who lived modestly and seemed to have little interest in material possessions.

Undoubtedly, Morton came to believe sincerely in his version of events. If the story was as he described, then it is not an implausible one. There may be no hard evidence to back up Morton's claim that Stern had warned publicly that, if captured, he would blow himself up, taking as many of his enemies with him as possible. His utterances and writings, though, were steeped in images of suicidal sacrifice. If his legend was to live on, he could not possibly come quietly when the knock on the door finally sounded. The massacre in Yael Street proved his organization was quite capable of rigging a bomb that could blow an arrest party to pieces. If Stern *had* made a desperate dash for the window it was not unreasonable to conclude that it might well have been that he was bent on detonating an infernal machine. But did he make that move? In the end we have the word

of one proud man against another and the truth will, in all likelihood, remain enigmatic and elusive.

For Morton, 12 February 1942 was the day when the path of his
professional life began to slope away, in a direction he had not
anticipated. He was ambitious and ending his police career in a
pleasant but inconsequential colonial backwater like Nyasaland
cannot have been in his plan. Back in England he lived quietly,
working and watching his children grow up. His job at the engineering company in Gloucestershire and later at the match company
Bryant and May must have been dull after the excitements of his
early life. Like his father he poured his extra energy into voluntary
work, serving as a comprehensive school governor and on local
committees. According to his daughter, Penny, 'there was always
some lame duck in tow that he was supporting or helping financially'.[9] Sam Chalmers, who worked with him in his garden at week-
ends before going on to an army career, remembers him as a 'special
person ... he was the opposite of a grumpy old man and had a
permanent smile.'[10] Around the bridge table, at meals with friends,
he spoke little about his past.

From time to time, Palestine would force itself into his thoughts.
The men he had fought were the masters now and a former 'gangster' a national hero. Twenty-five years after Stern's death, in 1967,
the anniversary was marked by a wave of publicity and events hail-
ing him as a patriot and one of the founding fathers of the state.
Roads were named after him in Jerusalem and Beersheba, and, in
Tel Aviv, Mizrachi Bet Street would come to bear his name. Postage
stamps bearing his image were issued and in 1981 a town in central
Israel was named Kochav Yair – 'Yair's Star' – in his memory. In
1980 the Israeli Defence Forces instituted the 'Lehi ribbon' honour-
ing its members and their struggle to establish the state. Three years
later Yitzhak Shamir became Prime Minister (a post that had already
been occupied by Menachem Begin), going on to become the
second-longest-serving premier after David Ben-Gurion.

If Stern had lived it seems unlikely he would have been thus garlanded. His self-destructive tendencies and inability to work with others as equals would have shunted him sooner or later to the sidelines or to oblivion. In death, though, he achieved the status of prophet and martyr he had yearned for when alive and his spiritual presence shaped events in a way that his physical one never could have. Yair's analysis – that British defeat was essential if the Jews were to have a state – became the prevailing wisdom.

Morton and his colleagues watched the triumphant march of Stern's disciples, some with dismay, some with acceptance and some with alarm. Even after many years the long arm of Lehi was still something to be feared. In January 1989, the *Spectator* carried extracts from an interview that the historian Nicholas Bethell had conducted with Yitzhak Shamir twelve years before. The Israeli Prime Minister had been remarkably frank about Lehi's programme of targeting Mandate officials. He said that Tom Wilkin had been killed because he 'was very dangerous for us ... he fought against us zealously, he was a fanatic.' Geoffrey Morton though was 'quite different. He escaped and he's still alive, but now it doesn't interest us. We're not going to kill him now.'[11]

'Jolly decent of him!' wrote Morton in a wry letter to the magazine. 'If only I'd known of this at the time of the interview I could have been spared twelve years quaking in my metaphorical shoes.'[12] But he remained on his guard. In 1992 he wrote to the chief constable of Gloucestershire following the publication of Ian Black's *Guardian* article which summoned Stern once again from his unquiet grave. The letter has not survived but the reply from the chief's deputy, Barry Shaw, has, noting Morton's concerns and reassuring him that a detective inspector has been put on the case.[13]

Geoffrey Morton died on 11 December 1996, aged eighty-nine. At Alice's insistence the cremation was a low-key event and not announced in advance. 'My mother was terrified that they were going to blow up the funeral – even then,' Penny remembered.[14]

Most of his old comrades had gone before him: Alec Ternent, Alec Stuart, Alex Shand, Dick Catling and John Fforde were all dead.

They had not seen much of each other in the latter years, but occasionally some would gather at a pub in London after an old comrades' get-together to swap old stories and sing 'The Holy City', the anthem of the Palestine Police. It is a wonderful hymn that captures perfectly the nostalgia and affection that seemingly almost every Briton who served there felt for Palestine, despite its dangers and tribulations. The place they had known, still linked physically and spiritually to antiquity, had long gone. But so, too, had the Britain that sent them there in a vain and finally tragic bid to stem the tide of history.

Acknowledgements

My thanks go first to my mother Kathleen and Sir Paul Beresford MP for their roles in the genesis of this book – an interesting process that would unfortunately take up too much space here to recount. I am especially grateful to Penny Brook for the access she has allowed me to her father Geoffrey's extensive archive and the unfailing helpfulness and generosity she and her husband Nigel have offered throughout the research and writing. I am frequently taken aback by the kindness people who are usually complete strangers to the author show when approached for help with a book. The response I got to my requests for information from those involved in this one was particularly impressive, particularly given the visceral animosities of the events described. In Israel I would like to thank Yair Stern for his insights into his father's life and personality and Amira Stern of the Jabotinsky Institute in Tel Aviv for her cheerful response to endless demands. Hannah Armoni gave me the run of the Lehi Museum's holdings and the benefit of her memories of life in the underground. I learned much from pleasant hours spent with Ze'ev Iviansky at his home in the Galilee and Azriel Weiss Livnat in his flat in Tel Aviv. In the course of my researches I was lucky enough to encounter – and, I would like to think, make a friend of – Uri Avnery, the former Irgun man and veteran of the independence war who went on to become one of Israel's great and eloquent liberal voices.

The same goes for Ilana Tsur, who as well as sharing her material sometimes shared a lunch table with me during breaks from delving in the Haganah archive files. Without access to these, the book could not have been written. This is a historical goldmine, largely unplundered by British researchers as far as I can tell. Panning and sifting the documents you are able to attain a real intimacy with the workings and thought processes of the Mandate's security forces. I was helped greatly there by Orly Azulay, Dorit Herman, Shimri Salomon and the former director Neri Arieli. Israeli academics have been busy there for some time, notably Dr Eldad Harouvi of the Palmach Musem in Tel Aviv, whose work has resulted in *Palestine Investigated*, the fullest account yet of the CID of the Palestine Police Force. It has yet to be published in English – an omission which cries out to be rectified – but he very generously allowed me access to the translation, for which a sincere 'toda raba'.

I would also like to thank Danny Eliav and David Shomron in Jerusalem and Mia Gepner in Tel Aviv for helping me access her extraordinary father's research material. Ram Oren talked to me about the background to his novel *Red Days*, a fictionalised account of the romance between Shoshana Borochov and Tom Wilkin. Sami Abu Shedadeh kindly gave me guidance on the geography of Jaffa in the period. Anyone writing about this place and time owes much to previous historians but I would like to express the debt I owe in particular to Ada Amichal-Yevin, James Barr, Zev Golan, Joseph Heller and Tom Segev.

In Britain, the memory of the Palestine Police is kept alive by the dedication of the indefatigable Edward Horne, author of *A Job Well Done*, the definitive history of the force, and a PPF veteran himself. Ted was endlessly patient with my inquiries. I hope he thinks the result is worth it.

The sons and daughters of those who served have been remarkably generous and encouraging. Dan Stamp spoke to me at length about his father Bernard and generously provided invaluable photographs and papers. Alex Stuart's daughter Linda lent me his annotated copy of Geoffrey Morton's book, and Ann Shand gave me an insight into the life of her father, Alex.

In Oxford I was given much valuable assistance by Debbie Usher at the Middle East Centre Archive, Saint Antony's College, and Lucy

McCann of Rhodes House Library. The staffs of the National Archives, the British Library, the Imperial War Museum and the London Library were their usual efficient selves. Jane Wells provided a fascinating insight into Geoffrey Morton's early days by allowing me access to the records of St Olave's Grammar School.

During a December 2012 trip to a freezing Suwalki, Avraham Stern's birthplace in eastern Poland, I was given a warm welcome and good advice by Ewelina Suchocka at the tourist office.

Old comrades from the Middle East press corps have helped in significant ways. They include Ian Black, Charles Richards, Don Macintyre and Jim Muir. Roger Boyes pointed me in the direction of some interesting Foreign Office documents and Robin Gedye translated passages of Otto von Hentig's memoir.

I would like to thank Tim Harris, Uri Avnery, Sir Sherard Cowper-Coles and Edward Fitzgerald QC for reading and commenting on the manuscript. The errors of fact and perhaps judgement that remain are mine, all mine.

I would like to pay special tribute to my friend and collaborator on the Israeli end of this venture, Ben Lynfield. Ben's gentle, courteous efficiency made the task so much easier. He is a great interpreter of a famously complicated place and whatever understanding I have of it owes much to his wisdom. Thank you.

At HarperCollins Arabella Pike has been her usual fantastic self, supported brilliantly by Steve Guise. A special thank you too, to Richard Collins for his meticulous editing. The picture research has been handled with great energy and enthusiasm by Sarah Hopper with much appreciated help from Esther Hecht in Jerusalem.

Finally to Henrietta and Honor – as always, my gratitude and love.

Notes

Prologue

1 See Chapter 11 for source notes of this account.

Chapter 1

1 M. W. Daly, 'Sir Harold Alfred MacMichael', *Dictionary of National Biography*.

2 Papers of Sir Harold MacMichael [hereafter MacMichael Papers], Middle East Centre, St Antony's College, Oxford University.

3 Ibid.

4 *Palestine Post*, 4 March 1938.

5 MacMichael Papers.

6 M. W. Daly. *Empire on the Nile*, Cambridge University Press, Cambridge, 1986, p. 273.

7 Papers of Sir William Battershill [hereafter Battershill Papers], Rhodes House Library, Oxford University.

8 *Palestine Post*, 4 March 1938.

9 Ibid., 6 March 1938.

10 Ibid., 4 March 1938.

Chapter 2

1 Geoffrey Morton, *Just the Job*, Hodder & Stoughton, London, 1957, pp. 48–52.

2 G. J. Morton Private Papers [hereafter Morton Papers].

3 Class reports, St Olave's Grammar School Library.

4 *The Olavian*, vol. XXI, no. 1, p. 114.

5 Class reports, St Olave's Grammar School Library.

6 Imperial War Museum [hereafter IWM] Sound Archive 12960.

7 Ibid.

8 Morton, op. cit., pp. 14–16.

9 Ibid., p. 17.

10 IWM Sound Archive 12960.

11 Morton, op. cit., p. 19.

12 Ibid., p. 20.

13 *Palestine Post*, 12 April 1938.

14 Morton Papers.

15 Morton, op. cit., p. 61.

16 *Eastern Evening News*, 13 April 1938.

17 *Palestine Post*, 14 April 1938.

18 Morton, op. cit., p. 63.

19 Ibid., p. 2.

20 David Ben-Gurion, *Recollections*, edited by Thomas R. Bransten, Macdonald, 1970, p. 36.

21 Howard Sachar, *A History of Israel from the Rise of Zionism to our Time*, pp. 25–266.

22 The National Archives [herafter TNA] FO 1093/330.

23 Ibid.

24 *Palestine Post*, 15 November 1937.

25 Morton, op. cit., p. 62.

26 Morton, op. cit., p. 62.

27 Morton Papers.

28 'The Irgun', Wikipedia, p. 5.

Chapter 3

1 Avraham Stern, *Letters to Roni*, edited by Aharon Amir, Yair, Tel Aviv, 2000, p. 182 (in Hebrew).

2 But then there are few plaques or monuments relating to any aspect of Suwalki's twentieth-century history. Perhaps it is too painful and contentious for anyone to want to remember.

3 Interview with Yair Stern, Jerusalem, 14 October 2012.

4 Leslie Sherer, *Memories of Suwalk*, Independent Suwalk and Vicinity Benevolent Association Yearbook, 1990.

5 Shmuel Abramsky, *Study of Suwalk Jewry, Jewish Community Book – Suwalk and Vicinity*, Yair-Avraham Stern Publishing House, Tel Aviv, 1989, p. 15.
6 Quoted in Abramsky, ibid., p. 19.
7 Interview with Yair Stern, Jerusalem, 14 October 2012.
8 Interview with Amira Stern, Tel Aviv, 28 February 2013.
9 This and many other details of Stern's early life in the following passage can be found in Ada Amichal-Yevin's exhaustively researched *In Purple: The Life of Yair – Abraham Stern*, Hadar, Tel Aviv, 1986, p. 13 (translated from the Hebrew by Ben Lynfield).
10 Interview with Yair Stern, Jerusalem, 14 October 2012.
11 *In My Blood Live Forever: Letters of Avraham Stern*, Yair, Tel Aviv, 1979, p. 228 (translated from the Hebrew by Zev Golan).
12 *Complete Poetic Works of Hayyim Nachman Bialik*, vol. I, edited by Israel Efos, New York, 1948, pp. 129–43.
13 Interview with Yair Stern, Jerusalem, 14 October 2012.
14 Quoted in Zev Golan, *Stern: The Man and His Gang*, Yair, Tel Aviv, 2011, p. 15.
15 Ibid., p. 16.
16 Ibid., p. 17.
17 Quoted in Golan, op. cit., p. 29.
18 Michael Ignatieff, *Isaiah Berlin: A Life*, Chatto and Windus, London, 1998, p. 80.
19 Joseph Heller, *The Stern Gang, Ideology, Politics and Terror 1940–49*, Frank Cass, London, 1995, p. 19.
20 Amichal-Yevin, op cit., p. 87.
21 Ibid., p. 91.
22 Yair Stern interview, Jerusalem, 14 October 2012. The detail of wild flowers blooming late in January seems to suggest some sentimental myth-making is at work here but in fact spring can come that early in Israel.
23 Amichal-Yevin, op cit., p. 120.
24 Ibid., p. 91.

25 Eliav, *Wanted*, pp. 62–4.

26 Haganah Archives, Tel Aviv [hereafter HA] 47/7.

Chapter 4

1 Amichal-Yevin, op. cit., p. 150.

2 Binyamin Gepner, interview with Sir Richard Catling, late 1970s.

3 Ibid.

4 www.genforum.genealogy.com

5 Details of the affair are taken from Ram Oren, *Red Days*, Keshet, 2006 (in Hebrew), a fictionalized account of Wilkin and Borochov's romance.

6 Binyamin Gepner, interview with Sir Richard Catling, Lehi Museum Archives [hereafter LMA], Tel Aviv.

7 Eliav, *Wanted*, p. 41.

8 Quoted in Golan, *Stern: The Man and His Gang*, p. 28.

9 HA 47/77.

10 *Manchester Guardian*, 24 May 1939.

11 *Palestine Post*, 18 May 1939.

12 *Palestine Post*, 19 May 1939.

13 Quoted in Amichal-Yevin, op. cit., p. 141.

14 HA 47/7.

15 Amichal-Yevin, op. cit., pp. 151–4.

16 Ehud Ein-Gil, 'Punish Those Responsible', *Ha'aretz*, 13 January 2009. The article is based on *The Birth of an Underground Organization* by Professor Yehuda Lapidot.

17 HA 47/59.

18 Quoted in Amichal-Yevin, op. cit., p. 154.

19 Eliav, op. cit., p. 72.

20 HA 47/59. Levstein/Eliav would later claim that the attack was aimed equally at British officials and Arab dignitaries who frequented the Rex. Eliav, op. cit., p. 67.

21 Translation attached to CID weekly intelligence report, HA 47/88.

22 Translation attached to CID weekly intelligence report, HA 47/87.

23 HA 47/89.

24 HA 47/77.

25 Ibid.

26 Eliav, op. cit., p. 77.

27 Ibid., p. 78.

28 Battershill Papers.

29 HA 47/59.

30 Interview with Uri Avnery, Tel Aviv, 28 February 2013.

31 Morris Gilbert, 'Jewish IRA Fights for Sovereign Palestine', 13 July 1939.

32 HA 47/59.

33 Eliav, op. cit., pp. 87–94.

34 Telephone interview with Edward Horne, 2 June 2013.

35 Binyamin Gepner, interview with Sir Richard Catling, LMA.

36 Telephone interview with Edward Horne, 2 June 2013.

37 According to Levstein's son, Danny Eliav, Zeroni held his father at least partly responsible for his sufferings. Shortly before the arrest, Levstein had borrowed Zeroni's car for a raid on a British arms dump and had not covered the number plates. The vehicle had been seen and the registration circulated. 'Zeroni came over to my father and he blamed him for all the torture he had from Cairns', he told me in Jerusalem in October 2012.

38 Eliav, op. cit., pp. 95–7.

39 *Palestine Post,* 27 August 1939.

40 Ibid., 28 August 1939.

Chapter 5

1 The Colonial Police Medal for Gallantry and the first ever awarded, according to Morton.

2 Morton, *Just the Job,* p. 110.

3 Ibid., p. 108

4 Private Papers of Alice Morton.

5 Morton, op. cit., p. 108.

6 Morton Papers.

7 Interview with Edward Horne, 10 January 2013.

8 Interview with Dan Stamp, London, 28 September 2013.

9 Morton, op. cit., p. 118

10 Nicholas Bethell, *The Palestine Triangle*, André Deutsch, London, 1979, pp. 72–4.

11 Ibid., p. 99.

12 Morton Papers.

13 TNA FO 1093/330.

14 Morton, op. cit., p. 121.

15 Eliav, *Wanted*, p. 112.

16 Ibid., p. 113.

17 Ibid., p. 114.

18 Quoted in Amichal-Yevin, *In Purple: The Life of Yair – Abraham Stern*, p. 217.

19 Stern, *Letters to Roni*, ed. Amir, p. 126.

20 Quoted in Heller, *The Stern Gang, Ideology, Politics and Terror 1940–49*, pp. 70–75.

21 Interview with Uri Avnery, Tel Aviv, 28 February 2013.

22 See Heller, op cit., p. 75, for a fuller expression of this philosophy.

23 Quoted in Golan, *Stern: The Man and His Gang*, p. 33.

Chapter 6

1 HA 47/7.

2 Baruch Nadel, interview with Nelly Langsfelder, Tel Aviv, 31 March 1976, Jabotinsky Institute Archives, Tel Aviv [hereafter JIA].

3 Quoted in Tom Segev, *One Palestine, Complete*, Abacus, London, 2012, p. 442.

4 He may have been acting in response to pressure from the Jewish Agency and the Haganah following a long-running

dispute resulting from a raid on an arms dump in Herzliya earlier in the year, for which IZL members were blamed.

5 HA 47/7.

6 Eliav, *Wanted*, p. 129.

7 Weekly Police Report, Morton Papers.

8 *Palestine Post*, 10 September 1940.

9 Eliav, op cit., pp. 130–33.

10 *Palestine Post*, 17 September 1940.

11 Weekly Police Report, Morton Papers.

12 HA 47/2 for this and subsequent quotes pp. 102–104.

13 Soffer, though, persisted with his enquiries, as is clear from his report cited above. Despite Wilkin's reluctance to cooperate, Soffer managed to renew his acquaintance with Ilin and pressed him for information about the robbery. Ilin stalled at first, then suddenly invited him to dinner and then lunch at the San Remo restaurant in Tel Aviv. Bluff came high on the menu, with both men prodding and pushing for a weak spot. Ilin did not mind admitting that Stern and Zeroni had organized the robbery as he was sure that the police had no solid evidence against them. Soffer countered that, on the contrary, the police had a lot. He claimed – untruthfully – that he had 'brought 20 detectives with me from Jerusalem and that they will not return until they arrest every one of the persons wanted'.

On Tuesday, 1 October, five days after the lunch, Soffer met Ilin and Rosenthal in Jerusalem where, despite his earlier bluster, he had returned. Ilin took Soffer to one side. He had a proposition for him from the perpetrators of the robbery. He 'hinted that to avoid trouble and fear of being constantly followed … they would rather pay a good sum of money to the police to put the file aside and not to extend the investigations to other corners'. Soffer decided it was time to up the ante. 'I told [Ilin] that I don't believe a word of what he said and that I am convinced he cannot get in touch with these persons as they do not trust him or David any more who are known spies of the police.' This challenge 'excited him very much and he protested. Then he said: "All right Mr Soffer, we shall be in your house on Saturday and you can see whether they have confidence in me or not."'

. In fact they turned up on Friday, just as the Soffers were about to sit down to their Shabbat supper. The hospitable policeman offered his guests a glass of wine and 'after receiving some refreshment [Ilin] requested to speak to me alone'. They moved into another room where Ilin told him that 'the offenders' would never surrender and it would be a 'dangerous undertaking' for Soffer to persist with his investigation. He suggested that it was his duty as a Jew to 'close the case like other hundreds of cases and be with my family in Jerusalem'.

Ilin now got down to business. 'He told me that he got in touch with the persons responsible for the robbery (would not mention names) and that they have offered and have given him 150 pounds to give it to me to close the case.' At this point he 'pulled out some notes from his pocket and said I have brought 50 pounds for you now'. Another fifty would come later. Ilin proposed to keep the rest for himself to pay doctors' bills following a bad car smash in Haifa.

Soffer joked that the money had perhaps come from the Anglo-Palestine Bank. He then confessed himself surprised and somewhat shocked by the approach. He had assumed that Ilin had come to 'give him a good report on the case' or to offer to 'persuade the offenders to surrender to the police and stand trial if they are really national heroes'. Ilin merely repeated the offer. The detective felt it was time to change tack.

'I then decided for the sake of progress of my case to adopt a different attitude and I told him that one should expect a better sum of money for dropping such a case and that I will reconsider.' Ilin took back the fifty pounds and said he would try to increase the offer. They agreed to meet again in Tel Aviv.

Before he left Ilin indulged in a little indiscreet bragging, designed, it seems, to undermine his host's loyalty to his employers. He informed Soffer that the IZL had paid agents inside the police force and as a result 'received copies of all secret reports'. Their left-wing rivals in the Histadrut (the powerful Jewish workers' federation) also spent a lot of money on spying and had gone so far as to 'compel a Jewish girl to sleep with an army captain to get his secrets'. Among the beneficiaries of the Histadrut slush fund was the late Inspector Cairns. Indeed, one of the reasons for his assassination was that 'he was bribed by the Histadrut and delivered many police secrets to them and as such he was fighting the Revisionists'.

The implication was that Soffer had better decide which side he was on. David Rosenthal had already delivered a similar message during the chance meeting in Jerusalem when he had told him, 'they know those officers who assist the Histadrut and that their time will come, and those officers who assist the IZL ... will be specially considered'. Immediately after the Shabbat eve encounter Soffer faithfully set off for police headquarters in the Russian Compound and gave a verbal report to Giles Bey, who requested the full written version which is quoted in the text.

14 HA 47/60.
15 HA 47/1.
16 Ibid.
17 Ibid.

Chapter 7
1 HA 47/10.
2 Eliav, *Wanted*, p. 145.
3 Ibid., p. 142.
4 Werner Otto von Hentig, *Mein Leben Eine Dienstreise*, Vandenhoeck & Ruprecht, Göttingen, 1962, pp. 338–9.
5 'Seven Days' section, *Yedioth Ahronoth*, 15 July 1983.

6   See Heller, *The Stern Gang, Ideology, Politics and Terror 1940–49*, ch. 4, for a full study.

7   Ibid., p. 86.

8   Eliav, op cit., p. 147.

9   Lubentchik's role in the story ended there. He decided to stay on in Lebanon and, when British forces swept in to drive out the Vichyites in the early summer of 1941, he was picked up and packed off to Mazra'a. Later he was moved to a detention camp in Africa where he fell ill and died.

10 Amichal-Yevin, *In Purple: The Life of Yair – Abraham Stern*, pp. 224–5. The friend was Yitzhak Tselnik.

11 Quoted in Heller, op cit., p. 87.

12 Interview with Yair Stern, Jerusalem, 14 October 2012.

13 Dr Kasriel Eilender, 'A Brief History of the Jews in Suwalki', www.kehilalinks.jewishgen.org. About 1700 Jews were murdered in a forest near Łomazy in August 1942 by the SS, abetted by Police Battalion 101, a formation of 'ordinary men' from Hamburg whose activities helped give the lie to the notion that only dedicated Nazis were involved in mass killings of Jews.

14 US Holocaust Museum Encyclopedia article 'Polish Refugees in Lithuania – Unexpected Rescue 1940–1941', www.ushmm.org

15 Yair Stern says she entered Palestine on forged documents arranged by his father's contacts in Kovno.

16 Quoted in Heller, op cit., p. 83.

17 HA 47/11.

18 HA 47/3.

19 Memorandum from unnamed 'British Inspector' at Tulkarm, 2 July 1941, HA 47/4.

20 HA 47/11.

21 HA 47/7.

22 'Life in the Lehi': interview with Moshe Svorai, www.eretzisraelforever.net

23 Testimony of Moshe Svorai, quoted in Amichal-Yevin, op. cit., p. 193.

24 HA 47/7.

25 HA 47/3.

26 HA 47/2.

27 HA 47/11.

28 Golan, *Stern: The Man and His Gang*, p. 33.

29 Heller, op. cit, pp. 87–8.

30 Papers of Alec Bowden Stuart, Imperial War Museum Documents Department 19259. This report is dated 10 December 1942 but it seems clear that these sentiments were already widespread a year earlier.

31 Quoted in Amichal-Yevin, op. cit., p. 236.

32 Quoted in Golan, op. cit., p. 34.

33 Quoted in Amichal-Yevin, op. cit., p. 273.

34 HA 47/4.

35 Eliav, op. cit., p. 147.

36 Ibid., pp. 246–50.

37 Eliav, op. cit., p. 149.

Chapter 8

1 The Attorney General v Nissim Reuven and Yehoshua Becker, 6 March 1942, Morton Papers.

2 *Palestine Post*, 11 January 1942.

3 Eliav, *Wanted*, p. 150.

4 Amichal-Yevin, *In Purple: The Life of Yair – Abraham Stern*, pp. 266–7.

5 Yitzhak Shamir, *Summing Up*, Weidenfeld & Nicolson, 1994, p. 35.

6 Eliav, op. cit., p. 15. When Levstein made these allegations in 1984, Morton was still alive. He did not challenge them, but given his proven determination to defend his reputation in the courts it seems unlikely the book, published in New York, ever came to his attention and there is no mention of it in his papers.

7 Morton Papers.

8 Morton, *Just the Job*, p. 136.
9 *Palestine Post*, 26 January 1942.
10 Edward Horne, letter to author, 12 March 2014.
11 Quoted in Amichal-Yevin, op. cit., p. 265.
12 Ibid., p 253.
13 Ibid., p. 261.
14 Interview with Uri Avnery, Tel Aviv, 28 February 2013.
15 Amichal-Yevin, op. cit., pp. 264–5.
16 Ibid., p. 258.
17 Ibid., p. 259.
18 Shamir, op. cit., p. 51.
19 Eliav, op. cit., pp. 152–3.
20 See *Palestine Post*, 12 February 1942, p. 3.
21 Eliav, op. cit., p. 154.
22 Ibid.
23 TNA HO 334/228.
24 Morton, op. cit., p. 137.
25 Ibid., p. 139.
26 Eliav, op. cit., p. 158.
27 *Palestine Post*, 21 January 1942.
28 *Palestine Post*, 22 January 1942.
29 Binyamin Gepner, interview with Alec Ternent, late 1970s.
30 *Palestine Post*, 22 January 1942.
31 Efrem Dekel, *SHAI: The Exploits of Hagana Intelligence*, Thomas Yoselof, 1959, p. 30.

Chapter 9

1 HA 47/3.
2 'Operations at 30 Dizengoff Street, Tel Aviv', Morton Papers.
3 Morton, *Just the Job*, p. 142.
4 The identity of the informant is unclear, but Morton reported to Giles that the gang assumed it was the owner of the flat (HA 47/3).
5 Morton, op. cit., p. 142.

6 'Operations at 30 Dizengoff Street, Tel Aviv', Morton Papers.
7 Binyamin Gepner, interview with Alec Ternent, late 1970s.
8 'Operations at 30 Dizengoff Street, Tel Aviv', Morton Papers.
9 Binyamin Gepner interview with Alec Ternent.
10 It can be read on p. 162 of Eliav's *Wanted*. It starts with the police bursting in and opening fire with cries of 'Bloody Jews! Filthy Jews!' and ends with Levstein delivering a stirring oration from his stretcher.
11 Baruch Nadel, telephone interview with Moshe Svorai, Haifa, 9 March 1976, JIA.
12 Exchange reproduced in 'The Murder at No. 30 Dizengoff Street: How Four Freedom Fighters Fell' (Lehi pamphlet), Morton Papers.
13 Binyamin Gepner, interview with Alec Ternent, LMA.
14 TNA FO 1093/330.
15 Ibid.
16 Eldad Harouvi, *Palestine Investigated: The Story of the CID of the Palestine Police Force, 1929–1946*, 2011, p. 221, translated from the Hebrew by Murray Rosovsky (unpublished).
17 Moshe Svorai interview with Ada Amichal-Yevin, JIA.
18 HA 47/9.
19 Ibid.
20 Morton Papers.

Chapter 10

1 Amichal-Yevin, *In Purple: The Life of Yair – Abraham Stern*, p. 278.
2 Ibid., p. 282, testimony of Roni Stern.
3 *Palestine Post*, 6 February 1942.
4 Amichal-Yevin, op. cit., p. 281.
5 Ibid., p. 276.
6 Eliav, *Wanted*, p. 166. Zak is transliterated as 'Jacques' throughout.

7 Another man was mentioned – 'Abraham Maeri' – but by the time the notice appeared the police had established that this was an alias of Avraham Amper, now dead.

8 HA 47/3, Alan Saunders, Report to the Chief Secretary, 20 February 1942, 'The Stern Group', p. 5.

9 Ibid., p. 4.

10 Harouvi, *Palestine Investigated: The Story of the CID of the Palestine Police Force, 1929–1946*, p. 225.

11 HA 47/3, Saunders Report, 20 February 1942, p. 4.

12 HA 47/3.

13 Amichal-Yevin, op. cit., p. 273, testimony of Binyamin Zeroni.

14 Ibid., p. 276, testimony of Yitzhak Tselnik.

15 HA 47/3.

16 Tova Svorai, *The Last Days of Yair-Avraham Stern*, Shaked (undated).

17 Amichal-Yevin, op. cit., p. 284.

18 Morton might have been better directing his anger at Binyamin Zeroni. According to Professor Eldad Harouvi in his study of the PPF CID, the Haifa bomb was 'prepared by Binyamin Zeroni and his men'. Harouvi, op. cit., p. 227. This work has not yet been published in English, depriving non-Hebrew-speaking scholars of a valuable source, an omission I hope will soon be rectified.

19 Morton, *Just the Job*, p. 143.

Chapter 11

1 Binyamin Gepner, interview with Alec Shand, late 1970s, LMA.

2 Morton, *Just the Job*, p. 144.

3 Levstein's testimony differs from the official account in some respects – he says that there was an Arab policeman guarding them initially and Daly did not appear until after Amper and Zak's death.

4 Eliav, *Wanted*, p. 119.

5 Morton's report 'Avraham Stern', 13 February 1942, in Stuart
   Papers, IWM 19259.

6 Ibid., p. 168.

7 Morton, op. cit., p. 144.

8 HA 47/3, Saunders Report, 20 February 1942.

9 Levstein claimed that his communications had been written in
   the same fashion though Morton's staff do not seem to have
   experienced much difficulty cracking the code. He also alleged
   that Svorai wrote his note in plain Hebrew. In the letter Svorai
   mentions other attempts to contact Tova from hospital, though
   he does not say through whom.

10 Morton, op. cit., p. 144.

11 HA 47/3, Saunders Report, 20 February 1942.

12 Tova Svorai, *The Last Days of Yair-Avraham Stern*.

13 HA 47/3, Saunders Report, 20 February 1942, Appendix D.

14 Amichal-Yevin, *In Purple: The Life of Yair – Abraham Stern*,
    p. 286.

15 Tova Svorai, op. cit.

16 Ibid.

17 Tova Svorai also claimed that he was wearing a grey suit, but
    this would be contradicted by the testimony of the policeman
    who found him, Bernard Stamp, who said he was clad in his
    underwear.

18 Many of the staff were Arabs, a fact that had alarmed Svorai
    when he was first brought in. He was reassured by an Arab
    doctor who 'spoke to me in English and said you have nothing
    to worry about, we won't harm you'. Moshe Svorai, interview
    with Ada Amichal-Yevin, JIA.

19 Eliav, op. cit., pp. 168–9.

20 Ada Amichal-Yevin, interview with Moshe Svorai, JIA. Svorai
    remained very sensitive on the subject. In 1993 he won a libel
    action against Anshel Spielman, director of the Lehi Museum and
    a former member of the group, for saying in his memoirs that
    Svorai's slip had led the police to Yair. In a convoluted judgement,

the president of the Tel Aviv District Court Eliyahu Winograd
found that Stern had been captured as a result of a routine search
and that 'based on the evidence placed before me, the British did
not arrive at the apartment on the basis of information
emanating from the slip of the tongue of the plaintiff'.

21 Svorai, op. cit.

22 Morton, op. cit., p. 145.

23 Svorai, op. cit.

24 Tova claimed that among his entourage was a Jewish detective,
the same man she had seen in the street three nights earlier.
He looked for a while at Stern then left the room 'as
restrained and quiet as when he entered'. The significance of
this figure is that his presence lends credence to the idea that
it was a police surveillance operation rather than Moshe's
indiscretion that led Morton to Stern. See *The Last Days of Yair
– Abraham Stern*.

25 HA 47/3, Saunders Report, 20 February 1942.

26 It was turned up by James Barr while researching his brilliant
account of Middle Eastern Anglo-French rivalries in the period,
A Line in the Sand. I tracked it down after noting the reference
and owe him a debt of gratitude.

27 The latter point would be disputed by Stern's supporters.

28 Svorai, op. cit.

29 Amichal-Yevin, op. cit., p. 290.

30 Ibid., pp. 289–90.

31 Ibid., p. 292.

Chapter 12

1 TNA KV 5/29.

2 Ibid.

3 Morton Papers.

4 Ibid.

5 JIA 3/112.

6 *Jerusalem Post*, 13 February 1942.

7 HA 47/3.

8 JIA 3/112.

9 TNA KV5/29

10 HA 47/3, Saunders Report, 20 February 1942.

11 HA 47/8.

12 HA 47/3, Saunders Report, 20 February 1942.

13 Morton, *Just the Job*, p. 147.

14 An honourable exception was Eden's private secretary, Oliver
    Harvey, who pleaded for the refugees to be given sanctuary.

15 Quoted in Bethell, *The Palestine Triangle*, p. 117. In October
    1941 a German Jew called Paul Falkenheim, who had been
    released from Dachau, was caught after being parachuted into
    Palestine. He was equipped with a wireless set and had
    instructions to 'find out as much as possible about troop
    movements and concentrations, the location of aircraft and
    their markings, new aerodromes and camp sites, shipping and
    the feeling among Palestinian Arabs and the possibility of their
    revolting'. He was warned that failure to obey orders would
    result in reprisals against his family. British intelligence were
    unimpressed by this operation and attempts to infiltrate two
    Armenians into the area and came to the conclusion that
    either the enemy espionage set up in the Middle East was
    'inefficient' or it was intended that the agents should be caught
    to distract attention from 'more important parachutists and
    seaborne agents'. See the file KV5/29 in the National Archives
    for more detail.

16 Quoted in Bethell, op. cit., p. 114.

17 Ibid., pp. 119–20.

Chapter 13

1 *Palestine Post*, 24 April 1942.

2 Morton, *Just the Job*, p. 149. Morton says that a watch was kept
   on the spot and 'before long a young Jew – a member of the
   Stern gang – was caught making his way towards the entrance

to the orange grove, carrying a sub-machine gun in a parcel'.
However, there is no mention of any arrest in police records or
in the memoirs of any of the Stern group.

3 Binyamin Gepner, interview with Alex Shand, LMA.

4 Morton, *Just the Job*, p. 149.

5 Gepner, interview with Shand.

6 Papers of Alec Bowden Stuart, IWM 93/58/1.

7 Ibid.

8 IWM 93/58/1. Reznitsky claimed that 'opposition was raised to
the attempt on the life of Mr Morton as apparently
Government had taken no steps against the Group for the
April 22 bombs [in Jerusalem]'. The shooting of Ezra Sharoni
in Jerusalem on 20 April 'once more angered the Group and
the bomb was exploded, happily without effect'.

9 Yaacov Banai, *Anonymous Soldiers*, Elisha Printing Press, Tel
Aviv, 1958, p. 112 (in Hebrew).

10 Quoted in Golan, *Stern: The Man and His Gang*, p. 91.

11 Yellin-Mor, *Freedom Fighter for Israel*, p. 86.

12 Morton Papers.

13 Ibid.

14 IWM 93/58/1.

15 TNA KV 5/29.

16 TNA KV 5/29.

17 Morton Papers. Morton described it as a 'secret document'
which he retained for his personal files.

18 Morton, op. cit., p. 147.

19 The *Palestine Post* reported on 21 April 1942 that Becker's
sentence had been reduced to life imprisonment.

20 KV 5/29.

21 According to Colin Imray, a Palestine policeman, there was an
officer called Richard Ballantine who had spent much of his
career in the Nigerian Police. Ballantine made it clear in his
report of the encounter that he was a new arrival in Palestine
so it could be that he was serving on secondment for a short

period. C. Imray, *A Policeman's Story* (unpublished MS, 1983), Rhodes House Library, Oxford University.

22 HA 47/12.
23 Shamir, *Summing Up*, pp. 39–40.
24 Morton, op. cit., p. 155.
25 Police report: 'Seizure of Ammunition at Givat Brenner', Morton Papers.
26 Morton Papers.
27 Morton, op. cit., p. 157.
28 Ibid., p. 172.
29 Morton Papers.
30 Ibid.
31 Morton, op. cit., p. 157.
32 Diary of Alice Morton.

Chapter 14
1 Morton Papers.
2 Diary of Alice Morton.
3 Morton, *Just the Job*, p. 164.
4 Shamir, *Summing Up*, p. 46.
5 Quotations from leaflets and poster are taken from CID translations in the Haganah Archive the Morton Papers.
6 It was assumed to have been the work of Yaacov Levstein and his star pupil, Moshe Bar Giora, who had escaped from Jerusalem Central Prison less than two months before. In fact, Levstein, with Shamir's approval, had disappeared on an extended sabbatical, teaching Haganah men how to build bombs in various kibbutzim. Eliav, *Wanted*, pp. 207–18.
7 IWM 19259.
8 Golan, *Stern: The Man and His Gang*, p. 105.
9 Quoted in J. Bowyer Bell, *Terror out of Zion*, Transaction Publishers, Piscataway, New Jersey, 1996, p. 112.
10 Ibid., p. 91.
11 Morton Papers.

12 Morton, op. cit., p. 173.

13 TNA WO 216/121.

14 Quoted in Bethell, *The Palestine Triangle*, p. 172.

15 Ben Lynfield, interview with David Shomron, 1 May 2013.

16 Segev, *One Palestine, Complete*, p. 7.

Chapter 15

1 Morton, *Just the Job*, p. 225.

2 Reported in *The Times*, 15 February 1967.

3 TNA FO 1093/330.

4 Morton, op. cit., p. 227.

5 *Daily Mail*, 4 February 1972.

6 Morton, op. cit., p. 314.

7 Ibid., p. 292.

8 Opinion of Helenus Milmo, 16 April 1952, Morton Papers.

9 The High Court of Justice, Queen's Bench Division 1952 M, No. 2157.

10 Morton, op. cit., p. 145.

11 *Daily Telegraph*, 3 February 1972.

12 Telephone interview with Richard Hargreaves, 10 April 2014.

13 Morton Papers.

14 Morton's counsel, Patrick Milmo, was the son of his first libel lawyer.

15 Morton Papers.

16 Ibid.

17 Gepner Tapes, LMA.

Chapter 16

1 Telephone interview with Ilana Tsur, 4 October 2013.

2 Interview with Dan Stamp, 28 September 2013.

3 Ilana Tsur, interview with Bernard Stamp.

4 Morton Papers.

5 Ibid.

6 Ilana Tsur, interview with Bernard Stamp.

7 Morton Papers.

8 Morton appears to have passed this on to his solicitor. Several copies were left in written and typed form in his papers.

9 Morton Papers.

Chapter 17

1 Binyamin Gepner, interview with Alec Stuart, LMA.

2 Translation from the Hebrew by Ben Lynfield.

3 In Alan Saunders's report, written eight days later, he writes that Stern 'was shot by two of the three policemen in the room'. HA 47/3.

4 Harouvi, *Palestine Investigated: The Story of the CID of the Palestine Police Force, 1929–1946*, p. 226.

5 My thanks are due to James Barr for this information.

6 Morton, *Just the Job*, p. 105.

7 Ilana Tsur, interview with Bernard Stamp.

8 *Maariv*, 10 November 1963, translated by Ben Lynfield.

9 Interview with Penny Brook, Hitchin, 21 October 2012.

10 Sam Chalmers, letter to author, 22 March 2014.

11 *Spectator*, 28 January 1989.

12 *Spectator*, 11 February 1989.

13 Morton Papers.

14 Interview with Penny Brook, Hitchin, 21 October 2012.

Picture Credits

Section One:
Page 1: (top) Jabotinsky Institute, Israel; (bottom) courtesy of Suwalk-Lomza Interest Group
Pages 2–4: Jabotinsky Institute, Israel
Page 5: courtesy of Penny Brook
Pages 6–7: Jabotinsky Institute, Israel
Page 8: (top) Lehi Museum, Tel Aviv/supplied by *Haaretz*; (bottom) courtesy of Gavriel Strasman

Section Two:
Page 1: (top left) © Dan Stamp; (top right) courtesy of Ram Oren; (bottom) © Dan Stamp
Page 2 (top left) Jabotinsky Institute, Israel; (top right) courtesy of Penny Brook; (bottom) courtesy of Penny Brook
Page 3: Jabotinsky Institute, Israel
Page 4: (top and bottom) Jabotinsky Institute, Israel
Page 5: courtesy of Linda Stewart
Page 6: Jabotinsky Institute, Israel
Page 7: (top and bottom) courtesy of Penny Brook
Page 8: (top) courtesy of Danny Eliav; (bottom) courtesy of Linda Stewart

Index

About the Author

Patrick Bishop has emerged as one of Britain's best-regarded military historians. He is the author of three works of nonfiction, *Fighter Boys*, *Bomber Boys*, and *3 Para*, and two novels. He lives in London.

http://www.patrickbishop.net